FORGIVE US OUR PRESS PASSES

FORGIVE US OUR PRESS PASSES

The Memoirs
of a
Veteran
Washington
Reporter

MYRON S. WALDMAN

St. Martin's Press
New York

Production Editor: Mark H. Berkowitz
Design by Judy Dannecker

Library of Congress Cataloging-in-Publication Data

Waldman, Myron.
    Forgive us our press passes : the memoirs of a veteran Washington reporter.
        p.   cm.
    "A Thomas Dunne book."
    ISBN 0-312-05992-2
    1. Waldman, Myron—Biography. 2. United States—Politics and government—1945–   3. Journalists—United States—Biography.
I. Title.
PN4874.W256A3   1991
070'.92—dc20
[B]   90-29169

First Edition: August 1991

10 9 8 7 6 5 4 3 2 1

For my wife, Jean; our sons, Morris, Danny, and Larry; my sister, Elaine; and for the memory of Margaret. And for all my colleagues in the great reporting game.

CONTENTS

ACKNOWLEDGMENTS

THE HELP AND THE KINDNESS OF MANY COLLEAGUES, FRIENDS, AND relatives went into the creation of this book. Some of those to whom I owe a particular debt are my fellow *Newsday* reporter, Michael Moss, whose assistance was beyond calculation, and Christine Merkle, *Newsday*'s Washington bureau librarian, without whose generous help this book could not have been written.

Larry Spinelli, author, college professor, congressional staffer, and good friend, cheerfully read an early draft of the manuscript and came up not only with encouragement but with expert advice and assistance.

So did three of my longtime friends, Martin and Lola Meisel, and Mark Talisman. And so did my sons, Morris, Danny, and Larry, and my wife, Jean, who had been telling me for years that I should write such a memoir and when I once began, never allowed me to become discouraged. My sister, Elaine, read a later version and provided good counsel as well.

At *Newsday*, Peter Gianotti, Dennis Bell, Jack Sirica, Patrick Sloyan, Pat Wechsler, and Earl Lane among others, also gave me valuable assistance. Many thanks are due to my *Newsday* editors, particularly Tony Marro and Stan

Asimov, for allowing me to integrate into this book some articles which previously appeared in the newspaper.

My agent, Jane Dystel, was my guide throughout, and my editor at St. Martin's, Tom Dunne, suggested key improvements, as did his assistant, David Meskill.

In the Capitol, my many friends in the press galleries of the House and Senate read excerpts of a work in progress, gave advice, and cheered me on. Some of them, but by no means all, are David Hess, Basil Talbott, Leslie Phillips, Tom Kenworthy, Susan Milligan, Frank Jackman, Jerry Gallegos, Kathy McShea, Finlay Lewis, Mary Deibel, Thayer Illsley, Elaine Povich, Bob Petersen, Frank Aukofer, Bill Eaton, Paul Houston, Mike Shanahan, Susan Feeney, and Peter Osterlund.

To all, my deepest gratitude and thanks.

FORGIVE US OUR
PRESS PASSES

1

THE FUNNY MACHINE

IT WAS THE NIGHT BEFORE ELECTION DAY OF 1980 WHEN I FOUND OUT that Bonzo the chimpanzee had tried to murder Ronald Reagan.

The story was told by the intended victim himself, who stopped to talk to a flight attendant as his presidential campaign jet sped north from San Diego toward Los Angeles. Reagan, nearing the end of a long political journey, began to reminisce, not about politics but about Hollywood and the 1951 movie that had been used to ridicule him in all of his campaigns, *Bedtime for Bonzo*.

Reagan leaned against the bulkhead of the plane as he spoke. He was without his jacket; his monogrammed, pocketless white shirt was immaculate. He was a candidate who never seemed to sweat. But though the last speech of the campaign was done, his pause on the plane stirred us, his grimy, weary chroniclers. A small crowd of reporters rushed to hear while TV cameramen struggled up the aisle in an unsuccessful effort to film the conversation.

Reagan was deep into his story. He said that during the filming of the movie, he realized that a distinct antipathy was growing between him and Bonzo. So he paid the monkey a visit to try to make friends.

But Bonzo, Reagan said, was not exactly hospitable. As Reagan bent over the monkey, the animal grabbed his tie and began to pull. Reagan tried to get away, but Bonzo was one strong chimpanzee. The monkey pulled and pulled.

"The knot got as small as that," Reagan said, pointing to his thumbnail. But fortunately for Reagan, Bonzo had hold of the tie in such a way that he was pulling the knot away from the star's neck instead of toward it. Still, things were kind of tight. When Reagan finally managed to get free of the monkey, he couldn't get free of the tie. "They had to cut the tie," he said.

And then thirty years later, right on the plane, Reagan finally took his revenge against Bonzo. "It's time to tell the truth about Bonzo," the Republican presidential candidate said. "Bonzo was a girl. She wore a piece of monkey fur to hide the fact."

To me, being on hand for this account could not have been more exciting or more amusing. It was my fifth presidential campaign, but every one was as fresh and dramatic as the first. I was there as one of *Newsday*'s Washington correspondents, the paper's senior Washington correspondent to be precise.

I had arrived at the Washington bureau in 1967 after being a reporter at *Newsday* on Long Island for four years. *Newsday* was in Garden City at the time, occupying a smallish building at 550 Stewart Avenue. It was right across from Roosevelt Field, where Charles Lindbergh had taken off to solo to Paris and fame everlasting. Now there was a shopping center, where poor reporters could buy dress shirts in Gimbels' basement for a dollar apiece. Alicia Patterson, *Newsday*'s founder and publisher, had wanted a Garden City address, I was told, partly so that she could put out this liberal paper that challenged the establishment right in the middle of the town where a lot of that Waspish, wealthy establishment lived. I thought *Newsday* was a great place to work, mainly because it had a deserved reputation in the business of being a writer's newspaper, a place where colorful and descriptive phrases actually were encouraged.

The circulation was about 350,000, which made it a major newspaper, but the city room seemed very small after my former place of employment, the 750,000-circulation *Philadelphia Bulletin*. Moreover, there didn't appear to be more than about seven or eight reporters working in it at any one time. Out front in the *Newsday* lobby there were a couple of cigar store wooden Indians—one of the many things Miss P. liked to collect—and their noses were all shiny because the reporters rubbed them for good luck on their way out of the building to an assignment. One of the first things the Times Mirror Corporation did when it bought *Newsday* was take out the cigar store Indians. There was a howl from the veteran reporters about that and the new management did its best to soothe them with understanding pronouncements. All the same, the Indians didn't come back.

Well, not for about twenty years, anyway. One day in 1991 I walked into the *Newsday* lobby and there they were, part of a little collection of artifacts set out to commemorate *Newsday*'s fiftieth anniversary. I rubbed the shiny nose of one of them as I went by.

I didn't know Miss P. She died in 1963 after an operation for ulcers two days after I came to *Newsday*. But I did know her spirit and her ways and the traditions she had established because they filled that paper for years after she was gone.

When I first got to *Newsday*, the editors put me on rewrite and then made me what they called the funny machine. It was Miss P.'s rule that there had to be at least one—preferably at least two—funny stories in the paper every day. She was dead but the rule was not. The editors wanted someone to write that stuff regularly.

Once, I made dandelion wine and wrote about that. Once, the editors parked me in a small woods in Suffolk County for a week without food but with toilet paper (I told them I wouldn't do it unless I had toilet paper), and that resulted in seven or eight funny stories about me, the man in the woods.

But mainly, just about every night someone—usually John Van Doorn, the night city editor—would dump a bunch of wire copy on my desk, or maybe a couple of releases from some public relations outfit, and announce to me, "Myron, this is a funny story."

I had permission to call anywhere in the world, to go out and interview people, to do anything but lie, to turn that stuff into something funny. I used to write my pieces with a combination of pride and fear that they weren't good enough—in fact, I still do—and I would show them, at least the ledes, to any of my neighboring reporters too slow to avoid me. I still do that today.

Once, Al Marlens, the assistant managing editor, told one of the cleaning men to walk up to me and ask to see my lede—that's *lede*, "not lead," a newsie's slang for the first sentence of a story. Everybody laughed when I showed it to him. I couldn't figure that out because he read *Newsday* regularly, so I really was writing for him.

Anyway, I guess I did all right at being the funny machine, because they kept me doing it for nearly a year. Whenever I wrote something John Van Doorn really liked, he would be my agent in pushing my stuff. John would yell out, "Hey, gang, listen to this."

Then the copy desk would stop work, and most of the reporters and editors would stop, and John would read my lede and then laugh. Often enough, everybody else would laugh and applaud too, even the people I had forced into reading it earlier. And then John, casting an eye at my portly frame, would say, "Everybody take a run around Myron." I guess he thought it would be good exercise.

I liked the appreciation, I liked seeing my name in the paper every day over stories that were my words instead of some editor's, and I sure did like the overtime. Because I wrote funny stories, sometimes when I wrote a check in a store on Long Island the clerk would recognize my name and ask for my autograph. I liked that too.

All my professional life I had wanted to work on a New York City newspaper, and Long Island's *Newsday* was close to it. I once had a shot at night rewrite on the *New York Journal American*, but there were a few drawbacks to working there. First of all, they had a very odd policy about rewrite men, who never went out on assignment but used the telephone or took notes from the reporters on the street. Rewrite men were the staffers who filled the paper, and the *Journal American* always needed one more person than Hearst had authorized. They got around that by taking on someone on a trial basis. Now, the union rule was that after ninety days, that person was permanently on the staff. So on the ninetieth day, the city editor would tell the tryout that he was very sorry but he just wasn't good enough. And the guy would be out.

I knew all about this when I came up Thursday and Friday nights from Philadelphia—my days off on the *Bulletin*—to moonlight doing night rewrite for the *Journal American*. I would work the midnight to eight shift, sitting at a long, scarred, U-shaped copy desk equipped with old typewriters, telephones, and headsets, with the smells of the Fulton Fish Market and the blares from the horns of the big steamships floating through the open windows. After the shift ended in the morning, I would go out for a beer with the other guys (there were no women).

Going out for a beer in the morning seemed the natural

thing to do because the night editor treated the darkness as if it were daylight. He would have us call up people at 3 or 4 A.M. as if it were high noon and quiz these poor folks, most of them the relatives of crime victims.

One night at around 4:30 he had a great idea. There was a judge named Kehoe who had been found guilty of some sort of crime and had been sentenced to a year and a day in jail. He was going to prison in the morning. The night editor decided it would be terrific if a rewrite man called up the judge right then and there and asked him how it felt.

I knew what was coming. I saw the editor looking at the rewrite bank and ducked under the table. The guy next to me, Fred Shapiro, wasn't fast enough. "Shapiro," the editor said, "call Judge Kehoe and ask him how it feels."

"It's 4:30 and you want me to call Kehoe?" Shapiro asked.

"That's right," the editor said. Shapiro gave an unhappy shrug, put on his headset, and dialed. He got the judge, identified himself, and asked the question. The scream at the other end of the line was so loud that Fred had to lift his headset to ease the pain. I put my ear next to his so I could listen too.

"Shapiro, eh?" the soon-to-be-incarcerated judge bellowed. "Shapiro. This isn't very Christian of you, Mr. Shapiro." And after a variety of threats, he hung up.

But waking people up wasn't the worst part of the job at the *Journal American*. One night a ferry boat captain fished three guys out of New York harbor whose small power boat had capsized. I was told to call them up at Staten Island Hospital and interview them.

To me, this was a snap. At least they were awake. And they were happy to talk. Now, the *Journal American* liked its interviews to be all in quotes if possible. So I wrote a story that began something like, "I thought sure as hell we were goners," gave a fast graf (paragraph) of explanation, finished the piece, and tossed it in the basket for the editor to read.

Since this two-night-a-week stint was a tryout, I was a little nervous—in fact, I was so nervous I could hardly sit in my seat. I watched the editor out of the corner of my eye as he read my story. I saw him begin to shake his head at about the second graf. Then he seemed to be shaking his head harder and harder at every line. Then he looked hard at the rewrite bank.

"Kid," he called to me. "Kid. Come up here." I went. "This story," he said. "It's no good."

"What's wrong with it?" I asked.

"It's terribly written," he said.

"How could it be terribly written?" I asked. "It's all quotes."

"That's the trouble," he said. "The quotes. They're no good."

"But that's what they said," I protested.

The editor gave me a look that was filled with pity. "Kid," he said, "that's not what they said. Sit down at this typewriter. I'll tell you what they said."

He raised my story and read from it. But now the quotes and the adventures of the three rescued men were very different. This was now a rescue straight out of the Perils of Pauline. "Write it," the editor commanded.

So I, who had trained and worked in the ordinary journalistic world where truth and accuracy were revered, still working at the *Philadelphia Bulletin*, where reporters could be fired for substituting a "but" when someone had said "and," completed my first piped story. That's what such news fictions were called—"piped," as in pipe dream. I was trembling when I handed the rewritten tale back to the editor.

He read it with great satisfaction. "Much, much better," he said. Then he looked at my face. "Kid," he said, "don't worry. No one will ever complain."

He was right. No one ever did. It was such an exciting story that it was on page one of the *Journal American* the next day. It was such an exciting story—and an exclusive, too—that it was picked up by the wire services, the Associated Press and United Press International. And on Saturday afternoon, when I returned to the rewrite bank of the good gray *Philadelphia Bulletin*, where the truth was valued over all, I saw a wire service version of my story, complete with the phony quotes, on the top of page three.

Another time at the *Journal American*, during the day, the city desk got a report of a terrible fire in a tenement in Brooklyn, with several deaths and many injuries. Eddie Mahar, the city editor, turned to his ace rewrite man and told him to get one of those all-quote interview stories.

The rewrite man, whom I will call Joe, got on the phone and took copious notes. Then he composed a wonderfully pathetic story, a first person account of the terror and tragedy of the fire as told by a survivor, whom I will call Genevieve Smith. It was a page one job for the late editions for sure.

The next morning the *New York Herald Tribune* came out with its version of the fire. "Among the survivors," the *Trib* article went, "was Mrs. Genevieve Smith, a deaf mute."

Mahar was beside himself. "Hey, Joe," he screamed, waving the *Tribune* at his rewrite man. "What about this?"

"I don't know, Eddie," Joe shouted back desperately. "She talked to me."

Mahar was not soothed. Later Joe stomped out of the city room and wandered sadly down the hall. "Jeez," he mourned, "some days you can't do anything right."

After a few weeks Mahar told me I was neither a good nor a bad rewrite man but that I would be acceptable for the ninety-day tryout. But even if this had been a real tryout I would have said no, despite the romance of a New York City paper on the waterfront, where the sudden toots from the great ocean liners made rewrite men on deadline leap out of their scarred chairs and where, after their shift ended at 8 A.M., the night team went out for a beer.

It was Rod Steiger, the actor, who convinced me to become a reporter. I was seventeen years old and he was five or six years older. He was an unknown then, just beginning his career.

At the time, Rod was dating my big sister, Elaine. I had introduced them. Rod and I had gotten to know each other the previous summer, when he was an entertainer at the Workmen's Circle Camp, near Poughkeepsie, New York, and where I also was working—as a waiter. Steiger got his job because of his talent; I got mine because my father was a member of this Jewish beneficial, fraternal, cultural, and politically active organization.

I loved to write but I loved to act on the stage even more. At De Witt Clinton High School in the Bronx, I was a reporter on the school newspaper and a contributor to the school magazine, but I also studied acting both in high school and dramatic school.

One night, as was getting more and more usual, Steiger came to our six-room apartment in the North Bronx to pick up my sister for a date. While he was waiting, I asked him to listen to me rehearse Hamlet's speech to the players. I had to give a recitation at school the next day.

"No, no, no," he broke in after the first few lines. "Give it to me."

And he began to read. "Speak the speech, I pray you, as I pronounced it to you, trippingly on the tongue. . . ." The apartment, filled with visiting aunts, uncles, and friends, became very still. It was then that I realized that although my mother, Hedwig, coached me in my roles;

although my parents had sent me to the Henry Street Settlement and later to Madam Piscater's dramatic school; although I had once been Ben Rogers, the sucker who traded an apple for the privilege of painting a fence in a production of *Tom Sawyer* that had run for more than a year; I never, never would become a real actor.

It was an immediate and total realization. I told this to Rod when he finished. He protested, insisting that it was to a degree a matter of training. But I knew.

From then on, I concentrated even more on studying and admiring the way stories were written in New York City's seven newspapers. The truth, I saw, could be written with drama and passion and feeling, even with poetic license. "The heat blisters the walls," I would read in the *New York Post*. "Saturday never ended for Jane Doe," I would read in the *Journal American*. "In her dreams and in her waking hours, she could still see. . . ." Obviously, good writers were treasured in the world of journalism.

At seventeen, I felt I could do almost anything with words except to sing or to be a good actor. My parents, neither of whom had gone to college, set great store on getting a good education. My father, Morris, was only a teenager when, a few years before World War I, he and his younger brothers and sisters fled czarist Russia for the United States and New York's Lower East Side.

His two younger brothers, Louis and Hymie, became lawyers, but my father had dismissed such a career. He was a great idealist and would say with a laugh that he had thought the millennium was at hand and that it would be a time when the world would no longer have any use for lawyers.

He was the smartest person I have ever known, a self-taught intellectual, a constant reader of books and newspapers, a labor organizer before I was born, and, as was my mother, an accomplished public speaker and a fine writer.

His brother, Louis, was a famous lawyer. In the 1920s, Louis was one of five socialist assemblymen kicked out of the New York State Assembly because they were socialists—a fact Louis could have hardly denied even if he wanted to, since he happened also to be chairman of the New York State Socialist party at the time. He was very radical, calling for such extreme measures as a guaranteed minimum wage, recognition of labor unions, and free college educations for the poor. After his colleagues removed him, he went back to his Lower East Side district and was re-elected and reseated in time to help lead the repeal of Prohibition.

My father was even tougher—organizing sit-in strikes and putting himself in physical danger for his beliefs. But these adventures of brothers who were socialists, yet also vigorous anti-Communists, all came before I was born.

In my lifetime, my father operated a small laundry supply business and was, as an avocation, a speaker for the Liberal party and an official of the Social Democratic Federation. My uncle Louis worked with labor unions, but also became rich enough to have an estate adjoining that of his friend, Thomas E. Dewey.

I saw my uncle Louis only on rare occasions, but intently followed news of his exploits. My father, who was still head of the family despite his middle-class income and the difference in economic circumstance, would sit at the dinner table every night and discuss domestic and international political events with his wife and two children.

Nearly all the time what he predicted would happen, actually happened. Because of my father, I won my first political bet—a ten-to-one shot that Harry S Truman would beat Dewey in 1948. I bet one dollar.

In and out of school, I did everything I could to improve

my writing techniques. I would join clubs and then edit their newspapers. At the Workmen's Circle Camp, where I was a waiter and busboy for nearly ten years, I was paid an extra ten dollars a season for editing the one-page daily mimeographed sheet. I had to write the paper in the mornings, which gave me a total of ninety minutes—the time available between serving breakfast and lunch. And at New York University, although I majored in history and minored in English, I became an editor and writer on just about every publication in school. At the University of Missouri, where I received a master's in journalism, I worked as a reporter on the *Columbia Missourian*, the journalism school newspaper where all the students had jobs.

To me, being a reporter and an editor was to have a front-row seat on events that affected my world. Also, I had attended an all-boy junior high school and high school, and was a little shy when it came to talking to girls. But being a reporter was to be granted the right to talk to everyone, no matter who and what the subject. Of course, I was still a little nervous about approaching people—both male and female—but time and repetition took care of that.

By 1962, when I declined the ninety-day tryout at the *Journal American*, I was fazed only by being ordered to make post-midnight calls and by being told to try to coax stories out of families who had been victimized by violence.

There were plenty of orders to do both at the *Journal American* and at the *Philadelphia Bulletin*. But the *Bulletin* had one clear edge—there, at least, there were rules about writing the truth.

So I stayed on at the *Philadelphia Bulletin*. Not that it didn't have some faults of its own. The paper was huge—a circulation of over 700,000—and it was the preeminent publication in the area. It was also the establishment newspaper. "The old lady of Market Street" was its nickname, and in both the affectionate and critical sense it was one that truly was deserved.

At the *Bulletin* there seemed to be a rule that murders and rapes and other catastrophes were to be written in lengthy and clinical detail, accounts exceeding one thousand words. But although the *Bulletin* had a group of fine writers and reporters, nearly all of them were governed by the strict *Bulletin* rules that resulted in stories being written in a dull way. A favorite technique was to begin the account with a description of the weather. When *Bulletin* readers saw the lede "It was sunny yesterday" or "It was rainy yesterday" they knew that somewhere in the ensuing paragraphs, probably pretty far down in the story, some calamity would be described. Some reporters, myself among them, would say that the *Bulletin* often confused dullness with respectability.

I was on night rewrite, working the 6 P.M. to 2 A.M. shift. One of the important duties of night rewrite was to write obituaries. We got the information on the telephone, sometimes from relatives who would call and sometimes from the funeral directors who would do the job for them.

The first week I was at the *Bulletin* I was ordered to take an obit from a grieving relative. Now mind you, I was a New Yorker and this was my first week ever in Philadelphia. So when the woman on the phone told me that the person who died was named "Clovia," or something like that, I asked her to spell the name.

She reacted with icy fury. "Clovia," she exclaimed. "Clovia. Where have you been living all your life?"

I tried to explain to her that I had been living in New York, but this did not seem to soothe her.

"Even in New York," she said, "they have surely heard of Clovia."

I assured her that I, at least, had not and asked

again—politely, I thought—if she would mind spelling the name.

"Clovia," she said. "Strawbridge and Clovia. Haven't you ever heard of Strawbridge and Clovia?"

"Madam," I said. "Could you please spell it?" The next sound I heard was the receiver slamming in my ear.

I hung up and strolled cautiously to the city desk. "Hey, Bill," I said to my night editor, Bill Grover. "You ever hear of Strawbridge and Clovia?"

"That's Strawbridge and Clothier," Grover said. "One of the biggest, if not the biggest, department stores in Philadelphia."

"Oh," I said. "I think the store just hung up on me." Then I told him what happened.

Grover turned a little pale. "It's Clothier," he said. "C-L-O-T-H-I-E-R. Did you get her number?" I had indeed followed regulations and gotten her phone number before all else. "You will call her back," he said. "You will hold your temper. You will get that obit."

I called the woman back and tried again to explain. It was not easy, but I managed to get her deceased brother's name and age. Then I asked cautiously if he had worked for the store or had some other profession.

"How dare you?" she said. "You have no right to ask about his occupation. My brother was at home. I shall report you to your employer. I shall ask him to dismiss you."

I wrote the obit as well as I could and it ran in the paper, on a page not very far from the big display ads the department store had placed in the *Bulletin*. Grover said he would do his best to defend me. Sure enough, the publisher was called, as was the editor. The city editor asked me what happened. A rumor had raced through the city room that the woman had called me anti-Semitic names, and he tried to find out about that. I told him that she had done no such thing but that she had grown angry when I tried to get the spelling of her brother's name.

The managing editor took his turn. He asked me if the rumor was true. I told him it was not. I was then reminded that I was still on trial at the *Bulletin*. I needed the job, but enough was enough. I told the editors that if they fired me then it would be for doing what I was supposed to be doing.

There was a high-level conference over my fate. They decided to keep me. Still, in the three years I lived in Philadelphia, I never shopped at Strawbridge and Clothier.

I wrote hundreds of obits after that, but none was quite so memorable—except, perhaps, the one that I began with this sentence: "John Doe, who as a trumpeter for the Fourth Cavalry chased Geronimo to the Mexican border before the turn of the century, received an arrow through his lungs and was sent home to die, did yesterday."

Not as good as the Chicago rewrite man who wrote, "Sam Smith, a window washer, died yesterday after he stepped back to admire his work." But not bad, either.

It had taken me nine months to get my first job as a reporter. I had come out of my draft time in the army equipped with a bachelor's degree in history from New York University and a master's in journalism from the University of Missouri, but the editors and newspaper employment offices were not impressed. Finally Oxie Reichler, the feisty editor of the *Herald Statesman* of Yonkers, New York, a daily with a circulation of fifty-five thousand, hired me for seventy dollars a week, warning me not to discuss my salary with other staffers because he was paying me more than anyone else.

I was thrilled with the job. I covered police matters and fires and the courts, wrote a business column, and was the sports editor one day a week. After a year, though, I felt it was time to move on, even though my salary had been upped to eighty-five dollars a week.

Now I was at the *Bulletin*. My assignments there were not limited to obituaries. The *Bulletin* gave me my first opportunity to cover politicians—in fact, my first opportunity to cover a president. Well, a former president, anyway.

It was the early 1960s and Dwight Eisenhower was coming to the Philadelphia suburbs, to the Valley Forge Military Academy, whose board had decided to honor him by naming a hall after him. I was given the assignment.

"What should I ask him?" I asked the city editor.

"Whatever the hell you want to ask him," he said. "Ask him," he suggested, "about wheat to Communist China."

The Chinese were suffering through a famine, and the big question in the United States was whether we should ship our surplus wheat there as a humanitarian gesture or, as the conservatives argued, let those lousy Commies starve.

I drove out to the campus trying to think of ways of phrasing this question. At the academy I walked with about six other local reporters to a given spot to meet the former president.

One of Eisenhower's aides approached us. "When he comes," he said, "there are to be no questions. Understand? No questions. If he wants to talk, he'll talk."

What nerve, I thought. Who is he to tell me I have to shut up? I watched with excitement as a limousine eased to a stop in front of us. Out stepped the old general, the old president, with a familiar smile crinkling his face. He waved at us for the photographers and then, without a word, turned to go into the building to see the place that would bear his name.

This would never do. "Mr. President," I shouted. "Do you think we should send wheat to Communist China?"

The smile left Ike's face and was replaced by a formidable scowl. "I won't answer that!" he shouted fiercely. "I won't answer that!"

What had I done? Would I be arrested? What would the Secret Service do? He was scaring the hell out of me. I jumped backward against my colleagues.

Eisenhower took a look at my face and walked toward me. He was smiling again. He put an arm around me. "You see, son," he explained, "I can't answer that. You have to understand. I was president of the United States. I haven't thought at all about whether we should send wheat. And if I gave an answer off the top of my head there could be worldwide reaction."

I nodded stiffly and said, "Yes, sir." Ike patted my shoulder and moved off. That evening I wrote strictly a feature story about the new Eisenhower Hall at Valley Forge Military Academy. No use getting people riled up about famines and wheat.

About a year later I got a lesson in political symbolism from another source. Dick Dilworth, the Democratic mayor of Philadelphia, was running for governor of Pennsylvania and Senator Joe Clark, the Pennsylvania Democrat, was running for reelection.

On a Saturday night I was assigned to follow Dilworth as he made the rounds from local union hall to local Democratic headquarters to local union hall. Clark was making the tour with him, but my editor told me that I should follow only Dilworth. The *Bulletin*, a Republican paper, had endorsed Clark's opponent, which I personally thought was a shame. As a private citizen I thought Clark was a fine senator and I admired him.

On this Saturday night, the mayor would speak first and then go to his next stop, leaving Clark behind to make a follow-up speech. At the first stop, when Dilworth left I obeyed orders and followed him. But at the second stop Clark caught up as Dilworth was halfway through his talk.

"Please stay," Clark asked me. "I have something very important that I must tell you."

"But I have to follow the mayor," I protested.

"Please," the senator said. "You simply have to stay."

Well, he was a U.S. senator and he was promising me something. Maybe a good story. So I let Dilworth leave and remained in my seat waiting for Clark to whisper some sort of revelation to me.

Instead the senator walked to the podium and began to speak. "I asked the reporter for the *Philadelphia Bulletin* to stay," the senator said, "because I have something very important to tell him. I want to tell him what a lousy, rotten newspaper he works for. What a terrible, awful. . . ."

I was sitting in the front. I promptly got up, turned around, and headed for the exit. It was a long walk because the hall filled with jeers and boos as I went.

But I knew *I* had the power of revenge. I would write about this outrage when I got back to the office, right?

Wrong. No, the city editor said, this is not the sort of thing to be printed in the *Bulletin*. So I did as I was told. I wrote about Richardson Dilworth instead. Joe Clark didn't get a mention.

2

BOBBY KENNEDY AND THE FLYING SOFAS

BY 1963 I WAS DESPERATE FOR A CHANGE. I ACHED FOR MORE important assignments, I yearned to be allowed to write stories in styles that were absolutely forbidden by the *Bulletin*. I wanted more bylines than the three or four a month granted by my editors. And I also missed New York.

I wrote to *The New York Times*, enclosing a few clippings. A reply came, written by the secretary to a *Times* editor. "Thank you for your interest in *The New York Times*," the answer went. "I regret to report that *The Times* is not interested in you."

One of my professors at New York University, Sid Towne, told me that there was an opening on the copy desk at *Newsday*. It meant I would be editing stories instead of writing them, but still, it would be a change and a return to the area I considered home.

I didn't know how much of a change until I took the train from Philadelphia to Long Island for my tryout. It was midafternoon. Except for one clerk and one editor, the newsroom in Garden City was deserted. "They've just gone out to play softball," said the lone editor on duty. "Dayside against nightside."

I couldn't believe it. I came all the way from Philadelphia for an appointed interview, and the guy who was supposed to talk to me was playing right field someplace? And who was putting out the paper?

"Here," the editor said, handing me some forms. "Sit down over there. You might as well take the writing test."

There were two stories to write. One was to create an article from a compilation of facts about a fictitious murder of a college coed. The other contained few facts—just directions to write an account about a successful businessman who was throwing away his career to buy a sailboat and set out to sea, wherever the wind might carry him.

I had plenty of practice in writing murders. For the other story I figured that if these people liked baseball so much, they really weren't all that interested in hiring me. Why not have a little fun myself? I wrote a parody of Alfred, Lord Tennyson's poem "Ulysses." I put the reporter in the story and had him ask the businessman why he was going to sea. The businessman answered with a slight misquotation of Tennyson's words: "To follow after a sinking star, to the utmost bounds of human thought." (It really goes: "To follow knowledge like a sinking star. Beyond the utmost bound of human thought.")

"The ball game's probably still on," the lone editor said when I'd finished. The copy boy drove me out to Eisenhower Park. Sure enough, Bill McIlwain, the managing editor, was playing right field for dayside. He interviewed me while dayside was at bat. When he was in the field, I sat and watched the game. Of course, one half inning I had to wait a little longer when he got on base with a single.

"I just hired that fellow last week," McIlwain said, pointing to a large young man playing left field for nightside. "Do you think you could hit like him?"

"No," I said. "But I think I can write and report pretty well." He asked me about my experience on the copy desk. I told him the truth—that I'd had hardly any.

McIlwain drove me to the Garden City train station after the game. I went back to Philadelphia thinking I had blown another one.

But a couple of days later McIlwain amazed me by phoning and asking me to come back for a tryout on the copy desk. "We really liked that writing test," he said. "Especially the piece on the businessman sailing away on his yacht."

Thank you, Alfred, Lord Tennyson.

I did miserably on the copy desk tryout. I was nervous, which made it especially hard to write clever headlines that fit. And I had little inclination to change perfectly good stories that reporters had worked so hard to write.

Worst of all, as I was working I knew I was a failure on the desk. After awhile the chief copy editor, Tony Insolia, told me to go to a typewriter and rewrite a wire service story. I wasn't sure of the *Newsday* style.

"What style do you want?" I asked, "*New York Times*? *Herald Trib*? *Journal American*?"

"Sort of like the *Times*," Tony said. I produced a straight, solemn story.

"No, no," Insolia said. "Can't you make it livelier?"

"Do you want *Herald Trib* or *Journal American*?" I asked.

"Definitely not *Journal American*," Insolia said.

So I pepped up the story to a moderate degree. "Better," Insolia said. "But still not quite right."

"Hey," I said, "you may not think you want *Journal American*. But that's what you want. I'll give you *Journal American*." And I sat down and wrote the liveliest—but most accurate—account that I could.

"Okay," Insolia said after reading it. "That's what we want, exactly."

"*Journal American*," I said. "You want *Journal American*."

McIlwain told me he would call with his verdict the next day and he was true to his word. "You're right," he said.

"You are a terrible deskman. But you're a pretty good writer. I'll hire you as a reporter if you want."

So in early July 1963 I came to *Newsday*. It was great fun. It was a place filled with talent and with people trying to pretend it was the living inspiration for *The Front Page*. Some of the desk drawers held scotch and bourbon as well as pencils, and there seemed to be parties in the newsroom just about every Friday.

One Christmas was celebrated for about two weeks, with each department—ranging from editorial to sports to society to the library—hosting a daily party to which all other departments were invited. This was climaxed with a grand paper-wide get-together that featured a wonderful snowball fight—inside the newsroom.

That was only one aspect of *Newsday*. There were also a crusading spirit and a striving to report and write the best stories in the business. Once, when I wrote an accurate account of a tense civil rights confrontation in Hempstead, Long Island, and one of the white participants protested my style of reporting, the attitude of the editors was quite different from those on some other papers. "Pretty strong stuff," the assistant managing editor, Al Marlens, said of my story. "But good. I sent that guy [the complainer] a nasty note."

Mainly, though, I was the funny machine. Good enough, yet I wanted to do other things as well. So in the fall of 1964, when Robert F. Kennedy was trying to take away Kenneth Keating's New York Senate seat, I asked if I could take a turn in covering the campaign. Permission was given.

It was very exciting. Kennedy was the brooding keeper of the flame, the solace of a nation still in shock and still mourning the murder of his brother John. It was hard for me to try to look calm and a bit bored, which I thought was probably the proper pose for a veteran, when I picked up Bob Kennedy with the political reporters from the other papers at Butler Aviation over at LaGuardia Airport. We got on board the *Caroline,* the then-famous jet-prop that had been JFK's plane. Averell Harriman, the distinguished diplomat, former New York governor, and advisor to Democratic presidents, got on the same day. He walked up the plane's steps toward Bob Kennedy, who was waiting at the door where JFK had once stood. Memories twisted Harriman's tongue. "Hello, Jack," Harriman said to Bobby.

Part of the cabin of the *Caroline* was fitted out like a living room, with sofas and individual chairs. There was one big easy chair set off from the others, a solitary seat for the master of the aircraft.

At night Kennedy would take off his jacket and put on one of the sweaters that had belonged to his dead brother. The sweaters were too big and hung in folds around him. Kennedy would sit in the easy chair, put his hand on his chin, and stare silently out the window. Then, suddenly, he would turn from the window to his watching cabin mates. He would either begin to speak to all of us or with a brisk gesture summon an advisor or a reporter to his side.

He didn't have any Secret Service protection. One of his press secretaries, Ed Guthman, and one of his retainers, a big guy named Dean Markham, were his bodyguards. Kennedy would ride in a convertible—on his orders preferably white, preferably a Ford or a Chevy, but never, never a high-priced car—and Guthman and Markham would lie belly down on the top of the trunk, hanging on to the backseat with the wind whipping through their hair and ballooning their suits, sometimes flipping up Dean's jacket and showing the pistol on his hip that he kept denying he carried.

Everywhere great throngs would gather to greet him. The campaign would come into some town with a population of twenty thousand, and thirty thousand would be there to listen to what he had to say, to see the brother of the assassinated president. Sometimes they would tear at his clothing as if he were a rock idol. Kennedy would talk while standing on top of a car. Markham would crouch behind him, holding onto the back of Kennedy's belt to make sure he wouldn't get pulled into the crowd by an overeager admirer.

More than a few times, though, the crowd was simply too close, dozens of them reaching out to the candidate in their emotion, clutching at his shoes, his trouser cuffs. Kennedy would escape then on his own, a political Errol Flynn leaping from parked car top to parked car top as he fled—leaving a dent in every roof.

"I think we can do better," he would say in his flat Boston accent, sticking his thumb out of an otherwise clenched fist for emphasis. He always ended his standard stump speech by quoting George Bernard Shaw's lines, "You see things and you say, why? But I dream things that never were and I say, why not?"

When he broke into that, the reporters would break for the press bus. One day Kennedy wound up his talk with, "You see things and you say, why? But I dream things that never were and I say, everybody head for the bus."

Harriman was on most of the flights. Once, we switched to a forty-passenger helicopter because airports at our destinations had runways too short for the *Caroline*. In one of those cities the helicopter broke down, and there was a wait of a couple of hours to get it fixed.

We all went to the airport bar. Harriman was a multimillionaire with a reputation of being tight with his money. But that night he announced that he would treat. Cheerfully he paid the bill for at least forty people and then turned to leave. Marianne Means, the Hearst reporter, stopped him.

"Tip," she whispered to Harriman. The former governor, former ambassador, took out his wallet again and laid

a bill on the bar. Then he looked at Marianne question-
ingly. She shook her head no. He put another bill on the
bar and looked up again. Again she shook her head. The
bills kept coming from Harriman's wallet until finally
Marianne nodded yes. And then we left.

In this campaign there weren't many issues. Keating
tried to make an argument that Kennedy was a carpetbagger from Massachusetts, coming into a state where he
didn't live to claim a Senate seat from a true New Yorker.
Kennedy kept saying he could do better.

I knew what he meant. I, for one, felt I was doing better
in my assignments because I was covering him. After two
weeks, however, I thought my political assignment was
over. But the editors let me continue, switching me to
Keating for a week.

With Keating, every afternoon at about four o'clock his
motorcade would stop. The senator would hustle off to a
phone in an office, a hotel, a gas station, even to a pay
phone on the street.

I was told that this was his daily call to Herb Brownell,
the old Eisenhower attorney general, who would counsel
him on what to do next. Marquis Childs, the great
columnist who was traveling with Kennedy, would shake
his head over Keating's efforts and ask, "How can you
fight a ghost?"

When I finished my week with Keating, I was told to
return to Kennedy. The first day back, Ed Guthman came
over to me. "Bob would like you to ride in the car with him
to the next town," he said.

"Gee," I said, "that's terrific. But I don't have anything
to ask him at the moment. Couldn't we save this at least
until the afternoon?"

"Now," Guthman said.

I got inside the convertible. "Hi," I said.

"Welcome back," Kennedy said.

"Thanks," I said. There was a silence that seemed to last for long minutes.

"Well?" Kennedy finally said.

"Well what?" I said.

"Well," Kennedy said, "How was it?"

"How was what?" I asked.

"Keating," Kennedy exclaimed in exasperation. "How was Keating?"

"Oh," I said, "he's just fine."

"But what's he doing?" Kennedy asked.

"What you read in the papers," I said. Then I told him the truth—that I could not and would not inform on either Keating or Kennedy, except in the articles I would write.

Later Kennedy, who was renting a house in Glen Cove on Long Island, told me he never read the Long Island newspaper, my newspaper, *Newsday*. "The carrier came around trying to sell me a subscription," he said proudly. "I ran him off."

That night, when the *Caroline* returned to Butler, I drove back to the office and collected a copy of every *Newsday* for the past two weeks. I put them in the trunk of my car. A couple of nights later I got my chance. The plane came back to Butler. My car was parked near Kennedy's limo. "Wait just a minute," I called to Kennedy. I ran to my car trunk and took out the stack of *Newsday*s and then hustled over to Kennedy.

"Hold out your arms," I commanded. Automatically, Kennedy obeyed. I stuck the stack of *Newsday*s in his hands. "Here," I said. "Great reading. Lots about you in there. Hope you take out a subscription. Good night."

I left him as his aides clustered around him, trying to relieve him of the pile of papers. The next day on the *Caroline*, Kennedy came over to me. "Don't do that again," he said. "I bought a subscription."

Usually in a political campaign it's the challenger who wants to debate the incumbent. Merely appearing on the same platform with the officeholder will elevate the person who is trying to take the job away. But Kennedy, the one-time attorney general, the brother of the slain president, the leader of a great and martyred family, didn't need that kind of device.

In this case it was the white-haired senator, Kenneth Keating, with his poorly fitted dentures bouncing around in his mouth, with his party bouncing around as the minority in Congress, and burdened by Barry Goldwater as its presidential candidate, who was in need of a lift. So Keating kept after Kennedy, trying to get a televised debate. And Kennedy, ahead in all of the polls, kept dodging.

To Kennedy's way of thinking, a debater had to be dull in order to be successful. "You should never win or lose a debate," he once told me on board the *Caroline*. "You should either barely win it or barely lose it." It was his idea that a convincing victory only created sympathy for one's defeated opponent.

As an illustration he pointed to Pierre Salinger, JFK's old press secretary and then an appointed senator from California, trying to get elected in his own right in a battle against the movie actor and song and dance man, George Murphy. "Look at Salinger," Kennedy said with contempt. "He knocked George Murphy all over the television studio and turned him into a candidate."

In New York Keating was getting desperate. Finally he bought thirty minutes' worth of prime time from CBS and announced that he would debate Kennedy. If Kennedy wouldn't show up, he said, he would debate an empty chair. Kennedy still wouldn't give an answer, but he declared that he was outraged. He promptly muscled the network into selling him thirty minutes of prime time directly after Keating was scheduled to speak.

On the afternoon of the appointed day, Ed Guthman and Debs Meyers, the other Kennedy press secretary,

quietly passed the word to the regular reporters covering
the campaign: be at the studio early, very early.

So, well before even Keating was to speak, the Kennedy
reporters were gathering at CBS, a warren of parallel
corridors and intersecting halls in midtown Manhattan.
The crowd doubled when the Keating reporters showed
up and began mingling with the Kennedy group—about
fifty in all.

Less than five minutes before Keating was to go on the
air at 7:30 P.M. and begin his debate with an empty chair,
the elevator door on the third floor opened. Out walked
Kennedy, Guthman, and several other aides.

"Please," a CBS producer said to Kennedy. "Your studio
isn't on this floor. Please go up."

Kennedy ignored him. He turned to me. "Where is
Senator Keating?" he demanded. I gestured toward the
correct corridor. Kennedy beckoned to me with his hand
and began to walk in that direction. I followed and the
other reporters fell in behind.

"You can't go there," the producer said. "Senator Keating is on the air."

And so he was, with an empty chair to symbolize his
opponent's absence and his friend and fellow Republican
Senator Jacob Javits in the studio to introduce him with a
powerful endorsement and a rebuke to the carpetbagger
from Massachusetts.

In the corridor two CBS guards blocked the way, making Kennedy and his entourage stop in their tracks. "You
can't go there," the producer repeated.

At that the burly Guthman grunted, lowered his
shoulders, and charged. He caught a guard on each
shoulder. Suddenly there were two private cops on the
floor. Kennedy was following Guthman, and the reporters
were following Kennedy down the hall. The cops screamed
vows of vengeance, and Guthman snorted his contempt.

In a couple of minutes the mob reached the studio door.

There was a sign on it reading PLEASE KEEP OUT. NO VISITORS. KEATING. Through the glass we could see Keating speaking and pointing at the empty chair, which had another sign on it. ROBERT F. KENNEDY that sign read.

Kennedy tried the door. It was locked. He pounded on the door, the television cameras recording his every knock. "Open up, Senator Keating," Kennedy shouted. "Open up. I'm here to debate you."

Richard Forsling, from the CBS studio legal staff, told Kennedy he couldn't go in, that it was a private show paid for by Keating. "I'm here," Kennedy said. "It's 7:30. I'm ready to go in."

Forsling told him that would be impossible. "Then this is a dishonest show," Kennedy said. "I'm here. Keating said he wanted to debate. He's going to have that empty chair in there. I want to fill it." He turned to the TV cameras behind him in the corridor and spread his arms. "I can't understand why he doesn't open the door," he complained. "I'm here to debate him."

"This is the worst day of my life," a CBS producer moaned, actually wringing his hands in his despair.

The reporters had no sympathy for his grief, though. We demanded that when Keating was finished speaking he should be made to come out and explain why he hadn't opened the door for Kennedy. The producer assured us that this would be done. After some more pounding for the benefit of the television cameras, Kennedy retreated and went up to his studio to make his own paid television speech.

Nearly all of the reporters, however, stayed near the Keating studio to await the words of the senator when he finished. CBS officials again promised they would make sure he would appear before us. We paced up and down. Suddenly, as I walked the corridor and looked down the maze of halls, I saw him.

Keating! An elderly man with two aides behind him,

tiptoeing with big silent steps toward an exit. They looked like the Marx Brothers at CBS.

"There he goes," I shouted. And the chase was on. Like mobile cannon, the shoulder-held TV cameras thundered along the corridor, dozens of reporters shouting and running behind. But I, who had seen him first, was leading the mob.

Keating and his men broke into a dead run. The two aides dropped behind. There was furniture against the corridor walls, easy chairs and sofas.

The Keating defenders were only two in number but they were young and powerful. They began flinging the furniture at us. A wooden-armed hardback chair came sailing down the corridor. I dodged it and kept running. I hurdled the next object, a small easy chair. But a spinning sofa was too large a missile for me to avoid. I fell over its top, somersaulting and landing on my back. I lay there without much regret, for I was out of breath, watching my thinner, more nimble, colleagues leap over the sofa and me like cattle maddened into a stampede. I didn't really have to get up because I saw my *Newsday* colleague assigned to Keating, Robert Caro (he later became famous as the biographer of Robert Moses and Lyndon Johnson) successfully soar over the sofa and rumble along the corridor after the senator.

I got up. One of Keating's aides was on the floor, bleeding from a cut across his nose caused by a wayward television camera. I helped him to his feet and to a water fountain.

Around the corner came Ethel Kennedy—a very pregnant Ethel Kennedy. "Goodness," she said. "Whatever got into Senator Keating? He was running and he nearly knocked me down. And he didn't even say hello."

That was the end for Keating. If he had had any hope, his performance after his empty-chair debate had finished it. Afterward, Kennedy went out to Toots Shor's restaurant to celebrate. Toots himself greeted him. "My, you're a little fella," Shor said to Kennedy. "Not tall like your brother."

Kennedy didn't even wince. "And I'm even shorter than that," he said. "I wear lifts." He picked up his foot to show Shor the cleverly thickened bottom of a shoe. Everybody laughed and went into the club for a drink.

The event really scared Keating. He did what is common practice today but was fairly unusual back then. He assigned an aide to spy on Kennedy so that he wouldn't be surprised again by any sneak attack.

The Keating spy was a young man who had scarcely turned twenty. He didn't try to infiltrate the Kennedy organization but just followed the motorcade in his own car as best he could. I knew him from my coverage of the Keating campaign but I never told the Kennedy people that they were being tracked.

But one night, at a rally in Westchester, the Kennedy motorcade was leaving in a hurry. From the press bus I saw that the Keating spy's car was hemmed in. He tried to back out and smashed into the auto behind him. He tried to pull forward and smashed into the auto in front of him. A policeman was going toward him. Drivers were screaming at him.

"Stop the bus," I shouted. "We've got to save the Keating spy." Once I explained what I was talking about, the motorcade was halted. Kennedy aides walked over and pulled the Keating man away from the policeman and the angry onlookers. They put him on the press bus. "It's easier for you this way," a Kennedy man explained to the secret agent.

Eventually Keating did get a debate with Kennedy, but it was on the radio, not television. And just as Kennedy said he would, the Democratic challenger was able to make it a dull dialogue indeed. He barely won, or maybe he barely lost.

But it was unimportant. On election day more New York voters cast their ballots for Lyndon Johnson than for his Democratic teammate Kennedy. But Kennedy still was a big winner, whipping Keating by more than 700,000 votes.

I thought covering politics was wonderful. It was a lot more fun than doing things like being the man in the woods or making dandelion wine. And it was at least as significant.

The next year, 1965, *Newsday* sent me to Albany to help cover the state legislature. And at the end of the session I was made the paper's political writer for Nassau County. It was an assignment with a big raise and it was about politics, but it was not one that I relished. I'd had a taste of covering a campaign of national interest—in fact, the editors had even given me a week at the top with the Goldwater presidential campaign—and I wanted more.

3

TO WASHINGTON

ALL THE SAME, I WORKED HARD AT BEING THE NASSAU COUNTY political reporter. It was an important beat for the paper and I was proud of my responsibilities. But frankly, I wasn't enjoying them very much. Covering meetings of the Nassau County Board of Supervisors may be important to *Newsday*'s readers, but to me they were less interesting than sessions of the New York State Legislature. And I knew that sessions of the U.S. Congress had to be still more interesting—to say nothing of the excitement of covering the president. Furthermore, I was working about sixty hours a week.

Finally I figured out that this wasn't making too much sense for anyone. I asked to be relieved of my beat. The editors didn't seem surprised and they didn't object. They put me on general assignment. It had been my move, but of course I felt that I had been demoted. I wasn't even a funny machine any more, evolving instead into an irritated and bored general assignment reporter.

Still, even a bored reporter has his moments. For example, when in October 1965 Pope Paul VI became the first pontiff ever to travel to the United States, I was assigned to cover him. But this time I wasn't alone. The editors were so excited about the pope that I was one of about forty-five *Newsday* reporters detailed to the visit. For any newspaper, this was an army.

My main job was to go to the United Nations and watch him there, then write a feature story of my choice.

He was going to give the children attending the international United Nations school a special audience, and I really wanted to watch that. But the UN press office said that all reporters would be barred from that event. One press officer did add, with a wink, that if I did manage to get in I would be welcome.

There didn't seem to be much chance of that happening. The police were, of course, especially worried about guarding the pope. And when police get worried about security, they take it out on the reporters. After all, although as far as I know physical assaults by reporters on public figures are not exactly commonplace, we are the only members of the public the cops can control. So I guess, like the rest of us, the police go with what they can get. And what they could get was us.

So when the great day finally arrived I still couldn't figure out how to get into the papal audience. I went down to the UN with more press ID tags around my neck than I could count. Among the most important were my Nassau County police pass, which I hoped would be honored by other police forces, and my United Nations pope pass, which let me into the UN building.

There were so many reporters inside that the police had also given us color-coded badges that limited us to the places we could stand. My area was next to the up escalator on the main floor. I was at liberty to walk anywhere in a space about ten yards long and three yards wide. After that I would cross into an area of forbidden color. I didn't think that my space would make much of a feature story.

No one seemed to know if the pope would even approach our space. All the same, there I was, pad and pen in hand, together with about fifty other reporters, all of us staring at the unpopulated up escalator while being held back by grim-looking police and security officers.

And then I saw them, the children of the United Nations school. They looked like fifth and sixth graders, freshly scrubbed preteens forming up in a long single line to go up the escalator to meet the pope. Behind every tenth child there stood an adult, presumably a teacher. Each grownup had a hand on the shoulder of the child in front of him. But not one of the adults, and not one of the children, was wearing an identification badge.

I looked again. The last child in line had no grownup behind him. I ripped my press badge–laden chain from my neck and stuffed the plastic into my jacket pocket. I tucked away my pen and pad. In front of me the police had turned their backs and were looking at the schoolchildren as well.

I ducked under the rope, circled around the mob. The feet of the last child were reaching the escalator. I walked briskly up behind him and clamped a hand on his shoulder. Startled, he turned around. "Hi," I said.

"Hi," he said.

"Eyes front," I said. He obeyed.

And up the escalator we went, unchallenged and triumphant. We marched down a corridor together into a room filled with UN officials and police. I eased away from the children and stood next to the adults.

Within a few moments Pope Paul made his entrance. He spoke kindly to the children in English with a heavy Italian accent, telling them about the things they should do to be good boys and girls.

He was charming. He was witty. But I would never remember all of this. There was nothing for it. My hand went to my jacket pocket and removed my notebook. I took out a pen and began to take notes.

But almost immediately, the implements of my trade

revealed me for what I was, a reporter, and therefore an uninvited, unwanted presence. A UN guard spotted me. He nudged a colleague. Silently and swiftly they closed in, bent on the instant removal of this danger to the audience—me. I was a dead reporter.

Then came a whispered voice. My friend from the UN press office, dignified, moustached, magnificent in a pinstripe suit, the most diplomatic-looking spokesman I have ever seen, moved even more swiftly to my side. "Glad to see you could make it," he whispered, holding out his hand for me to shake.

The guards paused. Grandly, he waved them away. So I whispered my thanks, took my notes, and covered the rest of the audience in peace. What a scoop! No other reporter had this! I exulted over my exclusive even though that silent little hullabaloo had seriously interfered with my notetaking.

After it was over, I went back downstairs and joined the other reporters in my ten-by-three-yard space. "Hey," one of them said. "Where'd you disappear to? You really missed something. They took us into a room and let us watch the audience the kids had with the pope on closed circuit TV."

Such adventures did not occur often enough for me. I wanted more fun from the business of being a reporter. And the most fun I'd ever had was covering the Kennedy-Keating campaign. Even before that I had decided I wanted to get to Washington some day and write about the people who controlled the country. It seemed to me that nothing could be more exciting than reporting about the most powerful politicians in America. As a general assignment reporter, I wasn't writing about important deeds or events very often. My job seemed so humdrum that it was only reinforcing hope for a change.

Once a reporter gets bored with the job, he may as well get into another line of work. Reporters may speak with slow southern drawls or rapid fire New York accents, but they are brothers and sisters in their drive to get the best possible story. Without that drive, the good stories and the elation at getting them simply disappear.

And on Long Island, I was getting bored. A change was necessary. To me there was, and is, nothing like covering politicians, an assignment which tickles a reporter's sense of cynicism and presents rich opportunities to write what really happens.

My friend Bob Caro, who had just been assigned to the Washington bureau, called me up. He told me that he had won a fellowship and was going to use the stipend to write a book about Robert Moses, the man who had built more highways and parks in New York than anyone in history. That meant, he said, that he would be leaving *Newsday*.

Bob informed me that he had yet to tell the editors. "Why don't you tell them again that you want to come to Washington?" Caro suggested. "Tell them that today. And tomorrow, I'll call and tell them I'm leaving."

And that's the way it was done. A couple of days after Caro had submitted his resignation, the editors called me in and asked if I still was eager to go to Washington. Of course I said yes.

But by the time I arrived, the editors at *Newsday* had decided to clean house at the Washington bureau, which gave an important newcomer to the paper the opportunity to shape his staff in the capital.

For Captain Harry—the late Miss P.'s husband, Harry F. Guggenheim—had just hired Bill Moyers, Lyndon Johnson's press secretary, as editor in chief of *Newsday* to bring some national renown to the paper. It was in some ways a strange move. *Newsday* was a liberal paper on its editorial pages, but Guggenheim was a conservative. He and Miss P. had had deep political differences—to the point that sometimes there were warring editorials on either side of the page, one written by her and the other by him.

And now he had hired a liberal to run the paper. Moyers would not and did not change his principles for Guggenheim—and Guggenheim, at first at any rate, let him go his way apparently unchallenged. Moyers made it plain that he wanted to change the paper in several ways.

He had an opportunity in Washington. There was only one other reporter in the bureau when I arrived, Martin Schram, and he had been ordered to Washington at the same time I had.

It was 1967. The bureau was on the sixth floor of the National Press Building at Fourteenth and F streets. There were individual offices for at least a half dozen reporters—a posh setup for newsies used to sharing desks in a city room. But Miss P. had wanted the bureau to be special. She obviously had wanted *Newsday* to look as good or better than any other newspaper bureau in Washington. And the National Press Building, she felt, was a star-status address for a newspaper.

The National Press Club itself was on the top floor. *Newsday* paid for the club memberships of all of its reporters in the bureau—all except the women, that is. That was because women were barred from membership, not even able to get a drink at the bar. On the door of the bar was a little brass plaque that made it seem as if one was entering a lavatory: MEN ONLY.

I knew absolutely nothing about Washington when I arrived. I knew I would need press passes but I wasn't sure how to get them. I didn't know that every department of the federal government had its own telephone book that the public could buy. Except for the Long Island congressmen and Senator Robert Kennedy, I knew no one in power.

In the office I would put in calls to the staffs of House members and senators and wait for them to call me back.

I waited for a very long time. Apparently *Newsday* did not have the influence in Washington that it had in New York.

So I used the technique that reporters who do not work for *The New York Times*, the *Washington Post*, or the *Wall Street Journal* are all compelled to employ on far too many occasions—phoning again and again until the secretaries and clerks were driven at last to ask the press assistants and legislative aides to return the calls. That was a system with mixed results. One press secretary to a southern senator who was nettled into getting on the phone informed me that I would have to make an appointment to call him.

Reporters are sometimes branded as putting a liberal slant on stories about politicians. This is absolutely false. What we really care about is access. Talk to a reporter, give him an inside story, and that newsie is in ecstacy. It doesn't matter if the source is a conservative or a liberal, as long as real news is involved.

The favor is almost sure to be returned. The source is likely to be quoted—or not quoted, if that is his pleasure—in one or more subsequent stories. Of course, if the source becomes involved in some sort of wrongdoing, all trade-offs are canceled. When that happens, it does the politician who is under a cloud little good to have been a source. A reporter's gratitude does not extend that far.

It is much easier for reporters to cover politicians than anyone else. We need each other, the pols for publicity and the reporters for news. And certainly, though sometimes we hate each other, more frequently we get to like each other—even to admire each other. It would be a poor reporter, though, who would allow his personal feelings to get in the way of any sort of a significant story.

As the years went by, I learned that the relationships between reporters and nearly all politicians change quickly with the changes in professional circumstances. There are senators and White House aides who will return calls to reporters from *The New York Times* or the *Washington Post*, but rarely perform such favors for the newsies representing lesser organizations.

Reporters for regional newspapers do manage to establish good relationships with politicians, but it takes a lot of effort. And repeatedly, reporters who have moved up to big-time newspapers and networks tell stories of how formerly distant politicians suddenly became warm and confiding dinner companions. Most but not all of those reporters understand that their cordial rapport with many of the powerful would vanish in an instant if they lost their jobs.

In 1967, however, I knew none of this. I was a Washington reporter in the worst fix possible. I was a Washington reporter with practically no Washington contacts at all.

In my first week in Washington, though, I did get one very important call. It was from my new boss, Bill Moyers. President Johnson was to hold a press conference in the afternoon. Moyers asked me to please cover it and write a story comparing how Johnson handled himself now, to how he had handled himself at previous conferences, when the Vietnam War had not beset him so.

It was a nice idea but there was a small problem. I had never been to a Lyndon B. Johnson press conference. Nevertheless, I hustled to the White House, where I tried very quickly to make friends with the regular correspondents there. I asked them how LBJ had behaved at previous press conferences. Apparently it wasn't something they had really thought about. They were helpful, but only a little.

I covered the conference. I remember Johnson prancing back and forth on a stage as he answered questions. But I wasn't sure if that was different from the way he had behaved on other occasions. Was this simply an old habit? Had he taken shorter steps at previous press conferences? Had he stood still? Could the presidential trot be a sign of nerves? Impatience? A full bladder? I went back to the office in a sweat.

I called up Al Marlens and asked him what to do. "Go with what you know," he said. "Forget comparisons. Just write a story about the press conference and make it colorful."

I followed Marlens's advice. As stories go, it wasn't much, but it was prominently displayed in *Newsday*. I heard not a word from Moyers directly. But the next week, in the press section of one of the national news magazines, there was an item about how Moyers was doing in his new job at *Newsday*.

It quoted him as saying that he was doing fine but that he still had to convince some reporters to obey his orders. Why, just last week he had told one of his Washington correspondents to go over to the White House and write a comparison story about the president, and the correspondent had ignored him, simply hadn't done it.

But the day after the item appeared, Moyers did phone me—to say he was sorry about it and to listen sympathetically to my explanation as to why I hadn't been able to follow his instructions.

Still, for all my inexperience in Washington and despite my flubbing of that assignment, the editors seemed to have great faith in my abilities. Only a week or so after the White House incident, Marlens called with new orders. The Johnson administration had negotiated a treaty with Panama on the Panama Canal.

The canal was always a touchy subject for the American people, and Johnson, for the time being, was keeping the terms of the treaty secret until he decided to submit it to the Senate for ratification. "You've got to get that treaty," Marlens told me.

I didn't know what to do. I made the only move left to me. Despite my previous failures on the telephone, I decided to call up the negotiators and ask them directly. And this I did.

"This is Mike Waldman with *Newsday*," I said on my first call. "I would like the terms of the Panama Canal treaty."

To my amazement I was immediately put through to the negotiator. I repeated my request. "Certainly," the negotiator answered.

Certainly? *Certainly*? This was incredible. "Just begin at the beginning," I said.

The negotiator gave the proviso that the information had to be attributed only to "sources" and then talked away. For more than an hour I took notes. Finally, when there seemed nothing more to offer, the negotiator said, "I have just one favor to ask."

"Anything," I said, "anything."

"Could I have an advance copy of the magazine?" the negotiator asked.

Newsday. *Newsweek*. Thank God nobody knew who we were. "Sorry," I said. "But you'll get a copy of the paper as soon as we get it here in Washington."

The next day *Newsday* led with my exclusive. But there are some disadvantages to anonymity as well. *Newsday* was important for state and local coverage, but when it came to national exclusives, in 1967 we were all but ignored by our competitors. Nobody outside of *Newsday* paid any attention to my scoop.

A week and a half later, a reporter for the *Chicago Tribune* got the treaty story on his own. His account was flashed all over the country by television, radio, and other newspapers. All of them credited the *Tribune* with the exclusive.

A couple of months later, though, a reporter came to the bureau who didn't need any kind of mix-up to get an exclusive. Flora Lewis, a world-class correspondent with a reputation to match, was hired by *Newsday* and sent to Washington.

Flora wasn't here but a couple of weeks when she got an interview with General Edward Lansdale, an officer so well known that he was the model for the protagonist of the novel *The Ugly American*. Moreover, he was considered to be the American who knew Southeast Asia best. Lansdale told Flora what he had never told any other reporter up to then—that in his opinion, the Vietnam War was unwinnable. Out of his mouth and under the Flora Lewis byline it was a sensational story, quoted everywhere.

The day after it appeared, Flora was out of the office and on to some other assignment. I was in the bureau and was designated to be the "garbage man." On newspapers the garbage man is the reporter who must write the follow-up on a big story—particularly if the follow-up isn't considered very important.

I was told to get a reaction from the White House and from the general himself. I called Lansdale, actually got him on the phone, and secured a few relatively meaningless observations. He had, after all, given the good stuff to Flora and there wasn't much left for him to say on the issue.

Then I decided to go all the way. Instead of phoning the White House press office I looked up the number of the National Security Council, that White House body that meets to advise the president on matters of intelligence and foreign policy. I called and asked if there might be a council spokesperson who could get back to me concerning a follow-up to the Lansdale story. I left my number with the sure feeling that no one would call back.

I was wrong. Within an hour the call was returned. It wasn't any assistant press aide who was calling, either. "Hold on for Mr. Rostow," the voice from the National Security Council said.

Walt Rostow? Walt Rostow himself? He was the president's national security advisor, the boss of the National Security Council, one of the president's closest aides. This was like never meeting Henry Kissinger and having him call you back; like not knowing Lieutenant Colonel Robert McFarlane and having him call you back.

"Thank you so very much, Mr. Rostow," I began.

But Rostow was not a happy man and he scarcely let me finish my brief expression of appreciation. "I am really browned off at you guys," he shouted. And then he began to holler that Flora's story was all wrong, that Lansdale would never say the things he had said, that his pal Bill Moyers, now my editor, had done him wrong by publishing the story.

I tried to tell him that he was only talking to the garbage man, but he wouldn't listen. So I figured, what the hell. I told him I had talked to Lansdale and that he had told me the same story he had told to Flora. I told him that if he was that mad, he should call up Moyers himself and tell him how he felt. What's more, I supplied him with the number.

"I will never, never give you a story again," Rostow said. "I will never talk to you again."

"Mr. Rostow," I said. "You never gave me a story before. In fact, you never called me before. So there's no loss."

On that cordial note we hung up.

But Rostow did give me another story. On Halloween afternoon, a White House aide who was a friend of mine tipped me that Lyndon Johnson planned to announce that night that he would stop the bombing of Hanoi and that the United States would meet the North Vietnamese in peace talks in Paris.

Our paper had long since been published that day, but I called the city desk and our man in Saigon was contacted so that he could get started on a story there. Our small forces in Washington were deployed to various positions. I was sent to the White House.

After the president made his speech, I was taken with the other reporters at the White House downstairs to the best available briefing room then in existence—the White House Theater. In 1968 it was a barren, cream-colored room in the White House basement with folding chairs and a wall texture that suggested it might best be used as a Laundromat.

Walt Rostow briefed us on the coming negotiations and then asked for questions. After awhile I raised my hand and was recognized. "Are these going to be four-power talks or two-power talks?" I asked. "I mean, will it be the United States and the South Vietnamese and the North Vietnamese and the Vietcong? Or will it just be the United States and the North Vietnamese?"

Rostow roared with laughter, but he was the only one. "Modalities," he chortled. "He's asking about modalities." Washington and Hanoi then proceeded to spend the next year arguing about the shape of the table to be used by the negotiators.

On April 4, 1968, Martin Luther King, Jr., was murdered in Memphis, Tennessee. Schram was ordered to Memphis to cover the events there and I was told to stay in Washington. At the time, we had a bureau chief, Nick Thimmesch, hired from *Time* magazine. Nick was not around that day, however, and Schram and I were taking our directions from Long Island.

As word of the assassination spread, the despair and rage of the federal city's majority black population boiled over. Mobs of black citizens roamed the streets. Stores were set on fire, windows were smashed, and there was widespread looting. Merchandise of all sorts that wasn't carted away was tossed on the streets in front of the shattered storefronts.

All night the riots continued, but in the early morning hours the city seemed to recede into an uneasy calm. The rioters went home to sleep, the fire department quenched the flames. But in the late morning of the following day the rage was building again.

Except for a receptionist, I was alone in the bureau, in a front office, looking out of a window. In the streets below, police cars equipped with loudspeakers began to drive up and down, broadcasting the ominous news to pedestrians, civil servants, and store owners: the rioters were coming again.

"Get off the streets," the loudspeakers boomed. "Go home."

There was panic on the sidewalks, in the office buildings, and in the downtown stores that were still untouched. Everyone—black and white—seemed to be running for their cars, locking the doors to their shops, looking for shelter somewhere, anywhere. The streets soon were jammed with autos heading for the suburbs, a mammoth rush hour at noon.

In the *Newsday* office the telephone rang. It was the day editor, whose name I will not reveal to save him from embarrassment. "I want you to go to the Capitol," he told me, "and interview congressmen and senators about last night's riot. Ask them what they think about last night, what should be done."

"Harry," I said (not his real name), "I don't think that's a very good idea. I was about to go out and cover today's riot."

"What riot?" the editor answered. "I've been looking at the wires [the stories on the AP and UPI tickers] and they don't say anything about a riot."

Just then, from the bureau window I saw the mob turn the corner, only about three blocks north on Fourteenth Street. Sitting at the window I could hear their shouts, see them breaking windows as they came. A line of outnumbered policemen retreated in front of them. Sirens split the air. And directly below, the loudspeakers were still telling everybody to go home.

"Wait a minute, Harry," I said. I opened the bureau's sixth floor window and dangled the telephone receiver down the outside wall as far as it would go. I let it hang there for about thirty seconds and then hauled it back inside.

"Did you hear that, Harry?" I asked. "Yeah," the editor answered. "It sounded awful."

"That's the riot," I told him.

Harry lost his temper. "There is no riot," he snapped. "Don't you understand? The wires say there is no riot, so there *is* no riot. Get your ass up on the hill right now."

I gave up and went. I put on my old raincoat and made my way outside. I threaded my way through the rioters, saying "Excuse me," nodding at a few angry faces and trying to ignore the hoots of "honky." I got to the parking garage where I kept my car. The guys at the garage assured me that it would be open when I got back.

I drove up Pennsylvania Avenue. It was only a little past midday, but I was in the middle of that terrible traffic jam of middle-class government employees trying to flee downtown Washington. In front of me I could see the Capitol.

The burning had begun again, and the red and gold flames danced behind the white iron dome. The fires were really a few blocks from the Capitol, but in the distance it appeared that the great symbol of the United States government itself was aflame.

In front of the National Archives the traffic jam brought me to a complete stop. I had the radio tuned to the all-news station. "Report of a sniper on the National Archives roof," the radio reporter said.

I ducked under my steering wheel and peeked up. I couldn't see a thing. I didn't hear any shots. But I scrunched down all the same, and as the traffic finally started up again I inched my car away while looking up from under the dashboard.

It was easy to find a parking space at the Capitol. There didn't seem to be anybody around. In the corridors of the House and Senate office buildings nearly all of the doors to the suites of the lawmakers were locked. Like the administration's civil servants, the senators, congressmen, and congresswomen also had fled.

I walked toward the Capitol building itself. And then, turning a corner and moving onto the Capitol grounds, I saw them—a convoy of army trucks, each truck filled with soldiers, pulling up next to the East Front steps, where so many presidents had taken the oath of office. This was no National Guard detachment. This was the regular army.

On the Senate side of the Capitol a squad of troopers hauled a .50-caliber machine gun up the outside marble steps to the first landing. "Take it up another flight, Sergeant," a lieutenant called. "It will widen your field of fire."

A few yards away a group of officers huddled over a map. It was a map of the maze of indoor corridors of the Capitol. They pointed out the twists and turns to one another, trying to figure out how the building could be defended, hallway by hallway.

A few blocks behind them the fires still burned. But on the grounds of the Capitol there was no sign of an enemy. I went to a telephone and called the bureau. Nick Thimmesch was there.

"Where the hell are you," he shouted. "Don't you know there's a riot going on here?"

I told him about my assignment from Long Island.

"Get back here right now," Thimmesch said. "Bring food. Bring water. We're barricaded in here."

I went back to my car. The traffic jam had disappeared; Pennsylvania Avenue was empty now. I kept stopping at restaurant after restaurant, but they were all closed and barred. True to the word of the attendants, though, my parking garage still was open. There were candy machines there, too. I gave the attendants bills. They gave me silver and I all but emptied their machines.

Outside, small groups of looters were still on the streets, carrying off various items. Clothing, appliances, and records seemed to be favored. But a block away there were more military convoys on the move, these made up of the National Guard.

I walked the two blocks toward the National Press Building, sidling past a few looters, my pockets bulging with candy bars. I walked with relief past the National Guardsmen, who eyed me curiously. Then I remembered what I had heard on the all-news radio. The guard had orders to shoot looters on sight.

My hands went to my pockets to hide the candy. Would I be taken for an Almond Joy thief, a Baby Ruth burglar, a Clark Bar criminal? The short walk suddenly seemed very long. But I reached the National Press Building without being stopped and the door was open. Mayor Walter Washington had imposed a curfew on his torn city, but it didn't apply to reporters.

On the sixth floor, however, the door to the *Newsday* bureau was locked. I pounded on it and shouted. Thimmesch unlocked it and pulled me inside. Then he locked it again. "I'm glad you're safe," he said.

I emptied my pockets of the candy and told him that the National Guard was on hand. Then I reported that I thought that the National Press Club restaurant on the thirteenth floor might be open and that I was going up there for dinner. It was indeed open and we did eat there.

Afterward we looked out the window. It seemed very quiet. I told Thimmesch I would go out and see what I could, and he said he would do the same. We went in opposite directions.

I didn't get far. At the corner of Fourteenth and F streets I heard a nasty voice. "Halt," the voice said. I had been stopped by a young guardsman on traffic duty in the intersection. He was holding a bayonet-tipped rifle.

"You're breaking the curfew," he told me.

"No," I said, waving my White House press pass, "reporters are exempt."

"You bastards in the press," he snarled. "If it wasn't for you none of this would ever happen. You're the ones who should die." He pointed his rifle at me. Then, inspired by his rage, he pressed the bayonet into my stomach.

Remembering the basic training bayonet course from my army days, I knew just what to do. My hands went into the air and I said, "Take it easy, son." I looked desperately down the street. There was a cop on the next corner.

"I ought to kill you now," the guardsman said.

I didn't know what to do now. "Take it easy," I said again.

The policeman turned in our direction. He took one look and came toward us on a dead run, shouting as he came. Hand on his revolver, he ordered the guardsman to put up his bayonet. He was obeyed. The policeman told the guardsman to leave the intersection. Again he was obeyed.

I left quickly myself. It was my closest brush with danger of the day. A few hours later the regular army marched into Washington in force, taking over from the National Guard.

That night tanks rumbled through the silent streets of the nation's capital. Soldiers and police were everywhere. There were no cars that were moving. Washington was under attack, and the downtown intersections of civilian streets were now military checkpoints.

On my way home after writing stories until almost dawn, I was stopped by soldiers at checkpoint after checkpoint and then allowed to go on. Once, when the light was red, I waited.

"What are you waiting for?" a soldier asked.

"For the light to change," I said.

"You've gotta be kidding," he said. "Get outta here." And I did.

The riots went on for a few more days before they finally subsided and the troops went away at last. The curfew was lifted, and the people in the black neighborhoods who had run from their houses during the disturbances went home from the churches that had put them up. Everything was pretty much back to normal, except in those poor black neighborhoods where most of the fires had been set.

The stores were gone there, literally up in smoke, and no one seemed willing to rebuild. For years the city politicians would complain about "the Fourteenth Street corridor" that had been the hardest hit by the fires.

At the bureau there was a change. Nick Thimmesch, who had been having personality differences with reporters and clerical help, was replaced as bureau chief by Joe Albright, an editor, reporter, and part owner of *Newsday*.

Joe decided to give his small staff definite beats. He made Marty Schram the White House correspondent, the most prestigious post for a reporter in Washington. He assigned me to cover Congress and a lot of politics.

It was a fine beat. For one thing, there was in the year of 1968—a year of war abroad and assassinations and violent demonstrations at home—a gray, pipe-smoking Republican member of the House of Representatives named Charlie Goodell. He was as anonymous as a politician could get, a moderately conservative congressman from Jamestown, New York, who basically did the bidding of the leaders of the Republican party and was popular enough to be a member of the GOP's exclusive Chowder and Marching Society, a House club whose members included Richard M. Nixon and Melvin Laird. He was, in short, a most solid and reliable member of the Republican establishment.

When Senator Robert F. Kennedy's quest for the Democratic presidential nomination came to its bloody, fatal, and shocking end in Los Angeles, it was up to the Republican governor of New York State, Nelson Rockefeller, to appoint a successor to serve in the Senate until the next election in 1970.

It was an opportunity for the Republicans to pick a safe replacement, someone who wouldn't rock the boat, someone Dick Nixon could count on should he win the White House.

So on October 10 Rockefeller rewarded old Charlie's Republican loyalty by appointing him to complete the remaining two years of Kennedy's Senate term.

Goodell, claimed Rockefeller without even a wink, "could give continuity to Senator Kennedy's effort." And Goodell, with an equally straight face, pledged that he would try to do just that.

Liberals snorted in outrage. Charlie Goodell, who up until the Rockefeller appointment had a voting record that the Americans for Democratic Action could approve only 33 percent of the time, the philosophical successor of Robert Kennedy? Those who could laugh, did. The others were bitter.

But Charlie Goodell, good old Charlie Goodell, did something totally treacherous to his party. He gave new meaning to political promises as most understood them. He actually was serious about his pledge.

For him, uttering the oath of a U.S. senator was like stepping through a magical political mirror. Charlie Goodell simply wasn't the same man. Almost immediately upon his arrival in the Senate he called for a halt to the bombing of North Vietnam. The other Republicans were trying to block the Supreme Court ambitions of Abe Fortas,

a Democrat, but for them Goodell was no help whatso-
ever. Kennedy-like, he sided with the liberals, vainly
demanding that Fortas be made the chief justice of the
United States Supreme Court.

Most Republican senators are not known for their
opposition to U.S. business endeavors, but Goodell broke
with the party philosophy again and became a leading
fighter against the manufacture and operation of a U.S.
supersonic transport (SST), arguing like a liberal that it
would pollute the atmosphere.

Worst of all he began to attack a fellow Chowder and
Marching Society member, Richard Nixon, with such
fervor that the GOP was beside itself. Clearly, something
was amiss with Charlie Goodell. His old Republican
buddies in the House had him over to a lunch to try to
bring him to his senses.

It didn't do any good. Instead, after long conferences
with the antiwar Vietnam Moratorium Committee, an
amalgam of liberals and radicals, he produced what was
the most extreme congressional proposal on the war to
date—a bill demanding the removal of all U.S. troops from
Vietnam within one year.

Never in his life had Goodell received such a reaction.
Rockefeller, the man who had made him a senator,
denounced him. Senator J. William Fulbright, one of the
leading Democratic doves, praised him. And the once-
unknown Goodell began to receive more mail than any
other lawmaker on Capitol Hill. His press conferences,
once clubby little affairs with a half dozen New York
reporters in his inner office, now had to be moved to
auditorium-sized committee rooms.

When Vice President Spiro Agnew attacked him by
calling him the "Christine Keeler of the Republican party"
after Keeler had undergone a famous sex-change operation, Goodell responded by wearing an Agnew watch.

"I have changed," Goodell said as he opened his campaign for a full six-year term in the Senate. "We have all changed. The problems of the country have changed. I believe in my country. I will carry my crusade to the people. I will tell them how proud I am in 1970 [that] I am not the man I was in 1959," when he first came to Congress.

But of course, something else changed too. Goodell did not exactly have the same Republican support in 1970 that he had had in 1959. Not only was Spiro Agnew coming after him but other Republicans were turning away, including the governor of New York. The country was beginning to veer to the right, and Rockefeller, up for reelection for governor in 1970, was quick to turn with it. Republicans in the state had their hearts set on taking revenge on their maverick conservative—by voting for James Buckley, the Republican who was running for the Senate on the Conservative party ticket.

Once, in New York City, Governor Rockefeller was dragooned into attending a Goodell fund-raiser. I was there, having been assigned to cover the New York Senate campaign. Rockefeller stayed a few minutes and then started to walk out. I knew he was scheduled to campaign the next day on Long Island, strong Buckley country. "Governor," I said, intercepting him, "when you're out in Suffolk County tomorrow, will you have a few kind words to say for Senator Goodell?"

Rockefeller stared at me. "Nice to see ya, fella," he said and kept walking.

I stepped in front of him again. "Come on, Governor," I said. "You can tell me. You going to say anything nice about Charlie Goodell in Suffolk tomorrow?"

"Good to see ya, fella," Rockefeller said and tried to walk on.

Again I intercepted him. "For the last time, Governor," I said, "do you have anything nice to say about Charlie Goodell?"

Rockefeller stepped up to me and grabbed the front of my shirt in one fist. "Listen, fella," he said, "I've got my own problems, see?" And for emphasis he slapped me firmly on my cheek. "I've got my own campaign to worry about, see?" And he slapped me again.

I couldn't believe this was happening. But I didn't know what to do. A reporter is supposed to be a neutral. What does a journalist do when he is being hit by a governor? How many years do you get if you hit back? I froze. I did nothing. I saw Attorney General Louis Lefkowitz, the chief law enforcement officer of New York State, standing behind Rockefeller and looking on in horror.

"So I don't have time to worry about anyone else's campaign, see?" Rockefeller said, administering a third slap. He stepped around me and walked on.

Lefkowitz stopped and rubbed my reddened cheek. "Ya gotta understand," he said to me. "The governor is a little excited, that's all."

"So I've noticed," I said.

Rockefeller was always very nice to me after that. But in 1970 he wasn't in a very good mood and he wasn't very nice to Charlie Goodell. There were reports that he donated some last-minute money to Goodell's campaign only after Charlie's wife called up Happy Rockefeller and asked her, "Do you know what your husband is doing to my husband?"

Goodell toiled his lonely way through the state. He took commercial flights, which no senatorial candidate of a major party ever does, but for Goodell there wasn't any money to charter a plane.

Dick Ottinger, the Democratic candidate, had a plane, but his campaign managers scheduled few appearances for him before large audiences. Instead, ahead of their time and behind in their techniques, they would fly him to closed industrial plants, pose him in front of the locked gates, and have him make a statement for the television

cameras without any voters around either to watch or to
be in the pictures.

On election day the liberal vote split, and both Ottinger
and Goodell lost to Buckley. After the election dozens of
reporters gathered around Goodell in a Senate room for a
final press conference. Even in defeat he was probably the
most popular politician in the Capitol. "Perhaps it wasn't
worth it politically," he said, "but what I was about in
those two years in the U.S. Senate was to try to speak out
in blunter terms than was natural and normal for American politicians. I tried to awaken the people."

Goodell became a Washington lawyer, and Ottinger
went back to the House as a successful congressional
leader of liberal causes. In private life Goodell did retreat
a little—but not very much—toward his conservative
roots. He even represented the French government in a
fight to establish routes for the SST in the United States,
something he had opposed as a senator.

Four years later President Gerald R. Ford, who had been
Goodell's Republican leader in the House, returned him to
GOP favor and capitalized on his relationship with the
antiwar forces by appointing him chairman of a presidential commission to arrange ways for the unpenalized
return of those Americans who had fled to Canada to
avoid the draft. When he wasn't doing that or lawyering,
Charlie would take long, leisurely lunches at the Palm
Restaurant, greeting friends in the Washington steak
house decorated with the caricatures of politicians. He
died of a heart attack in 1986.

Nearly everybody says that New Yorkers are terribly
provincial and snobbish, looking down their noses at
anyone who is not from their state. They are wrong. New
Yorkers like and admire people from out of state. At least
they did in the 1960s and the 1970s. Just look who they
have picked to be their senators. In 1964 they chose Bobby

Kennedy, a liberal from Massachusetts. And in 1970 they picked Jim Buckley, a conservative from Connecticut.

Buckley, guided by F. Clifton White, who had led Barry Goldwater to the GOP presidential nomination, had done everything right in winning the election. After he won, although he was the candidate of the very outside-the-loop Conservative party, he went right to the establishment, promising that he would give his first postelection interview to *The New York Times*. This did not make my bureau chief, Joe Albright, very happy. "You have to get that first interview," he told me. "I don't know how you do it, but you have to do it."

Buckley was coming to Washington to meet with Nixon at the White House, and F. Clifton White was coming with him. I figured it wouldn't do me much good to hang around there, because for one thing, there are too many ways to leave the White House and for another, I didn't know anyone really willing to talk at length to a lone and unknown reporter in the street.

But I also knew that Buckley and his guide White would be flying back to New York City later in the day. I knew Buckley was a millionaire so I figured he wouldn't fly the one-class Eastern shuttle. At the time that left American Airlines, which had a first-class section.

Of course, I still didn't know which flight he would take. But I guessed that just maybe he had made his reservations through the special travel office located in the Capitol for the convenience of members of Congress, even those members who had not yet taken the oath of office. Not wanting to lie, I tested my theory by going to the Senate side of the Capitol and making a call to the travel office from a pay telephone. "I'm calling from the Senate," I said truthfully. "Could you please tell me when Senator-elect Buckley is scheduled to fly to New York? I believe he's flying American."

"It's the 4:30," the agent said.

I took a cab to National Airport and bought a first-class ticket on the 4:30 P.M. flight. Sure enough, as I watched in the boarding area I saw Buckley and White walk right past me and get on the plane. I followed and quickly introduced myself. "I'm here to interview you," I told Buckley cheerfully.

"Oh no you're not," White said.

"Listen," I said. "I was always told that conservatives appreciate and reward ingenuity. I can't think of anything more ingenious than figuring out your flight and buying a ticket to New York just for an interview."

Buckley laughed. "Sit down," he said. "Clif, take his seat."

It was a terrific interview, lasting nearly all of the hour-long flight, and the beginning of a fine relationship with both Buckley and White. At LaGuardia Airport in New York I said good-bye, turned around, and took the Eastern shuttle back to Washington. By 9 P.M. I had filed a twelve hundred–word story on the interview. My editors seemed happy with the result. *Newsday* played it very big. A few days later the *Times* published its interview, which, I noted with satisfaction, seemed to be a partial reprise of mine. I also couldn't help but notice that the second paragraph of the *Times* story began, "In his first interview since the election . . ."

4

TEAR GAS

ONE OF MY ASSIGNMENTS AS A WASHINGTON CORRESPONDENT WAS TO cover demonstrations against the war in Vietnam. In the late 1960s and early 1970s it seemed as if there were marches and protests at least twice a month, almost inevitably turning violent and resulting in many arrests.

The reporters who went out to cover these events were divided on how to dress for the occasion. Some wore the jeans and T-shirt uniforms of the demonstrators, but others wore jackets and ties or dresses on the theory that this was one way to avoid arrest. We had a lot of debates on whether or not to wear army surplus helmets. There were an awful lot of rocks thrown, to say nothing of police clubs coming down on people. One fellow took a middle course by wearing a helmet on which he had painted the words: PRESS. DO NOT HIT.

I was a jacket-and-tie man myself. And of course, all of the reporters agreed to wear both their police passes and the passes issued by the sponsors of the demonstrations.

Newsday used to send down reporters from Garden City to help out. They were commonly the casual-dress kind. During every demonstration one of the *Newsday* gang was sure to manage to get himself arrested. We then would have to work at getting the reporter bailed out, which would take away from the reporting of the demonstration. It got a little annoying.

So one time I asked that *Newsday* send someone who couldn't possibly get arrested. The editors responded by assigning Les Hanscom, a man who looked far more like a journalist than a reporter. From the top of his distinguished head to the soles of his highly polished shoes, he was someone who emanated dignity, who demanded respect without saying a word about it. This guy could have passed for an ambassador. Although he dressed as if Brooks Brothers was his favorite store and spoke as if he worked for the State Department, he also happened to be a brilliant writer and a fine reporter.

He came down the night before the demonstration and decided to take an evening stroll before retiring to his hotel room. And there, before his eyes, right near the White House, he saw the Park Police chasing a group of young men, catching them, and tossing them into a couple of paddy wagons.

Les in his polite way asked the police what the young men had done. The cop he asked told him to leave immediately. Les said he was a reporter for *Newsday*. The cop was very impressed. He immediately arrested Les and took him along with the young men. I found out about it when a Park Police desk sergeant called me at home at about 5 A.M. He said that for some strange reason the prisoner from *Newsday* had not been at all cooperative. "When we asked him his occupation, he said he was an undertaker," the cop said. His real identity had been revealed to the authorities when they examined his wallet. I asked the desk sergeant to let him go, but he wasn't about to listen to me. It was several hours before our arrest-proof correspondent was released.

Probably the angriest of the protests were the May Day uprisings of 1971, which despite the name actually continued for several days. Thousands and thousands of young people descended on Washington, and every day thousands and thousands of them were arrested and scores of them were beaten by the police.

One of the wildest of the May Day days came when the protesters—there were easily more then ten thousand of them—jammed the area outside the House side of the Capitol to take their stand against the war. Facing the great throng were the Metropolitan Police and the Capitol Police, who were yet to become the professional unit they are today. For years the Capitol Police had been almost entirely a group of patronage employees who got their jobs through their favorite lawmakers.

Just two months earlier, on March 1, a Sunday, someone had blown up a bathroom on the first floor of the Capitol with a bomb so powerful that the great crystal chandeliers tilted, doors were cracked, and damage was estimated at $300,000. Since it was Sunday, security was at the barest minimum. In fact, except for the bomber, Capitol Police Officer Robert L. Bowen had the entire first floor of the Capitol to himself.

Once, a friend of mine who needed a job while going to law school was made a Capitol policeman by his congressman. The Capitol Police immediately gave him a uniform and a gun and badge. Without any training he was set to work directing traffic on the Capitol grounds. Things went okay for a few days until a tourist ran up to him. "Officer, Officer," the man exclaimed, "someone's broken into my car and taken all my stuff."

"That's terrible," my friend said.

"But Officer," the tourist said, "what should I do?"

"I suggest, sir," my friend said, "that you call a cop."

So the real cops were considered to be the Metropolitan Police, though by May 1971 the Capitol Police force was on its way to becoming somewhat more professional. On this day, both forces had set up barricades in front of the Capitol. After the reporters and the demonstrators had been pressed into these temporary pens, the police surrounded them. The demonstrators shouted and chanted. The reporters took notes. And on this sunny day Senator Lee Metcalf came marching into the no-man's-land between the mob and the Capitol steps. A Metropolitan Police officer in a riot helmet cut him off.

"You can't walk here," he said to Metcalf. Now, senators do not like to be ordered around by anyone. "I am a senator of the United States," Metcalf growled. "This is the Capitol of the United States. I can walk anywhere I damn please."

The policeman knew just how to handle this angry elderly man. "Leave now, or you're under arrest," he said. Well, one word led to another and finally it was all too much for the senator. Metcalf hauled off and belted the cop one in the chest. But the policeman was young and fit and Metcalf was neither. His fist bounced away without any apparent effect.

Two other Metropolitan Police officers grabbed the white-haired senator. "You assaulted an officer," one of the cops said.

"I'm not going to stand for this," Metcalf shouted.

One of the cops grabbed Metcalf's arm. A Metcalf aide came running up and began to wring his hands. "Oh, oh," he moaned. "I knew something like this would happen."

About twenty yards away the chief of the Capitol Police, James Powell, finally saw what was going on. Surely visions of lost jobs and vanished pensions swept through his heart and his head. His face seemed to turn about as blue as his uniform. "No," he shouted as the metro policeman took out the handcuffs. "No, no." He hurled himself between the senator and the Metropolitan Police, murmuring words of reproach to the city cops and elaborate apologies to Metcalf. Then he led the senator away toward a door in the Capitol.

While he was gone, several members of Congress walked out on the steps where a microphone was set up. The crowd was getting angrier. Congresswoman Bella Abzug went to the microphone. "Police," she said, "be nice and don't hit the demonstrators. Demonstrators, be nice and don't hit the police."

As she talked, a young male demonstrator walked up the steps a half flight above her. Clearly he was of a mind to appreciate such a beautiful day with every bit of his being. Silently he stripped to the absolute buff, posing naked in the sun while the unknowing Abzug continued to speak just below him.

Chief Powell walked back into the no-man's-land, this time holding a megaphone. With him was a man in civilian clothes whom I had seen at other times at the Justice Department. The chief came up to a few feet from where I was standing. "You have ten minutes to disperse," the chief said after the man in civies whispered in his ear. "If you do not leave, you will be arrested."

Reporters and some hundreds of demonstrators surged away from the police barricades. The police shoved us back.

"Can we leave?" I asked a policeman.

"No," he said with a grin.

"But if we don't leave," someone else said, "we will be arrested.

"That's right," the policeman replied.

Powell was standing very near me. The man in civies was whispering into his ear again. "You have three minutes to leave or you will all be placed under arrest," the Capitol Police chief announced into the megaphone. I leaned forward and whispered into the chief's free ear. "Except reporters, chief," I murmured.

"Except reporters," Powell repeated into the megaphone. The man in civies glared at me.

So the reporters were not arrested. The demonstrators

were, of course, but only 1,146 of them were taken into custody. That was a record low for the week. I remember that the last demonstrator to be arrested was twenty-three-year-old Mrs. Linda Puskas, who was carried kicking down the Capitol steps. I remember her because her four-year-old son Jimmy had been the youngest demonstrator, eating a Fudgsicle and waving a peace flag at the same time. As he was carried off by a cop, he hugged the officer.

The next day, as Bella Abzug walked out on the floor of the House, she was stopped by Congressman Richard Ichord, a conservative Democrat from Missouri. Ichord was holding a copy of the *Washington Post*. On the front page was a picture of Abzug addressing the demonstrators with the young man posing naked behind her. There was a black square in the picture where a family newspaper might put one.

"Look, Bella," said Ichord. "What do you suppose is under that square?" Abzug was in no mood to kid around. "Another Ichord," she said.

Earlier that May Day week there was a demonstration at the Justice Department. In all of the previous demonstrations at Justice—and there had been several over the months—a man had come out on the fifth-floor balcony and had raised the fingers of his hand in the V sign of the peace movement. Always before, he had been cheered by the demonstrators. But this time they shouted, "Jump, jump."

The police sprang a trap. They closed off both sides of the street and announced that the thousands they had cornered were under arrest. A lot of the demonstrators had to wait for a long time to be arrested. They waited so long that two of them decided to get married. I wrote the story like a wedding announcement.

Miss Joan Susienka, a former student at Fordham University, was married yesterday on the steps of the Internal

Revenue Service building across the street from the Justice Department to Mr. Thomas Fuller, who attends Fordham.

Both the 19-year-old bride and her 18-year-old husband streaked their faces with green paint for the occasion. Among the uninvited guests were Mr. John Mitchell, the attorney general of the U.S., who watched from the fifth-floor balcony; Mr. Jerry Wilson, the metropolitan chief of police, and several hundred policemen who were waiting to arrest the newlyweds and 2,200 other anti-war demonstrators for crossing police lines.

The police made their arrests of other protesters in hushed tones as a kazoo orchestra played "Here Comes the Bride" and the Rev. Mr. Harcourt (Harky) Klinefelter of Atlanta, a minister in the United Church of Christ, performed the necklace-and-ring ceremony. In lieu of a ring, the groom placed his rawhide necklace with a medallion reading "Love" over the bride. The bride fitted her ring to the groom's pinkie.

Mrs. Fuller, who is from Webster, Mass., was dressed in a brown-and-blue poncho, blue dungarees decorated with flowers, and suede shoes. In her blonde hair she wore a purple flower and around her neck dangled a white helmet, to be used as protection against nightsticks. Mr. Fuller, from Omaha, Neb., wore a brown suede handband, a brown leather jacket, blue dungarees, a red scarf and boots. Both were chewing gum but Mrs. Fuller discarded hers when the ceremony began.

The groom said that they had decided to marry about 10 minutes earlier. He added that they had been thinking about it for a long time.

The Rev. Mr. Klinefelter said after the ceremony that it really wasn't legal in the eyes of the law, because of the lack of documents such as a marriage license. But the groom said: "The people's ceremony is good enough for me." The bride said: "My mother is going to have a heart attack." The couple then waited for the police to take them to jail for the first hours of their honeymoon.

There wasn't anything funny at all about the opening day of the May Day protests, though. Thousands of young people stormed into the streets during rush hour to try to prevent the federal government from beginning another workday. They were met by ten thousand soldiers and three thousand policemen. To keep the demonstrators from blocking the cars of civil servants who were trying to get to their jobs, the cops and the troops used gas and chased the protesters down the streets. Yet they didn't try to arrest them.

But after the young people stopped trying to block the cars, there was a roar in the sky over the Potomac. Two big troop helicopters came growling into the federal city, landing on the grass near the Washington Monument. Soldiers doubled out onto Constitution Avenue, jogging into the street to form a picket line guarding the Justice Department.

It was 8:30 A.M. On Constitution Avenue the Metropolitan Police sergeant listened to his radio and then looked at his men standing near the troops on Constitution Avenue. He smiled. "We can make arrests," he said.

"Hallelujah," a patrolman answered.

All was quiet on Constitution Avenue. Then down the street came walking a young blonde woman in khaki and her big blue-jeaned escort. "You're under arrest," the couple was told.

The young woman's face twisted in fright. "We were just walking down the street," she protested. "Just walking along the street." Two cops hustled her over to a group of twenty other prisoners. Her escort went limp. Six policemen lifted him and carried him to the group. The young woman sobbed and ran to him. "Timmy, Timmy, oh, Timmy," she wept.

The other young people were taken captive swiftly. A young man in an Afro was dragged by his shoulders and hair to the group of prisoners. A single woman pedestrian was arrested. A second young couple came walking up Twelfth Street. "Them too?" a patrolman asked. The sergeant nodded and the arrests were made. "Well," the young woman murmured calmly to her friend, "it looks like I'm going to jail on an empty stomach." All of this was after the demonstration had ended.

That was the way it was throughout downtown Washington. There was a new crime in the capital—the crime of being young. Over the police radios the word was plain—arrest everybody under thirty who came walking down the streets. And arrest them they did. There were seven thousand arrests in the capital that day, more than any other day ever. By ones and twos, the young men and women were dragged, flung, or herded into the police wagons. A little later, as I stood with other reporters watching the soldiers guarding the Justice Department, I saw a woman I recognized walking on the sidewalk. She was about nineteen or twenty, and I had interviewed her the night before. She said that she had come to Washington with friends who intended to protest but that she didn't mean to join them. When she saw me, she stopped to say hello.

"Get off the street," I told her. "You'll be arrested."

She stared at me. "I haven't done anything," she said.

"Go into the museum," I said—we were standing next to one of the buildings of the Smithsonian Institution.

"No," she said.

"Have you had breakfast?" I asked desperately. "They have a good cafeteria there."

"I don't have any money," she said. I fished three dollars out of my pocket. "Here. Get in that museum." I handed her the money and gave her a little push. She stared doubtfully at me. "Go," I said. She turned and began to walk slowly toward the door.

Too late. A police paddy wagon came rolling past the line of soldiers, swerved on the curb and onto the lawn, and cut her off. Two policemen jumped out and grabbed her. They picked her up hand and foot, ignoring her screams, and tossed her into the back of the paddy wagon.

Reporters began to shout. "Let her go," we called. "She hasn't done anything." The police, having slammed the back door of the wagon, raised their fists at us and drove off to Robert F. Kennedy Stadium. Like any Latin American dictatorship making mass arrests of citizens, the federal government was penning its thousands of prisoners in a stadium.

There weren't too many reporters who enjoyed covering these demonstrations in Washington, but they certainly provided dramatic copy. It really didn't seem to be that dangerous to be on the streets as a reporter, and the only discomfort was the tear gas and the pepper gas that the cops denied they used but that always seemed to fill the air.

Once, after being caught by the gas I retreated to the *Newsday* office at the National Press Building in order to take a short time out. There was nobody there. As I sat at my desk I got a second reaction from the pepper gas. Suddenly I couldn't see. My eyes were burning. I needed water.

But I was disoriented. If I groped one way in the office I could find the door and get to the men's room. If I groped the other way I could walk out the window, six floors up.

I dropped to my knees and tried to feel my way on the floor. Just then the door opened. Al Marlens, my managing editor down from Long Island to see a demonstration for himself, walked in. He led me to a wash basin and watery relief. The next week there was a fifty-dollar bonus in my pay check. Combat pay! Marlens, I thought, should come down more often. I got gassed at every demonstration.

But when the time came to cover what was to be the last antiwar demonstration in Washington, I wasn't so blasé. I was reluctant to cover it. Maybe I had been lucky. I was really uneasy about going out on this one. My friend and colleague, Tony Marro, newly arrived in the bureau, volunteered to go out with me.

By the standards of the antiwar movement, this protest was small. There were only about seven thousand demonstrators, marching in separate contingents with their separate chants and their mix-and-match philosophies. There was the National Peace Action Coalition ("Out Now, Out Now"); the Vietcong flag–waving Anti-Imperialist Contingent ("Right On, Take Saigon, Victory to the Vietcong"); the Red flag–waving Communist party ("Dump Nixon, Dump Thieu, Vote Communist in '72"); and a contingent of gay demonstrators ("Hey, hey, Whatta ya say, Why Not Try It the Other Way?").

These groups marched up to the Capitol. On the grass the Anti-Imperialist Contingent unfurled large red and green banners, one of them reading "Youth Against War and Fascism." Holding a corner of the flag was a man who looked like youth had passed him by several years earlier. He said his name was Doug and that he was thirty-two years old. "Nixon's the tool of the corporations," Doug shouted. "It's an imperialist war."

I asked Doug what he did for a living. His voice dropped to a whisper. "I'm a market analyst in Manhattan," he said. For one of those imperialist stock brokers? "Unfortunately, we all have to make a living," Doug said and marched off to throw rocks at the Department of Health, Education and Welfare building.

Tear gas cannisters were tossed by the police. I began to choke. I looked for Tony and found him with a bruise on his cheek. "Chunk of wood," he said. We parted again to look separately at the demonstration. The kiosk where souvenirs were sold at the foot of the Capitol had been set afire. Then the rocks began to fly. Tony appeared again. His face was covered with blood, so much that I couldn't see one of his eyes. I should have stopped my work right there.

Instead I pulled him into the street and flagged down a car. "You have to take him to George Washington University Hospital," I told the frightened couple within. I shoved Tony into the backseat and went back to covering the demonstration.

A line of protesters had set up a barricade of burning trash and garbage cans and were throwing stones and bricks at the police.

I worked my way up the street to get as close to Police Chief Jerry Wilson as I could. He was certainly the center of attention. A rock crashed at his feet. Bricks sailed by his ear. Ice from soft drink cups spattered against him. Soda cans clanked against a nearby police car.

Wilson grinned. "It reminds me of World War II," the chief said. "You could see them coming in from every direction, from everywhere."

A rock knocked off his soft hat. He bent down and put it back on. Slowly he walked into the smoking kiosk and tried to stamp out the fire.

Then he backed out of the building. A rock smashed against his soft cap, denting the gold shield. Blood trickled brightly from under the cap, staining his eyebrow and running down his cheek. His right shirtsleeve became spotted with red.

Still the line of demonstrators kept throwing their bricks and rocks. "Are you insane?" a young woman protester shouted at them. Two young demonstrators ran in front of the chief and tried to shield him with their own bodies. He shouted them away. "We're going to move them out," Wilson told one of his lieutenants. "C'mon, Charlie, hurry it up." Immediately the gas-masked, helmeted Civil Disturbance Unit trotted up. They fired their tear gas guns in a volley. The demonstrators fled. I wept.

Back at the office I wrote two stories, one about Wilson that was headlined POLICE CHIEF'S RED BADGE. I put my name and Marro's on both of them.

For the first time, I had written an antiwar demonstration story from the vantage point of the police. Of course, it was the first time that I had the opportunity to do that. Like an umpire, I felt I was calling them as I saw them. When the police arrested thousands of young people walking down the street—not because they were breaking the law but simply because they were under thirty—I was indignant and I showed it in my articles.

As far as I know, there was no statute against being young. If the police could do this, then the United States simply wasn't a free country. Later, the courts said the same thing, awarding thousands of dollars in damages to nearly each and every one of the thousands who were arrested during the May Day protests.

But when the rocks started flying, the police did what they had to do and moved in to arrest the demonstrators—and on the day Tony was hurt they moved with a lot of tear gas and minimal physical force.

To me the stories were what was most important. And I felt that I was writing them not simply for the paper or for myself alone but for both Tony Marro and me. It was only after I finished, late at night, that I finally called the hospital to see how my friend was doing. Turned out that he had already left—the cut was above the eye. The next day, he made one of the Washington papers. The story said he was a photographer.

In 1971 riots and protests were far from the administration's only problems. Daniel Ellsberg was driving Richard Nixon crazy, the Justice Department crazy, the Defense Department crazy—so crazy that he is regarded as the touchstone for Watergate. What he did was cataclysmic not only for the president but for me personally. That was because he also was driving my national editor crazy.

In 1971 the one-time defense intelligence operative leaked huge sections of an enormous report on the Vietnam War to *The New York Times*. The Pentagon Papers was a chapter and verse account of colossal American errors in Vietnam and gave the very private opinion of the CIA that the war could not be won.

My editor got very excited when the *Times* started printing this stuff. He called down to Washington and ordered his bureau reporters to get on the stick. He said we'd better get ahold of at least one damn chapter of the Pentagon Papers.

We had scarcely gotten these fiery words when the *Washington Post* printed a couple of chapters. Good God, what was happening? Where was *Newsday*?

Martin Schram and I were detailed to get a chapter, half a chapter, any part of a chapter, any way, any how. I thought that the best thing to do would be to approach the former Republican senator from New York who was so close to the antiwar movement, Charlie Goodell. I called up and arranged for an appointment.

Schram and I went to see him. We sat down in his office. I felt embarrassed about asking him to give us some secret papers. I figured this would probably be a violation of the law on somebody's part. So I kept saying things like, "Well, how are you?" and "What do you think the peace movement will do next?" and "It looks like Ellsberg really destroyed Nixon."

Schram came right to the point. "We need a chapter," he said. Goodell puffed on his pipe and said he didn't know where one could be obtained. I asked him if he could look into it. He said of course. We shook hands and left. I felt more embarrassed than ever.

Days went by. Schram kept plugging away and so did I. And so did every other reporter for just about every other paper with a bureau in Washington. Schram got a lead. He went up to Boston, where perhaps someone might be willing to give us something. He left in the afternoon of June 29, fully thirteen days after the *Times* had published its first installment of the papers. That evening I got a phone call from a friend who was a congressional aide. I was told to go up to a hearing room in a Senate office building next to the Capitol.

I went. It was about 10 P.M. Senator Mike Gravel, a young, liberal Alaska Democrat, was sitting on the dais talking to a couple of his staffers. No other senators were around. But the room was filling up with reporters.

Gravel picked up a hefty block of papers, forty-one hundred pages worth of paper to be exact, and began to read into a microphone. He was the chairman of the Senate subcommittee on buildings and grounds but he wasn't reading anything about construction or landscaping.

As chairman he was calling a meeting of his subcommittee to read a statement into the public Senate record. It didn't matter that no other senators had come to the meeting. He was reading the statement anyway. And the statement was the Pentagon Papers.

Gravel read and read, but this new version of *War and Peace* was about six times as long as Leo Tolstoy's original. The senator broke down and wept. The very volume of the report was defeating him. He recessed the subcommittee for the night. But what of our deadlines?

A lending library was arranged. We stood in line in a corridor in front of a Senate office. Each reporter was given two chapters and had to pledge to bring them back the next day. I picked up my chapters, then raced for the bureau and wrote and wrote. I told the editor, Don Forst, that I would get more the next day. "Great," he said.

I kept my promise. The next day I brought back my two chapters, got on line at the slightly illegal lending library in the Senate office building, and waited to trade in my two chapters for two more chapters. It was quite a long line by now, with about twenty-five reporters waiting their turn. At the Justice Department and at the White

House there was rage and renewed threats of prosecuting reporters. But no one either at Justice or at the White House seemed to know about the lending library.

I brought the two new chapters back to the office and wrote again. "Great," Forst said. "Will this do it?"

"Oh, no," I said proudly. "There's lots more." In Boston Schram had picked up a chapter or two from his secret contact. But his skill at obtaining the material was all but ignored. Events had passed him by.

On the third day reporters on line decided they didn't have to wait to turn in chapters. We began to swap while standing in the corridor.

Back at the *Newsday* office I called Forst again. He seemed a little impatient. "Can you hold this to about six hundred words?" he asked. I tried.

On the fourth day, when I came back to the bureau with my two new chapters and telephoned, Forst was furious. "For God's sake," he shouted. "Will you cut it out? Enough already. No more Pentagon Papers. This is disgusting."

By this time the paper was no longer in the hands of an individual. The Captain had sold *Newsday* to the Times Mirror Corporation in 1970. Harry Guggenheim was in his seventies by then and was dying of cancer. He had brought in Bill Moyers to try to lift the paper into national prominence. To an extent Moyers had succeeded. But he also had moved the paper into a pose even more liberal than it had struck in the days of Miss P.

And Guggenheim, popular as a boss but lonely as a conservative in the Garden City newsroom, wanted to leave a paper that reflected his philosophy.

The Captain's wife was dead and he was dying and he didn't want his legacy to be a paper that largely favored Democrats. He would not let Joe Albright, his liberal nephew by marriage and my Washington bureau chief, have the paper. Joe owned about a third of the stock but the Captain owned 51 percent.

Albright and Moyers got together, though, and tried to block the Times Mirror bid. They made Guggenheim a counteroffer. The Captain was not interested, and Times Mirror, which wanted an East Coast anchor to balance its powerful West Coast newspaper, the *Los Angeles Times*, was hot after *Newsday*.

But Times Mirror did not want a small group of minority stockholders making trouble. The corporation kept trying to persuade Albright and the others to sell their stock.

Albright held out against the Times Mirror blandishments, ploys, and pressures. When I went to the bureau in the National Press Building in those days, it was like entering a bunker. For the first time I knew what it was to be a press spokesman, and I didn't like it.

My good friends, my fellow reporters, would call me up and ask me what I knew of Joe's latest maneuver. There were times when I did have an idea of what he planned. And against all of my reporter's instincts to tell everyone what I knew, I would say, like any spokesman whose boss was under pressure, "No comment."

In May Jim Bellows, an official of the Times Mirror Corporation, came to Long Island. I wasn't there, but the news quickly was heard in Washington that he had told *Newsday* staffers that Times Mirror wanted the liberal Moyers out and that it planned to replace him with a Republican. We also heard that this was a condition of the sale made by Harry Guggenheim—not by Times Mirror. Moyers gave up the fight and resigned in May.

The day that *Los Angeles Times* publisher Otis Chandler came to Garden City to inspect the new property and reassure the staff was the day the Pulitzer Prizes were announced. *Newsday* had won two, the *Los Angeles Times* none. Just before Chandler arrived Guggenheim called the paper. Obviously angry, he demanded to speak to Moyers.

"Captain, Captain," an excited secretary said to Guggenheim. "We've won two Pulitzers."

But Guggenheim's anger overcame his pride. "I don't care," I was told he shouted. "I want to speak to Moyers about this damn editorial."

After Moyers resigned, Times Mirror replaced him as publisher with Bill Attwood. He was no Republican. An ambassador under John Kennedy, an author, and a fine writer for the *New York Herald Tribune*, Attwood's most conservative move was to raise the price of *Newsday* from a nickel to a dime.

Joe stayed on as bureau chief for a couple of months, but Times Mirror would not have him at the paper. He too was forced out. Albright is the nicest, most democratic millionaire I have ever met. He could have retired. Instead he became an award-winning reporter for the Cox newspapers.

And I got my third bureau chief, Russell Sackett, the former head of the investigative team of *Life* magazine. A powerful, hard-eyed man of medium height, when I first saw him he looked awfully tough to me.

It turned out that he was—but not on the reporters who worked for him in the bureau. For us he became our defender in the ongoing tensions every bureau in Washington endures with its home office. One of the things he did for me was to act as my agent, negotiating on my behalf a seventy-dollar-a-week raise, by far the biggest increase I'd received since coming to Washington.

He knew that I liked to cover politics and that I knew the players in the Capitol, many of whom take leave to become activists in presidential politics every fourth year. More important, he liked the way I wrote about politics. So for this presidential election he clapped me on the back and told me I would be covering the 1972 campaign full time.

Both political parties arrange things so that presidential candidates and those who follow them around will suffer. In the winter they make the contenders campaign in places like Illinois and New Hampshire and Iowa. In the summer they make up for it by going south to hold their national conventions in cities that broil. I once suggested to a Democratic party official that for the sake of climate and comfort some consideration might be given to reversing directions. She laughed at me.

To me, the very best part of being a national reporter is covering presidential campaigns. When I'm doing this, it doesn't even seem like work. I'm watching a great show, filled with comedy and drama and heartbreak, and I'm telling people about the spectacle. The United States whizzes by. To see America from the vantage point of a presidential campaign excites me still—as much, I think, as when *Newsday* first gave me a sample by allowing me to cover Barry Goldwater's campaign for one week back in 1964.

On the campaign road, there are fourteen-hour days and little sleep and a lot of loneliness despite the camaraderie of reporters. But the sense of riding the cusp of history, and the wonderful stories a reporter can write, make up for it all.

Only once did I have a moment of deep regret. In 1976, I came home for a weekend and my five-year-old son, Larry, asked me, "Daddy, do you still live here?" I usually did get home on most weekends and tried without fail to bring toys for my children and a gift for my wife. Every night on the road, I tried to call home.

But after Larry said that, I spent a lot of time with him, and with my two other sons and my wife. But only for the weekend. On Monday morning, reasoning to myself that

I was away from home only one year out of every four, I was out again and having the time of my life.

In 1972, I spent the final week of the campaign covering Nixon. We went through the last couple of days in perfect climate, in San Clemente, California. Before 7 A.M. on election day Ron Ziegler, the White House press secretary, had all of the reporters and photographers lined up at Concordia Elementary School to watch Dick and Pat Nixon be the first voters of the Forty-eighth Precinct. About seventy neighbors of the Nixons were also at the school. They were the ones who applauded.

The Nixons walked inside the school, and the reporters and photographers went with them. We stood behind a rope to watch the show.

The voting inspector, an elderly woman named Wilma Wallington, was anxious to prove to the president and first lady that they were indeed the first voters. She pointed to the enormous cardboard carton that would be used to hold the paper ballots.

Nixon went along with it. The box came to above his waist, but the president picked it up and shook it. "Not even a mouse," Nixon said. Then he took a sample ballot and walked into a voting booth. His wife entered the booth next to him.

The ballots were huge, maybe twice the size of a page from *The New York Times*. This was because of all of the propositions and local resolutions Californians put on their ballot every election.

Silently we watched what we could of the legs of the president and the first lady. A minute passed. Then another. And then, from under the short curtain, the lower portion of the president's ballot, already marked, began to appear. It inched lower and lower as Nixon worked his way up to the top from the bottom.

The photographers were clicking their cameras wildly. The president was showing the world how he was voting!

Ziegler was beside himself. "His ballot is below the thing, his ballot is below the thing," the press secretary shouted while reporters tried to stifle their laughter and take notes at the same time.

"Stop your pictures! Stop your pictures!"

The photographers actually stopped. Then two minutes and thirty-five seconds after she had walked into the booth, the president's wife came out, holding her completed ballot.

Mrs. Wallington beamed. "Oh my, Mrs. Nixon," she said. "You beat your husband."

Pat Nixon held her head high, "I," she said emphatically, "studied it."

But in the presidential booth there was no sign of Nixon drawing the curtain. Three minutes passed. Four minutes. Then five. Finally, as the reporters murmured, five minutes and thirty-five seconds after he had entered, the president clearly wheeled around inside the booth to pull back the curtain.

He moved too fast. The ballot slipped from his hand. Nixon reached for it but it fluttered tantalizingly away, into the booth that had been occupied by Mrs. Nixon. With the curtain still drawn the president bent into the next booth to retrieve it, going after it briefly in an undignified crouch. The laughter from the reporters rang out. "Hold it, hold it," Ziegler shouted, warning the photographers not to take the ignominious picture.

Nixon picked up the ballot and stood up in his booth. He remained behind the curtain. I remember thinking he would be sure to be trying to calm himself, to tell himself not to let the laughter get to him, not to show us that he was upset in any way. Finally he pulled back the curtain and walked out of the booth. He posed, holding the folded ballot above the cardboard box so that there could be a photograph with dignity, then dropped the ballot into the box. "I wish you luck," he said to Mrs. Wallington and left, walking to the big black presidential limousine.

The third voter of the Forty-eighth Precinct arrived on a ten-speed bike. He was bearded and he wore sandals, which he removed before going into the voting booth. When he came out, some of us asked him how he voted. "Richard Nixon is not my candidate," he said. "He's ruined the neighborhood."

5

IMPEACH NIXON!

ON SUNDAY MORNING, OCTOBER 21, 1973, A FEW HOURS AFTER SPECIAL
Watergate Prosecutor Archibald Cox had been fired by
Solicitor General Robert Bork (Attorney General Elliot
Richardson and Deputy Attorney General William Ruck-
elshaus having resigned rather than obey President Nix-
on's orders to do the deed), the entire expanded *Newsday*
Washington bureau—all six of us—was on the job. Bob
Wyrick, our investigative reporter, and I began by trying
to reach all thirty-eight members of the House Judiciary
Committee by telephone.

We knew that only the House Judiciary Committee
would be able to begin a formal inquiry into impeaching
the president of the United States and then bring charges
against him in the Senate to compel his dismissal from
office.

Even before the Saturday Night Massacre there had
been a half dozen resolutions of impeachment introduced
on the floor of the House. But realistically everyone knew
that by themselves, they wouldn't go anywhere. Individual anger would not be enough to bring down a president.
If it was to be done at all, it would have to be done by the
House Judiciary Committee.

As reporters we were charged up. We could be onto the best political story of our generation.

So Wyrick and I began to work the phones. Since it was Sunday, it wasn't easy to find either members of Congress or their staffers. Still, we got a hit. I forget whether it was Wyrick or me, but one of us got someone to say that while there wouldn't be a special session of the Judiciary Committee, the next regular meeting was scheduled for Tuesday. Yes, our source said, of course the question of impeaching Richard Nixon would be discussed.

He spoke so calmly that we decided to write the story as if it were an item for club notes on a newspaper's society page. I was the one who wrote it. "The House Judiciary Committee will discuss the impeachment of President Nixon at its regularly scheduled meeting tomorrow on Capitol Hill," I wrote. It was an exclusive, but as far as I know only the paper in Rutland, Vermont, ever picked it up.

It was a time for threats and nobility, for jokes and for plots, for bribes and for boredom. The contest of politics had become war, and the battlefield was indeed the House Judiciary Committee.

On Capitol Hill the legislative branch just had to face it. No congressman or senator could get a word in the paper, a phrase on the nightly news, unless he or she mentioned the hottest story in the country.

Tempers were a little strained. On the night of November 14 Nixon called fourteen Republican senators to the White House. There were no arrangements for a press conference afterward, but we wanted to talk to those senators. There must have been thirty-five reporters and TV cameramen clustered at the South Gate in the back of the White House, where we figured they would leave.

We guessed right. One by one, the senators came driving out. Connie Chung, then a young Washington-based TV reporter, saw Senator Barry Goldwater behind the wheel of his car. She stepped into the roadway and waved. Goldwater gunned the motor and the car zoomed forward. Chung, shaken, leaped back barely in time. And Goldwater roared off past us.

We were all furious. How could anyone treat Connie like that? When the next car nosed warily through the gate, we actually leaped on it. We crowded to the hood. We grabbed the door handles. We snarled. The guy inside was alone. He sure didn't look like a senator. He looked scared to death. "Let me go," he said. "I didn't do anything. I'm a Secret Service agent."

Some of the other senators did stop, but they didn't say much. "There wasn't much good news," explained Senator Charles McC. Mathias, a liberal Republican from Maryland, from his rolled-down car window. And he pressed the accelerator.

We'd had more luck earlier in the day from Nixon's meeting with seventy Republican House members. There were so many of them that some were bound to talk. Those who did said that Nixon refused to appear at a joint session of Congress to explain Watergate, that scandal of burglary, money laundering, and political dirty tricks that was destroying his presidency.

"The Democrats would say 'The son of a bitch is lying,'" the president told the House members. "The Republicans would say 'Maybe he's lying, but he's our son of a bitch.'" Nixon also said on this November 1973 day that he would not resign, that he was ready to play the exciting highest-stakes game of impeachment. "If it comes to impeachment, so be it," he told the House members.

Every day I patrolled the offices of the thirty-eight members of the Judiciary Committee like a policeman on a beat. I tried to get to know them like I know my own family. I was such a frequent visitor to their offices that the committee Republicans gave me a nickname of which I was rather proud. They called me "Columbo."

Congressman William Hungate, a Democrat from Missouri who was on the committee, tried to ease the tension. At one point during a rare open hearing, when the Republicans on the Judiciary Committee loudly defended Nixon they were politely interrupted. "Some of my Republican friends could see an elephant walk through that door," Hungate said, "and they would say it's a mouse with a glandular condition."

Hungate was a songwriter in his spare time. Before the hearings began in earnest, he started working on an impeachment song. The working title was, "Put them all together, they spell I-M-P-E-A-C-H."

> "I" is for the income tax, he ducked it.
> "M" is for the money, make it cash.
> "P" is for the plumbers, they need helpers.

Then he got stuck. With an eighteen-and-a-half-minute gap on a White House tape bothering everybody, I volunteered—off the record, of course—the following lines: " 'E' is for erasures, eighteen one half."

Hungate was polite about it, but he didn't take it. He was getting a lot of other advice, anyway. Before "I-M-P-E-A-C-H" he actually had gotten a song on a record. It was called "Down by the Old Watergate."

> Come, come, come and play spy with me
> Down by the old Watergate.
> Come, come, come love and lie with me
> Down by the old Watergate.
> See the little German band,
> Haldeman and Erlichman
> Don't Martha Mitchell look great?

Come, come, come and play spy with me
I'll have the whole FBI with me
Down by the Water—
We'll make the police blotter—
Down by the old Watergate.

Somehow, early on I had a pretty good idea of how Hungate was going to vote when and if the committee decided to propose articles of impeachment against Nixon. In fact, I wrote a piece for the Sunday paper on March 24, 1974—more than four months before the vote finally was taken—saying that it looked as if the House Judiciary Committee was going to impeach Nixon.

My editors had pressed me to write a story about how I thought things would go, and I, feeling sure of myself, provided it. But a couple of weeks earlier, I did not think the House Judiciary Committee would take such an ultimate step.

I figured that the committee chairman, Congressman Peter Rodino, a Newark Democrat who was a big civil rights advocate, was too much a product of a party organization to have the iron it would take to go after a president of the United States. But when Rodino hired John Doar to be the special impeachment counsel for the committee, I and everyone else knew that the chairman really meant business.

Doar was the Justice Department guy who stayed with James Meredith on the bloody, blazing night the University of Mississippi was integrated. He was the lawyer who walked into Deep South towns with segregationist mayors and abruptly forced them into civil rights U-turns. John Doar, I knew, was one tough guy.

So while Jimmy the Greek was offering fifty-to-one odds that Nixon would not be impeached, I wrote a story that said that at least nineteen of the committee's twenty-one Democrats—or precisely half of the committee membership—would vote for impeachment. And I wrote that they would vote for impeachment even though they hadn't yet heard or read a word of evidence from the material being gathered by Doar and his staff.

Then I blithely named the nineteen. I also named the undecided and the ones I thought were opposed to impeachment.

The story moved on the *Los Angeles Times–Washington Post* news wire, to which more than a hundred newspapers subscribed. A couple of papers used the story and didn't treat it as analysis. In fact, in Congressman John Seiberling's district it was the lead article in the paper. The Ohio Democrat was enraged. He found me in the big corridor next to the House floor—the area is known as the Speaker's Lobby—and bawled me out for listing him as a sure impeachment vote. "How can you do this?" he said. "I don't know myself how I'm going to vote." My telling him that it wasn't supposed to be a news story as such did not cheer him. Of course, as it turned out I guess I knew his mind better than he did. Four months later he voted for impeachment.

To me, though, it was the impeachment Republicans on the committee who had a tougher time than the Democrats. To the Democrats Nixon was the obvious enemy. But to the Republicans Nixon was their political commander in chief.

There was Congressman Hamilton Fish, the Republican from upstate New York who knew Nixon personally and had campaigned both for him and with him. In a gesture of kindness Fish had written a letter in behalf of his defeated 1968 Conservative party opponent recommending him for a job in the Nixon administration. The chap he recommended got the job. He was G. Gordon Liddy. ("I made peace with myself," Fish told me in February 1974, shrugging off the letter for the man who became a convicted Watergate conspirator.)

Ever since the Civil War there almost always has been a Fish either in Congress or in a cabinet post. A namesake ancestor was the first to fall when Teddy Roosevelt led the Rough Riders in the battle for San Juan Hill. So Ham Fish had a tradition behind him. His father, another namesake and the very conservative congressman before him, was leading a committee in support of Richard M. Nixon. But the Hamilton Fish now in Congress would not be swayed, not by Nixon or by his own father.

Fish told his wife that they'd had a good time in Washington and that they should really try to appreciate the place now because they might not be there much longer. And Fish became a leading Republican force on the committee in the drive to impeach the Republican president.

Then there was Bill Cohen, a thirty-three-year-old Maine congressman who was the Republican who first came to mind when anyone speculated on who among the GOP members of the committee would vote for impeachment.

Fish and Cohen would sometimes comfort each other. Once, I was standing in a House garage with ABC's Sam Donaldson—he was covering Congress then—when we saw the two men.

"Say," Fish said to Cohen, "you weren't at the last Republican meeting." At that session of Republican members of the Judiciary Committee, Fish said, all present were informed that they had better vote against impeachment. The penalty for desertion would be that they would be turned into "non-persons." "And they just weren't talking about Congress," Fish said. "They said that they would make sure we wouldn't be in Congress again and they said they'd follow us into private life."

Cohen looked disturbed. "I only want to do what's right," he said unhappily.

I, of course, could not resist. "You can do no more," I piped up unbidden. "And the president can expect no less."

Fish draped a big arm around Cohen's shoulder. "Don't

worry," he said. "We'll get ourselves appointed impeachment managers [those House members who prosecute
impeached officials in the Senate] and we'll build a case so
strong that we will be sure to win."

"I only want to do what's right," Cohen repeated. As far
as I could tell, the threats may have made Cohen uncomfortable but never made him think of changing his mind.

One committee Republican who did change his mind
and came out for impeachment in the middle of the game
was M. Caldwell Butler, a tough Virginia congressman
who was a veteran of his state's legislature. But Butler had
a family problem. He had an aged mother-in-law who was
bedridden and who had been a fan of Nixon's for years.
There was no telling what would happen if she found out
on television that her son-in-law had decided for impeachment.

The story goes—and Butler only chuckled when I asked
him about it—that before announcing his decision he
made up his mind to break the news to her first. On a
Saturday he timidly entered her darkened room and stood
at the front of the bedstead. "Ma?" he said, trying to wake
her gently. "Ma?"

She rose up in the bed and flung out an arm, pointing a
finger directly at Butler. "Impeach him," she commanded.
"Impeach him."

In the middle of the night Congressman Tom Railsback,
a young Illinois Republican, would be awakened by night-
mares of impeachable offenses. "I used to think, what's an
impeachable offense, what's a high crime and misde-
meanor?" he said. It took him but a few weeks to figure out
what they were and that Nixon could be guilty of them.

It was tough on Railsback not only because he wondered whether a vote for impeachment would mean he
was "a traitor and disloyal" to his party but because both
he and Nixon belonged to the exclusive GOP congressional club, the Chowder and Marching Society. "He
knows me by my first name," Railsback told me back in

1974. "He thinks I'm from Rockford. I'm from Rock Island."

When the reporters began to sense his feelings, they started to follow him around. Two network camera crews trailed him back home to a basketball game between Moline and Rock Island high schools. They wanted to get a shot of him applauding.

They turned their klieg lights on him. Railsback wanted to applaud so that the lights would go off, but no baskets were being scored. The drought went on and on and so did the lights. Finally Railsback grew desperate. He and his wife turned to those around them and said, "Let's all clap." They did, and though the ball did not go in the basket, the lights did go out.

These men, of course, were the rebels. By far the majority of the Republicans on the committee were doing their best to defend the Republican president. In fact, when impeachment proceedings began, the GOP filled a Republican vacancy on the committee with Congressman Delbert Latta, a battler from Ohio who was selected not as a permanent member of the panel but for the sole purpose of saving Nixon from impeachment.

I liked Latta, but my favorite anti-impeachment Republican was Congressman Charles Wiggins, who was Nixon's hometown congressman from Orange County outside of Los Angeles. Three or four days a week the Judiciary Committee would have to break away from its closed door deliberations to answer the opening quorum call for the House, usually at noon.

This is the way the sessions on the House floor would open—with a taking of attendance. Miss too many of those and your opponent will have an issue in your next election, charging you with being an absentee congressman. So the Judiciary Committee would interrupt its meetings to allow the members to protect themselves.

After recording his presence on the House floor, Wiggins would come out of the Republican side of the chamber and walk across the broad corridor into the Speaker's Lobby.

He would sit at the head of a big mahogany conference table, with eager reporters seated in front of him. Those who could not find seats would form a second, and sometimes a third, row of standees. Then Wiggins would begin to talk about the particular anti-Nixon accusation of the day, saying it was false and arguing—brilliantly, it seemed to us—that the president was innocent of all wrongdoing.

A good friend of mine, a reporter who was an absolute Watergate expert, used to mutter, "That son of a bitch, twisting the facts again. Some day, some day, someone should take him on."

Now, unlike my friend, I did not know all of the Watergate facts. I knew some of them and I knew an awful lot about the impeachment process and I knew the members of the committee—but I did not think of myself as an expert by any means.

But one day, when my friend was standing next to me, I heard Wiggins say something that even I thought must be mistaken. What the hell, I thought, my buddy is next to me, itching to get into the action. If I stumble, he'll be sure to save me. So I interrupted Wiggins's monologue, challenging him on the point.

Wiggins came back at me with the ease of a great politician and lawyer. I parried—somewhat lamely, I thought—but comforted myself by knowing that my friend would jump in any second now.

Wiggins gave me another dazzling response. Where was my pal? He had stepped back in the crowd and was only listening. I did my best to insist that Wiggins had said nothing to disprove the accusations against Nixon. After about five minutes Wiggins uttered what to me were the most graceful and face-saving words I head heard in a long time.

"Mike," he reassured me. "You sure have a dirty mind."

"That was very interesting," my friend said to me a moment later. I think he was trying not to laugh.

There was other members of the committee who sometimes were more helpful than Wiggins. They went beyond talk. For example, after coaxing and pleading with one committee member for several days, he finally agreed to let me look at some of the confidential material being distributed by Doar, the Democratic counsel.

I went with this congressman to his office at eight o'clock at night. We were the only ones there. "Here's the stuff," he said. "You've got to lock it in my desk drawer when you're done. I'm going home now and you're on your own. Anyone comes in here and sees you, I don't know you."

He left, turning off nearly all of the lights. I began to write notes using only his desk lamp and crouching down whenever I saw the shadows passing the glass in the front door. He had laid more than fifty pages on me. I looked for the Xerox machine. I found it but it started up with such a loud noise that I turned it off.

In a sweat I returned to writing everything in longhand. I must have sat there for more than two hours. Finally I was done. I put the papers in a drawer and I turned off the light. I tiptoed out the door and walked boldly down the hall. I said good night to the Capitol cop at the door. Then I took a cab back to my office and in great excitement called the national desk.

"I got bad news for you," said the editor who answered. "The *Los Angeles Times* has the story. We're going to use their version."

I sputtered my protests but they didn't work. "Look," the editor said. "We're less than an hour from deadline and they have the story. Nice try. Go home and get some rest."

And so I did. But only after two double scotches.

On a dark, warm, rainy Washington day more than seven months after the Saturday Night Massacre the House Judiciary Committee finally began to hear formal evidence of its impeachment inquiry, evidence that had been gathered in such volume by John Doar and his special staff that the floor of the old offices in which they worked had to be braced against a possible collapse. On that same day, May 9, 1974, Washington's Republican establishment began to speak. They began to speak to Richard M. Nixon, and the message was: resign.

First it was House Minority Leader John Rhodes (R-Ariz.), who turned down an invitation to an economic meeting at the White House with Nixon. Instead he went to breakfast with reporters at the Federal City Club, where he told them: "The president ought to consider resignation as a possible option."

When Congressman John Anderson (R-Ill.), then the number-three Republican in the House and later to become the 1980 antiestablishment presidential candidate, heard what Rhodes had said, he wasn't about to disagree. He said it would be in the best interests of the country if Nixon were to quit. And the number-four House Republican, Congressman Barber Conable of upstate New York, said: "Obviously, the president does have to consider resignation as an option."

After that Senator Marlow Cook (R-Ky.), who was up for reelection, decided to say something as well. "I am now firmly convinced that resignation is a course of action which he must realistically contemplate," Cook said.

The White House gave the response it had given so many times. "The president will not resign even if hell freezes over," said White House Communications Director

Ken Clawson. But the advice wasn't coming from Democrats or liberals. The word to quit was coming from the president's own party.

At about 1 P.M. the thirty-eight members of the House Judiciary Committee, anonymities all, gathered in room 2141 of the Rayburn Office Building for the first day of hearing evidence. It was a beginning of historic importance but without grandeur.

James St. Clair, the president's impeachment lawyer, was the first to arrive in the green-carpeted, walnut-paneled room. Short, portly, and smiling, he posed for photographs at 12:45 P.M. directly in front of the portrait of Hatton Sumners, the long-deceased Judiciary Committee chairman who more than half a century earlier had presided at the hearing for Judge Halstead Ritter, the last American to be impeached and convicted.

"The president will not be impeached," St. Clair predicted as we clustered around him. "The House of Representatives will not impeach." But he would not say what the Judiciary Committee might recommend.

In the corridor outside the room more than one hundred people waited on line for a chance to sit in one of the eleven seats reserved for the public. Inside the hearing room St. Clair said that he was there "to listen and observe" and to abide by the rules of confidentiality set down by the committee.

A few minutes later Doar, the committee's chief impeachment counsel, and Albert Jenner, the bow-tied impeachment counsel for the committee's Republicans, entered the room. Smiling, they crossed over to St. Clair to shake hands. "You got the whole Red Sox with you?" Doar grinned at St. Clair, who was from Boston.

St. Clair, who did not follow baseball, glanced at his feet, trying to sneak a look at the color of his socks. "You got the whole Boston team with you?" Doar amplified. St. Clair smiled and murmured something inaudible.

We reporters scrambled for our reserved seats—the regulars crowding around the long rectangular press table to the committee's right while the overflow sat on chairs as part of the audience and held their pads and tape recorders on their laps. House employees gave the reporters texts of the statements the panel members planned to read.

At 1:08 P.M. the committee's chairman, Congressman Peter Rodino, brought down his gavel and began to read an opening statement which quieted the chatter of his audience. It was a businesslike speech.

> We understand our high constitutional responsibility. We will faithfully live up to it. For some time, we have known that the real security of this nation lies in the integrity of its institutions and the trust and informed confidence of its people. We conduct our deliberations in that spirit.
>
> We shall begin our hearings by considering materials relevant to the question of presidential responsibility for the Watergate break-in and its investigation by law enforcement agencies. This is one of six areas of our inquiry. We expect to continue our inquiry until each area has been thoroughly examined. . . .

The senior Republican on the committee, Congressman Edward Hutchinson of Michigan, was more dramatic. He emphasized that as far as he was concerned it would take "a finding of criminal culpability on the part of the president himself" to declare Nixon guilty of impeachable offenses.

"I trust that the members of this committee embark upon their awesome task each in his own resolve to lay aside ordinary political considerations and to weigh the evidence according to criminal law," Hutchinson urged. He asked that the members "seek the guidance of that Divine Providence which can be with us all" in making their judgment.

Then Congressman Harold Donohue (D-Mass.) moved that the hearing continue in closed session under rule 2, clause 27M of the House, which stipulates that "evidence that may tend to defame, incriminate or degrade" anyone under investigation should be taken in closed sessions.

Several liberal committee members objected to the motion. A roll call vote was demanded. By a count of thirty-one to six, the press was excluded. Congressman Walter Flowers (D-Ala.), the thirty-eighth committee member, was absent because he was presiding at a groundbreaking ceremony in his home district.

We reporters had known what the committee would do ahead of time but we were grumpy about it all the same. For only the second time in history hearings on whether a president should be impeached had begun in earnest, but they were beginning behind closed doors.

About three hours later the committee members came marching out of 2141. They were holding two thick black loose-leaf notebooks. One was an index of all of the materials gathered by the impeachment staff; the other dealt with the events ranging from the planning of the Watergate burglary operation to the actual break-in at Democratic headquarters. Doar had read an outline of the second volume aloud at the hearing as if it was a prayer book at a religious service.

"Quite boring," said Congressman Jerome Waldie (D-Calif.), one of the six House members who had voted to keep the hearings open. "If it had been on TV," Waldie said, "I think Americans would have fallen asleep watching it."

Impeachment was one of the most intense periods of my life. In six months I lost seventy pounds. I was up to seven cigars a day, not counting the half pack of cigarettes I sneaked in, but my angina, which had afflicted me since after about a year in Washington, had just about disappeared. I was so up, I brought a dead Canadian prime minister back to life.

I can explain how that happened. Every day I would stand with about eighty other reporters in front of room 2141 in the House Rayburn Building. We were outside 2141 because ever since that May 9 opener the Judiciary Committee had been meeting behind closed doors.

Just like the first session, in those meetings, John Doar would give each of the thirty-eight members of the committee fresh big black books of evidence and lead them through the pages, explaining and interpreting. All the while he was trying to speak in a monotone so that no one could accuse him of being biased against Nixon. Outside the hearing room Doar was so reluctant to talk to reporters that once, when I found myself walking with him in the sunshine toward Rayburn and remarked, "Nice day, isn't it, Mr. Doar?" he answered: "I wouldn't want to comment on that."

Despite being shut out, we reporters still hung around 2141, behind velvet ropes that the Capitol Police would set up sometimes in the hallway. That was because every so often there would be a vote in the House chamber over in the Capitol—one building and a congressional subway ride away. The committee members would come out of 2141 so they could vote, and we would grab them as they ran for the elevators that took them to the subway.

One morning, while walking into Rayburn, I saw a limousine pull up in front of me. It was decorated with a Canadian flag. A couple of guys got out and started to walk down the corridor. A reporter named John Pearson, who worked for the *Wall Street Journal*, broke ranks and chased after them. He was the only one.

"Hey," I asked my colleagues. "Who was that?"

"Pearson," a reporter answered.

"Not John," I said. "The guys he was chasing."

"Yeah," the reporter said. "That was Pearson."

Now, you have to remember that I was living in the world of impeachment. What was happening and what had happened anywhere else in the world was a little dim to me. So I said, "You mean the prime minister?" and my friend said, "Yeah." I thought nothing more of it.

But a couple of days later my *Newsday* colleague Tony Marro and I were told to write a story about why the news about impeachment was frequently confusing and contradictory. That was easy—everybody had different stories because the various members of Congress all told us different stories as they went running for the elevator.

So Marro and I sat down together to write this piece. As the senior man, I took control of the typewriter. Marro looked over my shoulder and made suggestions as I wrote. The first three paragraphs went okay.

> Washington—Three times, the bells in the Rayburn House Office Building resound. In their echo, one by one, three little lights on the clocks blink into golden life. Quorum call.
>
> Behind the invisible line marked by a police sergeant, 80 reporters stare down the corridor at Room 2141, a tantalizing, forbidden 30 feet away.
>
> Quorum call. The members of the House have 15 minutes to get to the floor. This includes the 38 members of the House Judiciary Committee. They are meeting secretly in Room 2141 to ponder the impeachment investigation of President Nixon.

So far, so good. But then I typed:

> Former Canadian Prime Minister Lester Pearson walks by the reporters, noticed but ignored.

"Wait a minute, wait a minute," Marro said, looking over my shoulder. "Pearson is dead."

I gave him a scornful look. "He is not, Tony," I said.

"You must of got him mixed up with someone else. I swear I saw him walk down the hall."

"He's dead, I tell you," Marro said.

But we were close to deadline. Pearson sure didn't look dead to me. I shrugged Marro off and kept typing.

Joseph Cardinal Mindszenty glides past in the midst of a priestly escort. No one follows.

Oh, it was a great story. Together we gleefully mixed our one-liners and descriptions of the scene, giggling all the way.

The far door of 2141 swings open. Rep. Joseph Maraziti emerges as if ejected by a catapult. It's Maraziti by two lengths as he speeds toward the reporters. Rep. Don Edwards is on the outside, closely followed by Delbert Latta. And here comes Robert Kastenmeier.

The reporters break for their favorites. To them, the race goes to the slower among the congressmen. Rep. Hamilton Fish does not seem to hurry. He strides from the hearing room to the elevator, not a racehorse but a flagship of a man with a dozen destroyers in his wake.

"What did you learn today, Mr. Fish?" one of the reporter escorts asks the towering Republican from Poughkeepsie. "There was nothing new," Fish says.

The corridor is bright with klieg lights. Fish is walking past the temporary television studio set up in a building entrance. "Can we talk to you for a few minutes?" a television reporter asks.

Quorum call. Quorum call. But the lights are bright and the television cameras of the networks beckon to the man from Poughkeepsie. Until the impeachment inquiry, Fish's basic contact with the press has been with the *Poughkeepsie Journal*, circulation 37,730. Yes, he will pause before the microphones for a few minutes.

But he knows it is all illusion. "I've been on the 6:30 news," he tells a reporter with a laugh. "I've been on the

7 o'clock news. Why haven't I gotten just one fan letter? All I get is the same old letters to send on to the F.B.I."

"What's new, Mr. Edwards?" "Did you discover an impeachable offense, Mr. Kastenmeier?" "Was there anything involving the President in wrongdoing, Mr. Latta? Or exonerating him, for that matter?"

One hundred and fifty-two steps from Room 2141 to the elevator marked "Members Only." A three-floor ride down to the House subway. A quick spin on the waiting train and up an escalator. Into another executive elevator and a three-floor ride to the second floor and the House chamber.

In pre-impeachment days, the congressmen could get from 2141 to the House floor in three-and-a-half minutes. Now some of them are missing quorum calls and votes.

A congressman hastens toward the elevator, reading aloud from notes he has taken during the session. Three reporters scribble as they run beside him. "That's who was present at that meeting, the way we heard on the tape," the congressman says.

"What was the date of the meeting?" a reporter asks. The congressman looks at his notes. "Oh, Jesus," the congressman exclaims. "You won't believe this. I don't know the date."

After the congressmen depart for the House floor, the reporters gather in small groups and try to fit the pieces together. They swap an Edwards for a Fish. A Kastenmeier for a Jerome Waldie. And often, they find they have been given contradictory information. To swap a Robert Drinan (liberal) for a Lawrence Hogan (conservative) is a sure way to get a contradiction, or at least a differing interpretation.

In the conversation about hush money, did the President say, "Jesus Christ, get it"? Or did he say, "For Christ's sake, get it"? Were there White House wiretaps on 17 persons, or was it 20? Different congressmen tell different stories.

The final versions reaching the public in the newspapers

and on television are either homogenized or incomplete. They are picture puzzles with many pieces missing.

At day's end, an official briefing is held. It consists of a laundry list of the events covered in secret, read by Committee Chairman Peter Rodino (D-N.J.). There is never any hint of what actually took place in Room 2141. The reporters' questions are evaded.

Rep. Edward Mezvinsky (D-Iowa), a committee member, says the fault lies with committee procedure. "It's an embarrassment for the press," Mezvinsky says. "It's an embarrassment for me as a member. You have to ask for something you know we aren't supposed to tell you, and we know that we're bound by confidentiality not to respond."

And so, the spectacle in the corridor of the first floor of the Rayburn Building goes on. Congressmen who are not members of the committee pause to watch in awe, amusement and disgust. A smiling Rep. Bella Abzug (D–New York) looks at the sight and chuckles, "vultures." Rep. John Seiberling (D–Ohio), who is a committee member, brings a camera to snap pictures of the scene for his own scrapbook.

"Why are you usually the first congressman out of 2141, Mr. Maraziti?" "In my school days, I was captain of the track team," the now-portly, 61-year-old Maraziti smiles. "I like to move fast."

Sometimes, congressmen walk away from the waiting reporters, toward a more distant and quieter elevator. Rep. Robert McClory (R-Ill.) says that this usually happens when there is a particularly sensitive topic discussed inside 2141.

But the sergeant in charge of the invisible line makes a policy change in favor of hot pursuit. "If they walk the other way," he tells the reporters, "you can go after them. But if they are coming at you, stay where you are."

Ah, the editors thought it was a terrific story. And Tony and I did too. It got great play the next day in *Newsday*.

Then at night I got a phone call from the national editor. "Mike," she said. "There's something you should know, something that really pisses me off."

"Yeah?" I said.

"Lester Pearson," she said.

"Yeah?" I said.

"He's dead," she said.

I couldn't help it. I began to laugh and laugh. When you've been working fourteen hours a day, laughing just seems to be the thing to do. Beside, I was thinking of all the other stuff in the story that was right. What's one little detail like revivifying a dead Canadian prime minister?

I laughed so hard that the national editor began to laugh too. When she stopped she reminded me that *Newsday* is a contributor to the *Los Angeles Times–Washington Post* News Service, which provides stories to many newspapers around the country. "What's also bad," she said, "is that it went out on the wire like that."

"Do me a favor," I said. "Try to flag the wire and get that line out of there."

She did attempt to do that, but someone at the news service—a key someone—did not get the message. This was such a good story that it was reprinted a couple of days later in the *Washington Post*, complete with Lester Pearson brought back to life.

But a funny thing happened—or didn't happen. Not one complaint was heard from the Canadian Embassy. And Tony and I got a lot of compliments about the story, but not one person mentioned Lester Pearson—at least not until I would bring it up.

For awhile Tony would get kind of upset whenever I talked about it. But I don't think he's angry anymore. After all, he got to be editor in chief of the whole paper. That's what happens when you know Lester Pearson is dead.

By mid-June the hearings seemed to be having a strange effect on many of those who were involved in them, including some members of the committee. On June 16 Congressman John Seiberling walked out of 2141 and accepted the assault of reporters with the stoic face of a hardened veteran.

"What did you talk about?" a reporter asked.

"Do you know the American eagle in the back of the room?" Seiberling asked as he stood in the corridor. "That plaster eagle up there has thirteen stars, thirteen stripes, thirteen arrows in one claw, and the olive branch in the other claw has thirteen olives. There are nine tail feathers, forty-six trailing edge feathers. . . ."

"Thirty-six trailing edge feathers?" a reporter asked.

"Forty-six," Seiberling corrected calmly. "It's interesting. . . ." His voice trailed off.

By the day Seiberling talked like this, each member of the Judiciary Committee had received twenty-seven black loose-leaf notebooks crammed with facts about alleged presidential offenses that might or might not be impeachable. Each notebook contained about a thousand pages. And the outlines of each had been read in the committee hearings by Doar in the deliberate Doar drone.

To break the monotony there were the tapes of the presidential conversations. "Listening to the tapes can be awful," a committee aide said. "The president is always opening and closing a drawer in his desk. Sometimes he is pounding on the desk, though this is not so bad. They are always drinking coffee and you hear the clinks of the cups and saucers. And they've broken through the speech barrier at the White House. They don't require sentences there."

Those committee members conscientious enough to search through their big black books never could find a flat statement that said, "The president did commit an impeachable offense."

"You can go through a whole loose-leaf book and not find one paragraph that states a crime," one aide said.

"You keep looking, asking where is the crime? It's like an Erector set. You're given the pieces one at a time, but you're not told how to assemble them. If you're not inspired to defend or to prosecute the president, then you're not inspired by anything you hear and it becomes deadly dull."

Less than a week later it was becoming more and more obvious that an edge of panic was being reached by the committee firebrands who were after impeachment. Was the creeping pace of the inquiry stalling the push to remove Nixon? Was committee secrecy exasperating the rest of Congress and the country into turning away from impeachment? Were they doing this all wrong? Was it all getting away?

In the caucuses of the Democratic committee members, Rodino kept reassuring them that everything was on target. To himself he sometimes would quote an Italian proverb: "He who travels slowly, travels surely and goes far."

But others weren't so sure. "I am disturbed by the delay and the postponement," said Senate Democratic Leader Mike Mansfield. All the same, Rodino and Doar stuck to their plan.

It wasn't the liberals but the Republicans and the conservative Democrats on the House Judiciary Committee who finally wrote the articles of impeachment that forced Richard Nixon to resign. The liberal and conservative Democrats tried to write them, but the pro-impeachment Republicans on the committee—big Ham Fish, and steadfast Tom Railsback and thoughtful Bill Cohen—wanted to do it themselves. And, with southern Democrats, that's what they did.

The Republicans on the committee who were trying to defend Nixon knew exactly what was going on. Thursday, July 25, Congressman Delbert Latta even told me what the vote would be two days before it was taken. "Strategy?

What strategy?" was Latta's answer when I asked him what was being planned by those Republicans who were still defending the president.

"When you've got the votes, you vote," said Latta, to whom the White House had assigned particular responsibility to ensure the loyalty of the six freshman Republicans on the committee. He knew when the game was up. "It will be twenty-six to twelve at least," Latta said of the coming vote for impeachment. "It might go to twenty-seven to eleven."

I asked him what effect the vote would have on the full House consideration of impeachment. "Certainly, an overwhelming vote in committee would have an effect," Latta said. Would twenty-six to twelve be considered overwhelming? "I would say it is," Latta said.

Everybody was talking about a smoking gun. Weeks earlier Marro and I had taken Francis O'Brien, Rodino's canny and imaginative administrative assistant, to lunch. He said that the problem the committee was having was to find "a smoking gun."

"Smoking gun," Marro said afterward. "That's pretty good. I like that."

I brushed him off. "What a cliche," I said. "How corny can you get?" And I did not use it when I wrote the story.

And now "smoking gun" was the catchphrase of the country. "My friends," Ham Fish had shouted at an emotional committee hearing, "we cannot find a smoking gun because there is too much smoke."

But everybody knew that the smoking gun was there, ready to be grasped by the pro-impeachment forces in Congress. And on the House Judiciary Committee the pro-impeachment Republicans and conservative Democrats were going to work. Six Democrats and Republicans went over to Railsback's office in the Rayburn Office Building and met there, trying to keep their sessions secret. They succeeded for a few hours, until some reporters, myself included, walking our incessant impeachment patrol from office to office, spotted Fish's shirtsleeved back as he tried to sidle unseen into the innermost room of Railsback's digs. Grinning at our shouts, they walked out to say hello, but they wouldn't answer any of our questions.

They worked hard over their alternative but they didn't have the pride of authorship. Instead they agreed with Rodino to have a liberal Democrat from Maryland, Paul Sarbanes, introduce the proposal of impeachment that they had drafted.

Sarbanes had never been in on any of the meetings of the pro-impeachment Republicans and conservative Democrats. He had been meeting secretly with the liberals on the committee in another part of the Rayburn Building who were drafting different impeachment propositions. And of course, the Nixon defenders on the committee had been huddling in a room of their own to plot their last stand.

Sarbanes didn't have much time to prepare for his new role as leader of the impeachment charge. The Railsback group shoved the piece of paper in his face about ten seconds before the committee began its meeting on Friday, July 26, 1974.

Poor Sarbanes, holding the paper in front of his nose, was still reading the charge to himself for the first time when he walked out into the committee room.

The television lights were on. All of the networks were there. Every seat was taken. There was no place left to stand. But despite the mob, I remember room 2141 was very still.

Sarbanes droned out the first article of impeachment, that group effort largely written by Congressman James Mann (D-S.C.).

Congressmen Charles Sandman (R-N.J.) and Charles Wiggins (R-Calif.) then demonstrated that the Nixon de-

fenders had not decided to give up after all. They immediately led a hard counterattack on the impeachment
article. Sarbanes tried but did not seem to know what or
how to answer. He was a Rhodes scholar but he neither
had written the thing nor had been given time to study it.

Sandman and Wiggins kept attacking, and national
television showed their assault live to the country. They
kept complaining that the charges were not specific. The
Democrats did not know what to do. They were scared
because they didn't want to look as though they were
being unfair. Once, Sandman went after Congresswoman
Elizabeth Holtzman, the New York liberal Democrat, so
fiercely that she was jumping in her seat for a chance to
answer.

"If the *gentle*woman would be patient," Rodino said
from his chairman's seat, "I'm sure that the *gentle*woman
will be given an opportunity to respond." Holtzman got
the message, but all the same, Rodino waited awhile until
she calmed down before giving her that opportunity.
Finally Rodino called a recess. The committee room was in
a turmoil.

Reporters rushed from their seats toward the raised
double semicircle where the committee held forth. I
headed for the Republican side and my favorite Virginian,
M. Caldwell Butler.

"I was in the state legislature," the pro-impeachment
Butler told me, "and I know all about filibusters. I hope
my Democratic friends don't panic in the next two hours."
He looked up at Wiggins, who sat in the upper tier of
committee seats. "Well, Charles," he said impatiently,
"how long are you all gonna' take on this?"

"Oh, Caldwell," Wiggins protested, "I'm all finished.
But you should ask Charles over there." He pointed at
Sandman.

"No," Butler said in an icy drawl. "Ah was addressin'
the um, uh, *in-tell-ectual* of the group."

Wiggins flushed but had no reply. If Sandman had

heard the exchange, he gave no indication. Butler went off to talk to Railsback.

It was 6 P.M. Railsback gathered his six Democratic and Republican allies. "Okay," I heard him whisper to them. "Let's try it. The card room of the Capitol Hill Club."

They tried to make it casual. One by one the seven plotters sauntered out of the committee room and walked the three blocks to the four-story building that really should be called the House Republican Club because that is what it is.

I sauntered right along with them. I followed them up to the card room. They opened the door. And there sat the counterplotters, the pro-Nixon Republican members of the committee. The seven waved feebly and backed off, finally settling for a table in a club dining room.

No reporters were allowed to sit in on any of these meetings, but Wiggins told us as he walked out of the card room that the pro-Nixon Republicans had decided to fight the impeachment article against Richard Nixon clause by clause on national television. In the dining room the Railsback group decided that the best strategy would be to let the Nixon backers have their time in front of the cameras.

So everyone went back to the committee room in the Rayburn Building, room 2141. And there they debated into the night. The Nixon forces lost every maneuver.

It was a day later, Saturday, July 27, just before 7 P.M., when Rodino finally was able to call for a vote on the first article of impeachment. There was dead silence in the room. All that could be heard was the voice of the clerk calling the roll of the committee and the members answering in soft voices.

The still photographers massed in front of the double tier where the committee sat. The television lights blazed. Every time a voice answered the clerk, the cricket clicking of camera shutters filled the room.

Railsback, sitting with the Republicans and waiting his turn, told me that to him the scene was petrifying. Every time there was a response of aye or nay, the camera flashes burst in the faces of the committee members, emphasizing each individual judgment. Railsback said that the flashes seemed to come nearer and nearer as the vote progressed. Finally, when it came his turn he voted aye, one of six Republicans to do so.

The vote proved that Del Latta was a fine counter. The committee was for the impeachment of Richard M. Nixon by a vote of 27 to 11.

The committee vote was over at 7:03 P.M. Down the corridor and around a corner from the committee hearing room was a big press room where the reporters who were covering the impeachment kept their typewriters. Since it was a Saturday night and all Sunday newspapers are strictly morning editions, deadlines for those of us who worked for eastern papers were already past or only minutes away.

Newsday was holding space until 7:30 P.M. With the other reporters I fled down the corridors to the press room and rushed for my typewriter.

But the paper! Somebody had swiped the writing paper from my typewriter case! A *Washington Post* reporter handed me a half dozen sheets of his stationery. By 7:28 the story was done under the *Washington Post* imprimatur and I was sending it on what passed for a fax machine to *Newsday*.

I called the national desk to tell them it was on its way. "You're late, goddam it," hollered Don Forst, my editor. But the story made the full run. Every Sunday newspaper that came off the *Newsday* presses had the tale of the impeachment vote. Best of all, it was my version, not a story from United Press International or the Associated Press.

In the days that followed, the committee approved two more articles of impeachment and defeated two others. It wrapped up its deliberations on Tuesday, July 30. But of course, the mortal blow to Nixon had been the first. Second and third strokes are always easier to deliver.

Senators and House members could speak of nothing but impeachment. I went to the office of Senator Jacob Javits (R-N.Y.) to try to talk with him and caught him unawares as I reached his threshold. "It is high time—" I heard him dictating to a secretary in his office. Then he saw me and stopped. "Get out of here," he shouted at me. He was only one of several Republican senators privately sending letters to Nixon, telling him that the game was up, that the moment for him to resign had arrived.

But other GOP lawmakers were planning a last desperate line of defense against impeachment. And the old hard-liners on the House Judiciary Committee were one group that was still standing fast.

With other reporters I kept walking from office to office, trying to pick up the latest intelligence. On Monday afternoon, August 5, I was just worn out. I had to take a break. I went to the House restaurant with Jimmy Breslin, who was writing a book on Tip O'Neill's part in the impeachment, an eventual best-seller called *How the Good Guys Finally Won*. We were having a cup of coffee when a House staffer came over to us and told us he had seen a member of the Judiciary Committee, Joseph Maraziti, one of the opponents of impeachment, tiptoeing down the second-floor corridor in the Capitol.

Breslin and I ran upstairs. I saw Maraziti walking along and then stopping to ask directions from a policeman. I got close enough to hear him say he wanted to go to the office of House Republican whip Les Arends. Since Breslin was writing a book rather than a column he gave up the chase at this point. But I followed.

It turned out that there was quite a little gathering at

Arends's office—eight of the ten anti-impeachment Republicans on the committee were there, being briefed by the president's lawyer, James St. Clair; White House Counsel J. Fred Buzhardt; and White House aide Bill Timmons. I hung around outside the door and waited. Very soon I had lots of company as my colleagues picked up the scent.

Inside the room St. Clair and Timmons were telling the congressmen that the transcripts of three more presidential conversations were about to be released. The president's men said the transcripts would show that Nixon himself had planned to cover up the White House involvement in the burglary of Democratic national headquarters at Watergate as well as other scandals. The smoking gun had been discovered.

St. Clair actually had called Wiggins, the president's most articulate defender on the committee, to tell him about the tapes three days earlier on a Friday afternoon.

After the Monday meeting in Arends's office Wiggins made a brief statement to the large group of reporters in the corridor and then rushed off. But I knew he had a story to tell. Together with only one other reporter I ran back with Wiggins to his office. He didn't protest. Instead he told the story.

When he got the call from St. Clair on Friday, he went to the White House to talk to him and to the president's chief of staff, Alexander Haig, face to face. Wiggins said he was stunned. He told St. Clair and Haig that he thought the three transcripts supported at least the first article of impeachment.

Wiggins was Nixon's own congressman, and he went back to his office where the walls were covered with Nixon photographs and thought about what he had been told. He did not tell anyone. Not even his wife. "I just thought about it," Wiggins said. "I got indigestion over the weekend." But by late afternoon on Monday Wiggins was ready. His press release had been roughed out even before the meeting in Arends's office.

Now, when it comes to impeachment the House of Representatives acts as a grand jury. If that body votes to impeach, then a trial is held in the Senate. There it takes a two-thirds vote to find a public official guilty of impeachable offenses.

Maybe, Wiggins said in his office, a defense could be made in a Senate trial that impeachment was not justified because there was only one instance of wrongdoing. Then he said he was not saying that such a defense should be made.

Before he talked with us in his office he had read his statement to the television cameras that made his position perfectly clear. "It is time for the president, the vice president, the chief justice and the leaders of the House and Senate to gather in the White House to discuss the orderly transition of power from Richard Nixon to Gerald Ford," Wiggins read in a choked voice.

His stoutest defenders in the Capitol had deserted him, but what Nixon would do next was uncertain. The Republicans sent a delegation to the White House to back up Wiggins, to back up their letters. Several reporters had an idea that this might happen, and we began to follow the Senate Republican leader, Hugh Scott. A half dozen of us trailed him down a second-floor corridor toward the House side of the Capitol. When he veered into a small unmarked room, however, I dropped off—but only because I knew what it was.

Sam Donaldson, who didn't, marched right in after Scott. Quickly there was an outraged bellow from the senator. "Out," he shouted at Donaldson. "Shut that door." Sam obediently retreated. Scott had walked into the Capitol's unmarked chapel to pray before going to the White House.

Scott, Senator Barry Goldwater, and House Republican

Leader John Rhodes were the three picked to tell Nixon the bad news in person. "The president was serene," Scott said afterward. "He had his feet up on the desk."

Scott, a big bald, moustached politician from Pennsylvania, said that Nixon asked for an assessment of his impeachment situation in Congress. "I said, 'gloomy,'" Scott recounted. "He said, "'You mean, damn gloomy?' I said, 'Yes, sir.'"

That was Wednesday, August 7. The next day, Richard Nixon resigned.

6

THE ADVENTURES OF JERRY FORD

NIXON'S RESIGNATION MEANT THAT THE FIRST APPOINTED VICE PRES-
ident in history now was the first person ever to become
president of the United States without having gone through
a national election. Of course, it also meant that Gerald R.
Ford in turn had to name the second vice president ever to
be appointed in the history of the United States. Ford
announced that Nelson Rockefeller was his vice presidential choice on August 20, 1974, but the former New York
governor was not able to win confirmation from Congress
and take the oath of office until December 19. The biggest
reason for the delay was that the Senate and House
committees holding the confirmation hearings had to
struggle with the fact that they were dealing with one of
the richest men in the world.

The day-by-day sessions lasted so long that Rockefeller
became uncomfortable while sitting at the witness table.
Hugh Morrow, one of the former governor's key assistants, would work his way up to the table bent double, as
if he was a soldier trying to take a hill held by the enemy.
When he reached the table, he would kneel and hand
Rockefeller something covered with a paper napkin.

Rocky would hold the package on his lap. After I saw
Morrow make the maneuver a couple of times, I stood up

to take a peek at the secrets he was passing to his boss. It was a strain, but I made out the contents of the package.

Morrow was sneaking his boss a stack of Oreo cookies. Discreetly, as he was being questioned, the former governor would pop them into his mouth one at a time and chew while holding his hand in front of his face.

Meanwhile the committees would be bugging him about what he was worth, and Rockefeller was answering between mouthfuls of cookie. Was he worth $97 million? Or was it $108 million? He didn't seem to be sure, exactly. He also had a maddening habit of giving gifts to his employees when they ran into financial difficulties.

He had given a guy named Henry Diamond $100,000 in stock because he did not have a pension plan and was worried about "making provision for his family." He'd given New York State judge Fred Young $5,000 because he had problems with his son. He'd given former New York State Housing Commissioner James Gaynor $107,000 in gifts and loans because he had problems getting rid of some property. And he'd given Henry Kissinger $50,000 to set up a trust fund for his two children.

Besides all of this, to members of a federal commission on which he served he had given Christmas gifts that he seemed to consider pretty tokens and nothing more. They were hand-blown Steuben Glass figures worth about a thousand dollars apiece.

Politicians investigating other politicians usually get suspicious about this sort of philanthropy. But Rockefeller was just a generous guy.

I have to say that most of these hearings were a bore. But he was one of the most important New York figures of our time, and *Newsday* demanded a daily story no matter what.

One desperate Friday, as the drone of dull questions and answers was driving reporters from the hearing room of the House Judiciary Committee, I simply did not know what sort of a story I could provide. Then I thought that perhaps I could write a kind of feature—how the committee members handle Rockefeller and how Rockefeller handles them.

Before the hearings had started, each of the committee members had received a big loose-leaf notebook that distilled the obligatory FBI report on the vice presidential nominee plus other inquiries into his background.

Well, I thought, the committee handles Rockefeller as though they have a book on him, which they do. Then I thought of his techniques—harsh and tough with Congressman Robert Drinan (D-Mass.), the liberal congressman–Jesuit priest; soft and cautious with the tough Congresswoman Elizabeth Holtzman from New York. And I suddenly realized what was going on.

I tiptoed to where Morrow was sitting. "Okay, Hugh," I said. "I want to see the book Rockefeller has on the committee."

Morrow was stunned. "You know about that book?" he exclaimed.

For me this was a grand moment. I actually had guessed right! "Yes," I bluffed. "And I want to see it now."

"Okay," Morrow said. He edged up to the witness table, picked up a big black loose-leaf notebook, and brought it back to me.

There was a little bio of each of the thirty-eight members of the committee, each illustrated with a photograph. But alas, there were no dark secrets in the pages—only whether each was liberal or conservative and whether he or she supported Rockefeller's vice presidential confirmation. Drinan was listed as someone who did not support Rockefeller's confirmation. The bios also listed the questions each had asked of Gerald Ford when he had gone through the same confirmation process.

All in all it was kind of disappointing. But it was

something no one else had, it was getting late in the day, and a reporter goes with what he's got. And I went with it, truthfully of course. "They're just short descriptions," said Morrow accurately.

Finally Rockefeller got the okay by the Senate and the House, despite his riches. On the night he took the oath in the Senate chamber, more than two hundred members of the House crowded into the room to watch the swearing in of the second appointed vice president in history. President Ford came down the aisle to see the ceremony close up—and stumbled on a step leading up to the dais. A few minutes later Rockefeller walked down the aisle and stumbled on the same step.

All his life Rockefeller had been number one. Now all of a sudden he was number two. I asked Hubert Humphrey, back in the Senate after his stint as vice president, what he thought of the situation. "I want to wish Nelson the best," he said, "but something about the office seems to keep vice presidents in check, no matter how talented."

The next day Rockefeller fulfilled a pledge. He went to a party in his honor given him by reporters who had once covered him in Albany. I was one of them, long since having reestablished friendly relations with the former governor.

I was standing near the front door when he walked in, and by happenstance I was the first to shake his hand. "Congratulations, Mr. Vice President," I said.

"Oh," he said, "we've known each other for so long. To you, I'm never Mr. Vice President. To you, to you—"

"Yes, yes," I interjected eagerly.

"For you, just call me 'governor,'" the new vice president said.

Jerry Ford is not only a likeable man but also was the most loyal politician in Washington that I can remember. It is true that funny things seemed to happen to him once he became president, but all the same, he was loyal.

Some of what happened to him came about because he just did not watch where he was going—like the time he fell down the steps of Air Force One in the rain after the plane landed in Salzburg, Austria. Other times things happened to him because his mind played tricks on his mouth, like when he accepted a lantern from a group commemorating Paul Revere's ride and said, "I'm not much one for history, but who can forget Paul Revere's words as he held this lantern high and said, 'One if by day and two if by night.'"

Sometimes things just happened to Ford that were not his fault. Like the time when he was about to hold a nationally televised press conference in the East Room of the White House and stood waiting for his cue in a side room.

"Ladies and gentlemen," the announcement came, "the president of the United States." All of us reporters stood up and waited for Jerry Ford to come out.

On our side of the East Room we saw the doorknob of the side room turn. But the door did not open. We saw the knob turn again. And again the door did not open. There was a great rattling and banging on the door. Then, on our side, the doorknob fell off.

A couple of minutes later a red-faced Ford was led out of another door in the side room and brought in through a different entrance to the East Room.

But Ford was a nice guy, a terrific guy as a matter of fact. He got his start on the Washington power ladder when he challenged Charlie Halleck, the Illinois congressman, for the job of House Republican leader. He won, beating the incumbent, and one of his supporters in his big victory was a Long Island Republican congressman named Jack Wydler.

Ford never forgot Wydler and always tried to do favors for him. For example, one way Wydler raised money for his campaigns was by forming an organization he called the Congressional Club.

Wydler got a bunch of Long Island businessmen to contribute one thousand dollars apiece to his reelection campaign. And this entitled them to become members of the club. As members, they and their wives would be invited by Wydler to Washington once or twice a year. He would give them lunch, courtesy of the caterers in the Capitol, a tour, and a guest speaker. The speaker was always Jerry Ford.

Ford addressed the Wydler Congressional Club when he was the House Minority Leader and he addressed the Congressional Club when he was vice president.

On the evening of May 14, 1975, Jerry Ford had been president of the United States for less than a year—and on this night he had his work cut out for him. The U.S. merchant ship *Mayaguez*, with thirty-nine hands on board, had been seized by Cambodia in the Gulf of Siam. We had just been kicked out of Vietnam by the North Vietnamese and were not feeling very good about it. Now Cambodia had given us another shot. To Ford, enough was enough.

Throughout the day he had been meeting with his intelligence advisors, with Secretary of State Henry Kissinger, with the specialists of the National Security Council. Reporters rushed to the White House. We paced on the lawn, trying to see through the windows of the executive mansion so that we could at least figure out who was talking to Ford in there. What decisions was he making with the help of the greatest military and diplomatic minds of the country?

I, for one, did not have to look very long. A side door of the White House opened. Out walked Jack Wydler, leading a string of about twenty Long Island businessmen and their spouses. Everybody seemed to be quite happy.

"Jack," I said. "What are you doing here?"

"This is the Congressional Club trip," Wydler told me.

"I took everybody to the White House. Jerry promised me a long time ago he would speak to them."

The topic was supposed to have been energy. But Wydler said that the president seemed to be preoccupied with something else—the capture of a ship named the *Mayaguez*.

"He called it 'an absolute act of piracy,'" Wydler told me. "He said, 'They are not going to get away with it.' He said, 'We're going to see that this type of activity is not going to prevail.'" And cheerfully Wydler and his Congressional Club sauntered toward the White House gates.

A little later Ford had a final session with the National Security Council. Then he called in congressional leaders and told them what he was going to do. When he walked into the Cabinet Room to tell them, everybody got up and applauded. But after he told them, some of them were very worried.

What Ford did was to send in the Marines, send a couple of destroyers, and order our jets to bomb the hell out of a Cambodian airfield. The Marines fought the Khmer Rouge, got pinned down on a beach, suffered heavy losses, and found the *Mayaguez*. But there were no crewmen on board. A little later they found the thirty-nine—the Cambodians had put them on a fishing boat and let them go.

Ford decided to tell the reporters about the whole thing himself—at about 12:30 A.M. at the White House. First he changed out of his tuxedo into a blue business suit. He had not only been chatting with Wydler and his friends but had also been entertaining the Dutch prime minister at the White House with a state dinner in the middle of all this. He had carried on with the dinner just so that everything would look sort of normal. And of course, as with his treatment of Wydler, the president did not want to disappoint his guest from overseas.

Ford was quite proud of the whole episode. He had the

wheel of the *Mayaguez* mounted and put in the Oval
Office. It was his greatest military victory.

Just after Ford won his war against Cambodia I found
myself in a small conflict of my own. The union published
the salaries of every editorial employee at *Newsday*. I
discovered that although I was the senior reporter in the
Washington bureau, only one other *Newsday* correspondent was being paid a lower wage.

I was, of course, furious and made that very plain to
Marty Schram, who by then had become the bureau chief.
But my anger came after he had already used up his 1975
budget for merit raises for other reporters in the bureau.
So Schram tried to placate me in another way.

Ford was going to Europe to meet with NATO leaders
for the first time. Then he was going to Austria for a
conference with Egyptian president Anwar Sadat. Schram
was the White House correspondent and I covered Congress. But he assigned me to make the trip.

It was the first time I had ever been to Europe, and I was
very excited. It was also practically my first time to cover
diplomatic meetings. I thought about that a lot, but I
figured this was Jerry Ford's first time doing this stuff too.
Maybe we would learn together. Of course, he had Henry
Kissinger along to help him, but I thought I would do all
right on my own.

When the plane landed in Brussels on May 29, I was a
little disappointed. The suburbs there looked something
like Queens. Moreover, there wasn't much of a crowd to
wave and applaud as the presidential motorcade sirened
through the streets. But that was because of unfortunate
White House timing. Ford landed just as the telecast of the
championship game for the European Soccer Cup was
about to start.

At the hotel I wrote and filed a quick story about the
airport greeting and the soccer game and then hit the

streets with a few other reporters. We polished up on foreign affairs by staring at the prostitutes sitting like statues in easy chairs behind plate glass windows of small establishments that looked like bars. We made faces at them to try to make them laugh but had no success.

The next morning I was ready for real diplomacy. I also discovered that covering most important or grand presidential events is done without being there. What happens is that a half dozen reporters plus television cameramen are chosen by the White House press office to cover a particular event. This little group is called a pool. The reporters in this pool are obligated to write an account of what they have seen and heard. This "pool report" is distributed to the hundred or so other reporters who were not lucky enough to be in the pool. Everybody then writes his story from the pool report, perhaps with an assist from private conversations with White House aides.

Different reporters are chosen for each event. Ford was to meet with seven heads of state, one at a time, but all of them in a single day.

I looked at the list of pools provided by the White House and to my delight found my name as a pooler for a couple of the first meetings.

In the morning I was given a special White House pass that read "pool," taken to the U.S. Embassy, and led into a small, elegant reception room. In front of me, like a stage set, were a couple of blue velvet chairs and a red velvet sofa.

Ford entered and sat down in one of the chairs. Constantine Caramanlis, the Greek premier, sat in the other chair. Kissinger came in and sat on the sofa. Aides of both leaders clustered along the walls. I stuck out my tape recorder and waited for the words of diplomacy.

"The first job I ever had," Ford told Caramanlis, "was given to me by a man of Greek background in his restaurant. I was very lucky."

That was it. After those words the reporters were tossed out of the room. An hour later Caramanlis left. The pool was allowed to go back into the room. There was Ford, sitting on the velvet chair. In walked the Greek adversary Suleyman Demirel, the premier of Turkey. He sat down in the same chair that just before had been filled by the premier of Greece.

"What kind of weather have you been having?" Ford asked Demirel.

"We have been having lots of rain," the Turkish premier said. "That means a good wheat crop."

So much for the Turks and the reporters. Again the pool was asked to leave. Demirel got his hour with Ford and then left.

Back the pool went into the room. There was Ford, still in the chair. In walked the Portuguese premier, Vasco Dos Santos Goncalves. He sat in the same chair that had been occupied by the Turk and the Greek. The Portuguese were a little peeved because they had just had a sudden change of government and Ford had said that if the country went Communist it should get out of NATO.

Still, Ford is a friendly man. "Do you have a busy schedule too?" he asked Goncalves.

"I do not speak English too well," Goncalves said.

Ford sat silently and clasped his hands in front of him. Goncalves sat silently and clasped his hands in front of him. Ford leaned toward Goncalves. Goncalves leaned slightly away from Ford.

Other Portuguese officials were entering the silent room. Suddenly Kissinger made a master diplomatic stroke. He slapped the empty seat next to him on the red velvet sofa. "Put one Portuguese over here," he called. "This is just to confuse the situation."

Everyone laughed at that. Even Goncalves got the drift of the joke and grinned.

It was easier when West German chancellor Helmut

Schmidt sat down in the blue velvet chair. In fact, it was Schmidt who began the negotiations that surely would lead to a great diplomatic breakthrough. "How many pipes do you have?" Schmidt asked Ford. "I have about fifty," Ford said. "I should stop pipe smoking but I thoroughly enjoy it."

"Oh," Schmidt said, politely ignoring the warnings of the American Cancer and American Heart associations. "I don't think it does any harm."

I understood that one and realized that Ford and Schmidt would be friends and perhaps even reach some agreements as a result of the chancellor's words. I had seen diplomacy in action, and even I knew that diplomacy is the art of tact.

We flew off to Salzburg the next day to watch Ford meet Anwar Sadat. It was raining when we landed, a little more than a fine drizzle. We had to wait awhile for Air Force One to land, and in the meantime I gaped at the snowy grandeur of the Alps—we were within spitting distance of Adolf Hitler's mountain retreat, Berchtesgarden. I thought of that as I also stared at the Austrian soldiers in their gray uniforms, looking just as if they had stepped out of a B movie about World War II.

Those guys were simply wearing the wrong outfits to be on our side. I didn't feel any happier when I heard that the veterans of World War II—the German and Austrian veterans—were having a reunion and a parade in the city to coincide with the Ford-Sadat meeting.

I wasn't the only one who was uneasy. Ron Nessen, Ford's press secretary, also said the scene gave him the creeps. "These are the people who killed the people," said another American newsman.

But the Austrian and German reporters were crowding around, friendly, hospitable, offering pens and pins as small tokens of amity. I talked to them and tried to take notes of first impressions, but by this time my pad and pen were too wet for writing. As Air Force One landed I hurried inside the terminal to try to buy a pencil. As I rushed outside again I heard a roar. I could not see over the mass of reporters in front of me. "Ford just fell down the stairs," a taller colleague told me.

Damn, damn, damn! I had missed it. "Is he hurt?" I asked.

"Naw," my friend said. "He's up again."

I got as many details as I could and then mournfully turned to follow the directions I had been given for the walk in the rain to my assigned place, a room in the Mozart Hotel.

I had a suitcase in one hand and a typewriter and a bag crammed full of pads, pens, tapes, and papers in the other. On my chest hung pieces of plastic declaring that I was a White House correspondent as well as a big tag reading "Newsday."

As I began to walk down the street, looking at gray uniforms and German signs, a pretty blonde woman ran up to me. "*Newsday!*" she exclaimed and threw her arms around me and kissed me. Salzburg was definitely looking up.

It looked up even more when I got to the hotel, with her help, and found that Austrian television was running superb pictures of the Ford fall sequence over and over, priceless to any reporter who desperately needed to write an eyewitness account.

As for my new friend, she was an American. In fact, she was from Long Island and I was the first sign of her hometown that she had seen since coming to Austria to try her luck as an opera and night club singer. And, great fortune, she had been asked by the State Department to escort reporters in need of assistance.

For the three days that we were there, she guided me through the streets of Salzburg and to the finest restaurants in the area, translating for food and for interviews all the way. Just to make this relationship clear, the two other male reporters who always went with me on these excursions joined with me in also treating her boyfriend to lunch.

Still, it really was almost like the start of a B movie. There were the Alps, the soldiers in gray, the president of the United States, the president of Egypt, Arab diplomats whispering fragments of information to American reporters, American diplomats clamming up when approached by American reporters—and a pretty young woman to act as our guide.

I thought she was just about the only Salzburg resident who would be willing to speak to me in English until I was about to check out of the Mozart Hotel. Then the concierge, a large, heavy man with a white handlebar moustache who wore a grand uniform with gold shoulderboards, approached me.

"Herr Valtman," he said.

"Yes?" I said.

"Is it true that you work for *Newsday*?" he asked.

"Yes," I said.

The concierge beamed. "For three years I work on Long Island," he said. "I work in a restaurant. Please give my very best to all the people in Rockville Centre."

Sadat, too, was happy. He and Ford worked out a good deal giving Egypt economic help and the Israelis limited access to the Suez Canal, where they had had none before. And Ford was happy because he nearly fell down a marble staircase, but Sadat caught him in time.

We flew on to Madrid, where Generalissimo Francisco Franco welcomed the president. I had never before seen so many soldiers and civil guards holding so many different kinds of tommy guns at a public ceremony. The soldiers also were wearing Nazi helmets which Hitler had donated to Spain a couple of generations earlier. The

Spanish had de-Nazified (though not beautified) the helmets by painting them brown.

Ford had a hard time shaking Franco's hand because the
old dictator was in the last stages of Parkinson's disease.
The great and irreverent correspondent Peter Lisagor took
one look at Franco's trembling arms and promptly gave a
loud snort. "Franco," said Lisagor, "is the best martini
mixer in Madrid."

Still, some of Franco's aides had a point to make too. At
a Ford-Franco banquet open only to a press pool, one of
them turned to his American counterpart, gestured toward the reporters, and murmured, "Those are the real
dictators of the earth."

7

THE YEAR OF THE CHICKEN

BILLY CARTER WANTED A DRINK. HE NEEDED A DRINK. IT WAS APRIL 6, 1976, a shivery Democratic presidential primary day in Wisconsin, and Billy yearned for a warm-up. But his big brother Jimmy said no. Jimmy was running for president and was ahead of the pack, but this primary was a really close one. It was as close as Mo Udall, that pesky, never-say-die, funny Arizona congressman who was Jimmy's toughest rival for the nomination, might get. With reporters paying close attention, Jimmy Carter wanted the people around him to be sober, most of all his own brother.

Billy, however, saw no harm in a snort, particularly in Milwaukee, the city that may not have made beer famous but surely didn't do anything to run it down either. Now, whether Billy and Jimmy actually had an argument about it I don't really know, but I do know this.

Billy got very mad about not being permitted to have a pop; so mad, in fact, that he walked out of his brother's headquarters hotel in uptown Milwaukee and went across the bridge and past Macy's to the downtown hotel that was Mo Udall's headquarters. He walked right into the room where the Udall staffers were getting ready to go out on their last-minute get-out-the-vote drive and volunteered to help.

The Udall people couldn't really figure out what to make of this. A few of them thought that Billy could be a spy, maybe, but they quickly put that idea aside. That would be just too dumb. So they went along with their newest volunteer and put Billy to work.

All day he helped them put up Udall posters and assemble literature that urged Democrats to vote for Mo Udall instead of brother Jimmy. At night Billy helped the other side decorate the Udall primary celebration ballroom. At that point some of the Udall aides gently suggested to him that with the polls about to close he might like to get back to his brother's headquarters. But Billy said no. He knew there was no way he could get a drink there.

Instead he and a half dozen of the Udall staffers and a couple of reporters, including me, went to the Bombay Bicycle Club, which was in the hotel, to wait out the results of the primary. Billy seemed very happy, swapping jokes and hoisting his glass for various toasts.

Every so often a couple of us would duck out to the ballroom to see about the returns. It was very close, with Udall in the lead. It got later and later and I kept switching back and forth between the ballroom and the bar, alternately checking on the vote count and on Billy. Mo was still ahead, and Billy, with his glass in front of him, did not seem to be losing his good cheer.

As my deadline began to close in I went up to Udall's suite and knocked at the door. He opened it, stood in the doorway, shirtless and shoeless, and invited me in. He walked barefoot into the living room and with relish recalled his fun playing basketball during the campaign.

"This is the Carter blind spot," chortled Mo, flipping his hand over his head. "I should be playing basketball," the former forward for the old Denver Nuggets said. Even though he was leading in Wisconsin, he was figuring on second place there and also in New York, which was holding its primary on the same night.

"Forty-one to thirty-nine in Wisconsin," he said. A close second would not be so bad. Two strong seconds and he could go on, keep on challenging Carter.

His daughter Bambi came in and embraced him, telling him he was winning Wisconsin. Udall shook his head and told her it was still a tie. The 5:30 news on television had reported that it was close, so close that his aide, Terry Bracy, had written two statements for him, one a speech of victory and the other a concession. Bracy had written the victory statement first because it came so easily and sweetly to mind.

I went back downstairs to the Bombay Bicycle Club. Billy Carter was still there with his new Udall friends. I took out my typewriter and started writing at the table, raising a glass of wine whenever another toast was being made.

A Udall man came running into the bar. "They're calling it for Mo," he shouted. Billy looked up, his face impassive, and took another sip. His Udall pals shouted their glee.

I headed for the elevator and the Udall suite. Mo answered the door again. He wasn't smiling anymore. His face was tense. His body was rigid. He did not seem to know what to do with his hands.

Victory in Wisconsin was staring at him from the television set in his hotel bedroom, and it seemed to make him more nervous than the prospect of defeat. What was worrying him so?

"CBS," Udall said to me. NBC and ABC had already projected him as the winner of the Wisconsin Democratic primary, a triumph that would have defied all polls, including his own. "I feel great," Udall said, looking grim.

Then he said: "It looks fairly sure, but I've seen elections turn."

Then he began to think about victory and how he could have possibly won. "We had good media," he said. "It got my name around." He said the endorsement of organized labor in seven of Wisconsin's nine congressional districts had been a key factor. "They really turned out," he said. He began to smile. "Maybe *Time* magazine will put me on the cover," he said. "We'll be very much in the delegate picture."

Still, he didn't want to go down to the ballroom. It was very late at night. The final returns from the conservative dairy area of the state were yet to be announced. But aides in the ballroom were phoning him, telling him he simply had to make an immediate appearance to show himself all over the country on the networks. The national TV audience was shrinking as they were telling him this.

Udall put on his jacket. He grabbed Bracy's victory speech and rode down to the Marc Plaza Crystal Ballroom. By the time he climbed on the platform he was in a good mood. "When the story of the '76 campaign is written," he told the cheering crowd and the television cameras, "it will have turned . . . on the critical decision by the people of Wisconsin—the people of Wisconsin who had the judgment and common sense to choose issue over image."

All of the reporters raced to phone their papers and file the story. I rushed with them and then went back to the Bombay Bicycle Club. Billy Carter seemed to be in a terrific mood. He was laughing with the growing group of proud Udall staffers. Udall himself went upstairs to bed.

In the club, victory drinks were being served all around. The laughter and the chaffing went on for more than an hour. It was early morning when another Udall aide walked into the bar. He wasn't smiling. The dairy districts had been counted at last, and they were conservative areas where Udall was not strong. And the votes from those districts had been enough to change things around. Jimmy Carter had won a narrow victory over Mo Udall.

There was a collective groan at the table—and a shrieking rebel yell of triumph from Billy Carter. "Yooohah," Billy hollered. "Yoooohaa." But Billy was a nice man. He looked at the stricken faces around him and immediately patted the shoulders of disconsolate Udall men and women.

Ronald Reagan was in Rock Island, Illinois, waiting for the result of the Republican presidential primary in Florida. His staff had a pretty good idea of what the result would be, which was the main reason he was in Rock Island instead of Miami or Orlando or some other Florida city to take the bows for the outcome.

Even though he was insulated by distance, he accepted the result badly. To get pasted by Jerry Ford in a southern state was no fun for a conservative who was playing all the right-wing notes, rhyming slogans before Jesse Jackson even thought of doing it, catchy little couplets like "Welfare queens in designer jeans."

And now, in a linchpin primary, he was a loser again. Reagan was a natural optimist, but he and his staff were having trouble smiling after this one. All the same, Lyn Nofziger, Reagan's press secretary, decided that he would try to make the best of the situation for his boss.

On March 10, 1976, the day after Florida had voted, there was to be a Reagan motor caravan through Illinois, driving for a win in that next primary state. Instead of having Reagan ride in his customary comfort—a limousine—Nofziger decided to put him on the press bus, just to show the reporters that his man might have lost but that he was neither down nor out.

Nofziger even arranged for about fifteen reporters to interview Reagan one at a time, one-on-one, with ten minutes allowed for each tête-à-tête. I asked to be one of the reporters, but I was new to the campaign and, furthermore, had the bad luck not to be working for a paper considered to be able to influence the outcome in Illinois. Lyn told me I had put in my request too late.

But I wasn't done yet. The next morning I made sure I was the first reporter on the bus. The seat that Reagan would be occupying was plainly marked and was toward the rear. I took the seat directly in front of it and waited, the only person on the bus besides the driver.

Soon Reagan was led on board and seated by Nofziger. The bus began to load up. I turned around in my seat and began to talk to Reagan. It was a cold, rainy morning. Reagan, his face glum, stared out the window and said something about the weather.

I tried to comfort him. "This isn't so bad, Governor," I told him. "Washington just had a heavy snow."

"Washington deserves it," Reagan growled.

In the fields, red tractors stood silent and empty. "They're from Russia," he said.

"What's from Russia?" I asked.

"The tractors," he said.

"From Russia?" I said.

"They're red," he said.

I did not know whether he was referring to color or country of origin. But I decided it would be prudent to stop talking about red tractors.

Instead I kept sitting half twisted in my bus seat, staring over the back of it at the candidate. In turn, Reagan looked across the Illinois border at the low skyline of Davenport, Iowa. "I got my first job there," he said. "Station WOC. That's where it all began."

WOC. The call letters stood for "World of Chiropractic." More than two generations earlier, as a radio announcer on his first job, one of the lines Reagan had had to say there, over and over, was: "WOC, Iowa, where the tall corn grows."

It had been the beginning of his public career. And now, on a bus rolling through the rain, he might be approaching its end. Reagan pointed to the trees and talked about how bare they were in Rock Island, and how green the trees were in California, a mere plane ride and universe away.

But then Reagan tried to cheer up. "Our campaign organization people see a reasonable possibility of having enough delegates to be close," he said to me.

The bus was five minutes on its way. Ted Knap, the Scripps Howard political correspondent who also had been shut out of an interview, took the seat next to me.

Nofziger came back with a reporter and cut me off. The reporter sat down next to Reagan and had his interview. Ted and I leaned our ears against the crack between our seats and furiously took notes. When the reporter's time was up, we turned around and asked Reagan to explain some answers further.

Then Nofziger brought the next reporter back and we did it all over again. This was great. We had the best seats on the bus—and the most complete interview of any newsie on board.

Sometimes instead of amplifying, Reagan would stare out the window and make remarks. The bus cruised beside the brown flatland, past a junkyard, and Reagan marveled at the discarded autos. "You look at these junkyards and wonder what other country in the world throws away cars of such recent vintage," he said.

He began to compare himself to Barry Goldwater, crushed in the presidential campaign of 1964. "I have never believed that Barry Goldwater was defeated by his positions," he said. "But they tried to portray him falsely. For example, Barry Goldwater was never against Social Security."

Now, Reagan said, Ford was running around the country claiming that he, Reagan, wanted to invest Social Security funds in the stock market. Reagan said he would never do that. "They're trying to do the same thing to me," Reagan said. "Goldwater was no wild-eyed monster. He wasn't going to push the button."

Reagan said Goldwater was smeared by Bill Roberts and Stu Spencer—two political consultants who had been Reagan's close advisors until they were wooed and won to Ford's side for the 1976 campaign. Now Reagan was blaming Spencer and Roberts for his defeat in Florida.

The bus stopped in Ottawa, Illinois, and Reagan got out to make his standard speech about Ford selling out the Panama Canal and selling out on detente. The crowd seemed to turn him off. He kept flubbing his lines. But at the next stop, in Joliet, the faithful turned out, eight hundred strong, to cheer him and have a torch singer belt out, "Everything's Coming Up Reagan."

"The way you're acting," Reagan beamed. "I find myself in the night thinking maybe people like yourself might get discouraged. Then I come out and find out you're worried I'm going to get discouraged. Well, neither of us is discouraged. We're going all the way . . ."

Reagan was right about going all the way—at least as far as the Republican National Convention. He didn't win the Illinois primary, but in North Carolina Senator Jesse Helms, the crafty right winger, threw out the Reagan operatives and ran the former California governor's campaign himself. And with Reagan denouncing Henry Kissinger and talking about the president betraying the true believers of the right on the Panama Canal, Helms and his political operation took the measure of Ford in North Carolina. So March 23, North Carolina primary day, was a turning point in the Reagan campaign and certainly a turning point for his morale. By May 5 Reagan had stormed past the president of the United States in primary contests in Georgia and Alabama and Indiana and Texas.

The other side rallied, but with only a couple of weeks

to go before the 1976 Republican convention President Gerald Ford still hadn't locked up his race for the nomination against Ronald Reagan.

Back in 1976 the right wing hadn't yet taken over the Republican party. At the time there were still a lot of moderate Republicans who had some political clout. To them Reagan looked like a brainless, inexperienced Hollywood weirdo, a right-wing nut who mouthed sinister slogans. So Reagan's handlers, particularly his campaign manager, John Sears, decided that they would execute a maneuver that was brand new to presidential politics and would catch the GOP moderates off guard.

They had Reagan select his running mate in advance of the GOP convention. And the guy they had him pick was Senator Richard Schweiker of Pennsylvania, a bona fide moderate-to-liberal Republican. With a partner like that Reagan might be able to stun Ford by picking up some moderate delegates.

It was a great idea. The only trouble was that the right-wing delegates to the upcoming Republican National Convention who had been for Reagan were absolutely furious. They went bananas. In particular the sixty Mississippi delegates and alternates, each with a half vote and all until now in the Reagan camp, were up in arms.

Clearly a rescue operation was essential. So on Wednesday, August 4, 1976, Reagan, Schweiker, and an assortment of aides flew down to Jackson, Mississippi, to meet in the Ramada Hotel with the Mississippi delegation. They were going to convince those sixty conservatives that Schweiker was a nice guy after all, just about as far to the right as any of them.

Reagan made no secret of the mission, and the hotel also was filled with reporters, buttonholing delegates and alternates, Reagan aides, and just about any passerby in the halls.

Since there are many Mississippians who are cautious when approached by a Northerner, in this situation it definitely pays for a reporter to have a regional accent. Having been born in Brooklyn, I quickly forged an alliance with a Mississippi reporter.

The two of us soon discovered that the delegates were receiving mysterious notes. Could they come to room 1065 after seeing Reagan and Schweiker? And could they not tell the Reagan people or anyone else about the invitation?

Now what in the world could be in room 1065? There was only one way to find out. Press passes around our necks, the two of us marched on over to the room and knocked firmly.

The door opened. A dozen Mississippi delegates were inside. They looked at our press passes and blanched. "I'd better go out another way," one delegate shouted and bolted for the window. Except it was sealed.

On the bed, red-haired Harry Dent sat and laughed. Harry Dent. He was Gerald Ford's chief operative in the South and a familiar face to every reporter covering the presidential race. "Please leave," he said between chuckles.

There was nothing for us to do but step outside. But we didn't go far. We lingered in the corridor and watched as delegate after delegate went from sitting down with Reagan, Schweiker, and Mrs. Schweiker to room 1065 to speak with old Harry Dent. They were ricochetting from Reagan to Ford and Reagan didn't even know it.

After awhile Dent opened the door and told us to come in. He was still laughing. "If Ronald Reagan can sell Richard Schweiker to this delegation, then we should send him to the North Pole to sell iceboxes to the Eskimoes," he chuckled.

Dent was resting on the bed in a room he had taken under another name. "I got what I wanted," Dent bragged to us. "I have reported back to the White House and to the

Ford committee that the Reagan-Schweiker mission was a failure."

Mississippi probably would vote as a unit at the convention. "Thirty golden votes," Dent exulted.

The delegates had gone into the closed meeting with Reagan and Schweiker carrying a list of Schweiker's votes. Why was he cosponsor of the Humphrey-Hawkins jobs bill that Reagan had labeled "a blueprint for fascism"? Why was he supporting the Kennedy national health insurance bill? And why, oh why, had he favored time and again the voting rights act that gave the ballot to the blacks in Mississippi and elsewhere in the South? Schweiker had a lot to answer for.

"Schweiker wouldn't get a bid to any major college fraternity in the state," James T. Speed, an alternate from Meridian, said. "He'd be blackballed."

Tupelo mayor Clyde E. Whitaker announced that he was switching to the president. Thomas Giordano of Pearl, the popular secretary of the Mississippi GOP, made an emotional statement at the closed Reagan-Schweiker meeting, saying he was disappointed in the choice of Schweiker. "Oh, I love that Tommy Giordano," Dent said. "Oh, he will speak."

I managed to talk to some of the delegates, but only about ten of them. But I was given a complete list of the delegation, together with the phone numbers. It was past midnight. I wrote my story, phoned it in, and went to bed in the Ramada.

I had to be back in Washington the next day. Still, I wanted to find out how effective Harry Dent really had been. So another alliance was forged—this time with my colleague from the *Los Angeles Times*. After all, the same corporation owned both of our papers. We split the list between us.

In the two hours left to us before we had to board a plane, we reached forty-two of the sixty Mississippi delegates. Eighteen of them said they now were for Ford. Thirteen said they were undecided. Only eleven said they were sticking with Reagan. Dent was right. It had been a good night for him and for President Ford.

Nearly every candidate has a stump speech, a talk that he repeats word for word throughout his or her campaign. Reporters assigned to cover these people every day get so that they also memorize the words. They can—and some-times do—speak them right along with the candidate.

The politician most faithful to the stump speech that I ever covered was Ronald Reagan. Particularly Ronald Reagan in 1976. With only a few updates it was just about the same speech he had been giving for years as an employee of General Electric. And at nearly every stop his wife Nancy was part of the act. She would sit below him, almost literally at his feet, staring up at him time after time with the same adoring smile, as if she had never heard this stuff before and it was just *wonderful*.

Reagan would tell people how when he was governor of California he returned tax money to the people. Watching him would be like watching the same movie over and over. He would get to the part where "they said it'd never been done before and I said [chuckle, let a smile crease the rosy face], 'Well, they never had an actor here before either.'"

The hour could be early and the hour could be late, but the laugh never dragged and the smile was always the same. You could set a watch by the timing of his dramatic pauses. And there was never an ad-lib to break the rhythm. It was driving the press crazy. I asked Reagan if it didn't drive him crazy too.

"Now this is the same question—I was never on Broad-way as an actor—it was the same question I used to ask my fellow actors who had played maybe a two-year run in a play," Reagan answered. "They said something to me then that I couldn't understand, but now I understand— the same lines, but they were a different audience.

"You anticipate, you will come to know they are going to appreciate certain portions of the speech, whether it's a joke or whether it's a positive line. So there is a stimulation from the audience itself. Now I understand what those people were telling me about doing a play."

Reagan's critics laughed at him and said he was an ideological ignoramus on foreign policy, a hard-line right winger who was a tool of the rich, whose selfish proposals would destroy the old, the poor, and the weak. But in the area that counted most—the technique of appealing to the voters—the other politicians running for president were fumbling amateurs. No one could ever perform the rituals of publicity with the dash and the presence of Ronald Reagan.

All his adult life Reagan had been a public man: radio announcer, movie actor, television host, governor of California. "I've been accustomed to being recognized wherever I went," he said. "I've wondered sometimes how someone straight from private life—what a strain it must be to get accustomed to that, to everything, photographers and so forth."

On board the campaign plane he always kept his attaché case at hand, containing hundreds of four-by-six unlined index cards bound together with rubber bands in separate decks, as though he were a professional gambler with words. His speeches were on those decks, handwritten in summary form. Each deck was a separate speech, but he would shift cards, separate, and combine from deck to deck. Yet the basic speech was always the basic speech, and the television cameras were always on hand to broadcast different excerpts.

Although he kept giving the same speech, sometimes with familiar variations, depending on the cards, he never trusted his memory. Every time he would make an appearance he always had his deck of cards in front of him.

One of the favorite stories told by my friend and colleague Pat Sloyan is of the time the attaché case Reagan was carrying opened and the cards, bursting from their rubber bands, spilled all over the sidewalk. Aides and reporters were on their hands and knees, helping Reagan pick up the cards

He stacked them together hurriedly and then entered the building and walked to the podium to give the talk. Pat said it was the strangest speech he ever heard. The cards were out of order and Reagan kept interrupting himself by saying, "No, no, that's the wrong card."

Still, he did stick to the script. Even in the five-minute individual interviews he granted to reporters on the campaign plane, questions on national issues invariably evoked the same responses—virtually word for word— that he gave at mass rallies.

Whenever I was granted a one-on-one session I tried to think of questions that did not involve anything in his stump speech. Once, I asked him if he ever had any doubts about his abilities to do the president's job.

"Oh, I think that any man who would deny that would be a liar," Reagan answered. "Of course, you realize that it's an awesome task. But I suppose I probably had more concern that way when I became governor of California. But now, after eight years [as governor] I've discovered we do have a system that works and you are able to call upon the people."

I asked him what he meant by "the people." He didn't say he meant the voters. He said he meant his advisors.

"The people" never put Reagan in shopping centers or had him shaking hands at plant gates or walking the sidewalks of the downtown of some big city. He spoke only at rallies. He was nearly sixty-five and physically it was easier; the TV coverage was the same and it allowed him to keep his distance.

"The people," his people, couldn't win him the Republican nomination for president. But on the night of August 18, 1976, while Reagan wept and the Republican National Convention was picking President Jerry Ford as the GOP choice, Reagan's people already were planning his campaign for 1980.

After he lost, Ronald Reagan went back to California and I went back to Washington. There I was told by my editors to forget Congress for awhile and concentrate on Jerry Ford at the White House. There was nothing really unusual in this—every fourth year many smaller bureaus turn away from the senators and House members on Capitol Hill to have their Washington reporters go after the bigger, more interesting, and flashier story—the fight for the presidency. Usually the congressional correspondent chases the challengers. But this time, with Jimmy Carter holding a double-digit lead over Ford, bureau chief and White House correspondent Marty Schram assigned himself to Carter as the likely winner.

This was okay with me. It was just after Watergate and Ford had given I-really-mean-it orders to his cabinet and to his White House aides that they must cooperate fully with the press. For the first time since I had arrived in Washington, top-level administration aides were returning my calls on a regular basis. As a class, not all nonpress people who have worked for various presidents have given me a terribly hard time—just most of them.

But there were some in the White House who were very friendly. Once, I was interviewing a senior presidential aide—-which president I promised never to tell—in his White House office just down the hall from the Oval Office. We were about halfway through our talk when his secretary called to tell him that he had some visitors.

"You can stay," he said. "But this can't be in your story."

A couple of seconds later, in walked two chubby little guys on either side of a big handsome man. "Well," one of the little fellows said to the White House aide, introducing him to the Adonis, "here's your new [he named a southern state] FHA director."

Hands were shaken. "I've got the forms you filled out right here," the aide said. "Everything looks just fine. Yessir, you'll make a fine Federal Housing administrator."

The handsome man gulped. "Federal Housing?" he said. "I thought I was going to be the Farmers Home administrator."

His two small sponsors stepped into the painful silence. "Hell," one told the aide, "FHA and FHA. What's the difference? He'll be a great Federal Housing administrator."

The handsome man grinned. "Besides," he chimed in, "the Federal Housing building is only fifteen minutes from my house. I'd have to drive nearly forty minutes to get to Farmers Home."

I was sitting on a sofa listening to this. I began to laugh and could not seem to get myself to stop.

"No," the White House aide said, giving me a reproachful look. "It will have to be Farmers Home. Since we processed you for Federal Housing, we'll just have to do it all over again."

The three visitors protested but not very hard. They took some more blank forms and headed for the door.

This was one of my more intimate encounters with White House aides at work. I didn't often get to see anything like that up close.

And I didn't under Jerry Ford. But all the same, his reign was a golden age for me when it came to getting telephone responses from White House aides. Sometimes they were sulky about doing this, but their moods didn't bother me. The bureau phone was ringing for me, which made me happy even if there were callers who were not.

The Ford election team had told reporters that the president wanted to have a formal campaign kickoff and that he wanted to have it at his alma mater, the University of Michigan. In 1935 Ford had been named the most valuable player as the center on the school's football team.

But it soon became obvious to me that there was something strange going on with this campaign opener. Nobody, not James Baker III, who was Ford's campaign manager, or Ron Nessen, who was Ford's White House spokesman, would give an exact date for this so-called kickoff speech. Already it was early September and the days for campaigning were bleeding away.

The national desk gave its permission and I flew off to Detroit, rented a car, and drove to Ann Arbor, home of the University of Michigan Wolverines.

I visited the university publicity office. They were polite, they were even helpful in a lot of ways, but they said they didn't really know anything about why no date had been set for the campaign opener. I stopped at the offices of university administrators, I chatted with members of the faculty, and I finally persuaded a couple of people who seemed to have an inkling of what was going on here to go out with me for a drink. Or two or three.

After an hour or so they softened and gave me a few hints—hints that I quickly was able to check.

It seems that at the end of August, Red Cavaney, whose job was to set up trips for the president—he worked in what is called the White House advance office—telephoned Robben W. Fleming, the president of the university.

Fleming was vacationing in Wisconsin, but the White House operators know how to track down almost anybody. Cavaney told Fleming that Ford would like to speak at the university.

"Mr. Fleming responded that he obviously is always delighted to have the president back," one university official told me, "but that equally obvious was the political nature of the visit."

In other words, was the president of the United States being told that he was not welcome at his own alma mater just because he was running for election? Not at all, not at all, the university official said. Apparently, Fleming informed Cavaney that all it meant was that the university itself could not extend the invitation. It did not mean that some *organization* on campus was barred from inviting him.

No sweat, Cavaney thought. A couple of days later he led a team of White House advance men to Ann Arbor. They found off-campus space to set up an operation. The university provided them with a list of student organizations.

Very soon the White House advance team discovered that there was one big problem. The University of Michigan was a liberal school. As a club the Young Republicans on campus had gone out of business a long time ago. In fact, from the anthropology club to the zoology society, the advance team could not find a single group at the university willing to invite the president of the United States for the purpose of making a speech or for anything else.

Then Frank Ursomaso, who was one of the advance men, remembered. Specifically he remembered twenty-one-year-old Cecilia Leslie of Grosse Pointe, who had been a White House summer intern until only a month before, working in fact in the advance office.

Even better, back in Washington the president had posed for a picture with CeeCee Leslie. And while she had been working at the White House, the young woman had invited Ford to come back to her campus for a visit—the campus of the University of Michigan, where she was now a senior.

Would that invitation stand? Well, CeeCee Leslie was a person, not a club—not a club yet, at any rate. But that might be changed. Ursomaso went to the campus telephone books. He found CeeCee in Martha Cook dormitory and explained the problem.

Immediately she agreed to be the founder of a brand-new campus organization—the University of Michigan Students for Ford. But a club has to have more than one member. Swiftly she enrolled her fiancé, Franklyn Kimball, a law student; Bruce Sisler, who also had worked in Washington as an intern; and Susan Smereck, a dormitory friend.

This was terrific! An organization to invite Ford! But then the advance team ran into yet another problem. To extend an official invitation the University of Michigan Students for Ford had to be an official organization.

And how could it be an official organization if fall classes weren't going to start until after Ford spoke? The team consulted with university administrators. There was an out. Provisional recognition as a club.

But that could only be obtained if Calvin Luker, the president of the Student Assembly, would approve.

Luker was not the kind of a guy who looked like a Republican. When I met him he had long hair, and judging from what he was wearing at the time, he didn't seem to be the type who would favor ties and jackets as everyday attire. He was also a former sergeant, a veteran of Vietnam.

CeeCee Leslie hustled over to the office of Henry Johnson, the university vice president. The White House advance team was waiting there.

"They asked me to come over," Luker said. "They gave me a recognition form with four signatures." Luker said that since the University of Michigan Students for Ford pledged not to discriminate against anyone and had even gone over the minimum membership requirement of three signatures, he saw no reason not to grant provisional recognition.

Luker said he didn't like Ford or Carter. "This was purely pragmatic," he said. "I would be every bit as helpful to a Carter organization."

The President Ford Committee—the big one back in Washington—gave their new campus organization three thousand dollars to pay for the use of Crisler Arena and more money to pay for leaflets and posters to be put up around the campus. The university refused to allow posters to be hung inside the arena.

Still, the president had his invitation. Ford delivered his formal opening talk there on the night of September 15. The Michigan Republican organization made sure that the fourteen-thousand-seat arena was jammed by sending busloads of young Republicans from all over the state rolling onto the campus. But there were also enough students on hand to boo and to heckle the president. Toward the end of his speech, someone exploded a firecracker. All the same, Ford was able to have his opener when he wanted it, though he might have liked a little more glitter to the crowd. Bo Schembechler, the school's fabled football coach, was too busy to hear the president speak, so Ford went to him, watching him direct the team practice and then joining the players for a training table dinner before he spoke. A second-string center, Steve Notta, asked Ford whether he had ever centered the ball over someone's head. "Many times more than I'd liked to," the president replied.

Jerry Ford was campaigning so fast and so hard that there were days when he did not know where he was. This could be difficult because he liked to start off his stump speech by saying "it's great to be in ———," and then half the time he would say the wrong town name. He also tried to use every minute; thus the installation of a loudspeaker in the presidential limousine.

While motorcading from the airport to wherever he was

going to speak, he would talk into the microphone in the limo, saying, "Hello, hello. Nice to see you. Great to meet you." The only trouble was that the people on the sidewalks couldn't see through the shadowed windows of the president's automobile, so all they got was this voice with no body attached. Riding in a Jerry Ford motorcade felt a little like acting in an old TV episode of "My Mother, the Car."

Everybody on the press bus laughed a little about this, and some decided it would be good to laugh at other things as well. When the San Diego Chicken, the guy in a chicken outfit who entertains at San Diego Padres baseball games, showed up in his costume at a Ford rally, both the reporters and the president were delighted—but for different reasons. "The chicken—I love it," Ford hollered.

Jim Naughton, then a reporter for *The New York Times*, figured that if Ford really loved the chicken that much he should not be separated from it. So when the rally was over he went up to the guy wearing the costume and bought the chicken head. It cost him a hundred bucks.

Naughton carried the chicken head on the bus and on the press plane. Now, Ford had a habit of holding planeside press conferences. The next day, in Portland, Oregon, the president took questions standing near the plane while the reporters crowded around.

Naughton was in the crowd, but he had crouched down. In that position he put on the chicken head. And then he reared up and raised his hand, trying to ask a question.

There was no missing Naughton. The chicken head was three feet high. The president didn't know what to do. He was trying not to laugh. Naughton managed to ask his question through the chicken head, and Ford managed to answer it without breaking up. But it was tough.

The conference ended and everyone got on Air Force One and the two press planes. Once aboard the planes, reporters and staffers—and even the president—giggled and whispered together.

Dick Cheney, then the young White House chief of staff, and Bill Greener, the campaign press secretary, conferred with a few reporters. Then the two presidential aides telephoned Ford's advance staffers, who were in Cleveland to prepare for the president's appearance there.

Two days later the planes landed in Cleveland. And when Naughton opened the door to his hotel room he heard strange noises. He looked down. There was a rooster—a large, live rooster—running around his room and doing what nervous animals do when they are locked in strange places.

Naughton ran after the rooster, caught it, carried it to Greener's room, managed to open the door, and threw it inside. By this time his luggage had been delivered to his room. Naughton opened his suitcase, stuck in his hand, and cracked the raw eggs that had been placed inside.

He cleaned up the mess as fast as he could. Then he located Cheney and Greener, who still hadn't gone to his room, and invited them in for a drink. There—that would show them their little trick hadn't worked. Of course, Cheney and Greener accepted the invitation right away.

They looked around the clean room, took their drinks, and sat down in the only two chairs. Naughton sat on the bed. Again he heard the cracking of the shells of several very raw eggs. Greener and Cheney cackled and left.

When Greener discovered the rooster in his room he shooed it into the hallway. I found it there, strutting along the corridor. I did not know what to do with it so I took out my pad and pen and tried to interview it. A television crew came along and began to film me talking to the rooster. But the rooster stonewalled, refusing comment on anything. It just tried to keep walking.

Television cameras always draw crowds, particularly when roosters in hotels are involved. This was no exception. Soon the corridor was filled with reporters, Ford staffers, and civilian guests.

Then the hotel detective came rushing up. "Sir," he asked me, "is that your rooster?"

"No," I replied.

"Well, whose rooster is it?" the detective demanded.

"There are those who would say that it is the rooster of Mr. Jim Naughton," I answered, "but both I and Mr. Naughton would deny that."

The hotel detective called for assistance. The rooster was placed in a makeshift cage and carried to the front desk. Reporters kept walking up to the desk clerks all evening and remarking that it was very odd for a hotel to keep a rooster on a reception desk.

I was not a witness to this, but I understand that the next morning, as Air Force One sped through the sky toward the next stop, Ford called a reporter up to his forward compartment and asked him to come in and shut the door.

"Okay," the president said to the reporter. "This is just between us. Now tell me what happened to Naughton and the rooster."

Kent County Airport was dark when Ford came home to Grand Rapids, Michigan, on election eve, Monday night, November 1. A three-quarter moon illuminated only the clouds, and the crowd at the gate was hidden in the shadows. Air Force One rumbled up to the waiting motorcade and the stairway was pulled up to the plane. The door opened and the president started out, his arm around his wife Betty.

He quickly descended the stairs, shook hands with his half-brothers Dick and Jim, and kissed their wives. A porter asked him if he was tired. "I'm fine," Ford said. "We've got a couple of more gigs tonight." He was terribly hoarse. He grinned and said, "I can't tell you how nice it is to be home." He put his arm around his wife and hugged her. "I've got my little mama here," he said.

The polls had showed that Carter was plummeting like a stone. They showed that the Democrat was still ahead, but the Ford staff was talking victory all the same. Without the help of Ronald Reagan to reunite Republicans after a bitter primary season, and without the support of Reagan's followers, they thought they still had a chance of winning.

Downtown the election eve welcoming parade through Grand Rapids had already started. There were bands and Boy Scouts and a procession of 1948 automobiles to mark the year Ford first began to serve the Fifth District as congressman. At the airport the president did not shake hands with those at the gate—perhaps in the dark he hadn't seen them. He got into his limousine to join the parade.

In front of the Pantlind Hotel on Monroe Avenue a small stage had been set up. Jerry Ford's people were there on the sidewalk, thousands waiting for their hometown president. "Ford, Ford, Ford," they were chanting.

The president got on the platform and encouraged them to keep it up. "Let's go, let's go," he shouted in his hoarse voice. "Let's go, let's go, let's go. All right."

He began to speak and his eyes filled with tears. He made gentle fun of his own words, saying, "I conclude these totally prepared remarks." A high school band struck up the University of Michigan fight song and over and over, the president croaked the words right into the microphone: "Hail to the victors valiant; hail to the conquering heroes; hail, hail to Michigan; the champions of the West."

So with a song and with hope and with the comfort of his friends, the last day of his campaign came to an end. The next morning Ford got up early, voted before 7:30 A.M. and then hung around the hotel with nothing to do until

11 A.M., when he went back to Kent County Airport to be honored at the unveiling of a mural depicting his life. He cried there again as he spoke of his stepfather and mother.

Then he flew back to Washington, ending a trip that had taken him 15,705 miles to 25 cities in 22 days. I rushed home to vote and then went back to the White House to write how Ford would be spending his election night. Of course, neither I nor any other reporter in the White House was able to see him—we had to stay in the press room while Ford was upstairs in the family quarters.

We had to rely on his White House press secretary, Ron Nessen, to tell us what he was doing. We found out that he had a dozen or so guests to wait with him; that he had hugged one of them, singer Pearl Bailey; and that after awhile his running mate, Senator Bob Dole, and his wife Elizabeth had left to watch the returns from their own home. We also found out that the White House doctor had treated him for laryngitis.

But the most important thing we learned was that he went to bed on election night without conceding to Carter, even though he was trailing by 2 million popular votes and more than 150 electoral college votes. We found this out from Nessen shortly before 4 A.M. in the morning. That was because Ford had gone to bed at 3:15 A.M.

I wrote a story on a typewriter at the desk reserved and marked for *Newsday* in the White House press room. I dictated and then walked the block and a half up Pennsylvania Avenue to the bureau office. At 5 A.M. I was the only one there. I called the national desk and asked if the early morning shift could phone the bureau at 8 A.M. so I could take a nap on the couch and then get back to the White House and not miss anything.

I would have stayed at the White House, but all of the few comfortable chairs already were occupied by sleeping reporters. It turned out that a call wasn't necessary. I was so on edge, I couldn't get to sleep on the *Newsday* sofa.

At 7:30 A.M. I went back to the White House. I had a long wait. Then, at 12:15 P.M. the president himself walked into the press room with his wife. Their three sons, daughter, and daughter-in-law were with them. Ford's face was puffy, his voice was down to a whisper, and the pants of his blue-striped suit looked as though he'd slept in them.

"It is perfectly obvious that my voice isn't up to par," Ford said. So his wife read the congratulatory telegram that was being sent to Carter. Behind her, the president bit his lip as she spoke.

After she finished, all of the Fords walked off the platform and began shaking hands with all of the reporters, trying to make small talk as they worked their way around the press room. Ford finished and with difficulty turned to try to make his way through the mob to the door. "I never was a good broken-field runner," he said a bit sadly. "I guess you all knew that."

A couple of weeks later Dick Cheney called Jim Naughton, who had long since stowed away his San Diego chicken head, and told him that Ford would give him an exclusive interview at Camp David. Jim made the two-hour drive to Camp David. But Ford was at the White House at the time. It was the last practical joke of the campaign.

A few years after that, though, Cheney, by then a new congressman from Wyoming, suffered a heart attack. He was in a hospital still in critical condition when his wife Lynne walked into his room. For the first time since he had been stricken, she was smiling. She opened a telegram and read it to her husband. "I didn't do it," she read. "Signed, Naughton."

8

LIZ

IN THE LATE 1970S AND EARLY 1980S SENATOR BOB PACKWOOD WOULD host an annual weekend for Republican politicians in the Tidewater area of Maryland. He was chairman of the Republican Senate Campaign Committee then, the panel that did just what its name said it did—help Republican Senate candidates win election.

Packwood figured that one way Republicans could get to know one another better and compare ideas would be to have these two and a half days together in an informal, relaxed atmosphere. During the day ties, suits, and jackets were discouraged. Republican elected officials from all over the country were invited, although it was mainly senators and congressmen who attended. The Washington press corps also got invitations, and everyone was encouraged to bring his or her spouse.

We all had to pay, of course, but reporters didn't care because the bills were footed by the newspapers. It wasn't a weekend where much news was made, but it was a good place to talk with politicians and establish relationships and contacts that would be helpful in the future.

So in 1980 my wife and I went to eastern Maryland for the weekend, held as usual in the Tidewater Inn, an old and elegant establishment that served simply wonderful crab cakes.

Another couple that went out for the weekend was the nearly new Republican senator from Virginia, John Warner, and his wife, the actress Elizabeth Taylor. Naturally they were the center of attraction. All of us—governors, senators, congressmen, spouses, staffers, reporters—were looking out of the corners of our eyes whenever Liz walked by.

Now, in the mornings the pols and most of the newsies played tennis or jogged and probably would have wanted to laze or exercise or shop all of the two and a half days away. But Packwood figured we all should put in some work for the weekend.

He would set up big round tables in the ballroom and name them after famous Republicans—like the Wendell Willkie Table, the Abraham Lincoln Table, and so on. He would assign Republican politicians to each and then give them topics to discuss.

After the pols talked about their topics they would vote on giving reports. Then one of them at each table would stand up and give that table's report to the whole ballroom. We reporters—or at least the reporters embarrassed into doing some work—would roam from table to table, trying to pick up something that would turn into a story.

Well, on this particular Saturday, which happened to be February 1, the topic was whether the Republicans nationally should get behind the idea that only men should have to register for the draft. The Republicans began talking about this hot topic and I, dressed in tennis shoes, jeans, and a black turtleneck sweater, was yawning as I wandered from place to place. Then all of a sudden there was a commotion at the table where John Warner sat with his bride Liz.

A half dozen reporters rushed the Taylor-Warner table,

tape recorders pointed ahead of them in anticipation of history.

Warner had just announced that he thought women should not be allowed to register for the draft.

"Booo," Liz mouthed at her husband. "Boooo."

Warner's face crimsoned. "You don't have a vote here," he told his wife.

Delaware Governor Pete Du Pont and Congressman Bob McClory knew their politics and they knew their actresses. They sided with Taylor. They told Warner he was discriminating against women.

Warner told them that when he was secretary of the navy there were more jobs opened for women than ever before.

"What kind of jobs?" Liz demanded of her husband.

Warner didn't answer straight on. He said that women could always volunteer for the armed services.

Liz became sarcastic. "Would they be going back to being Rosie the Riveter?" she demanded.

"No," Warner said wearily. "They won't go back to being Rosie the Riveter." He turned away from his wife, looking at Du Pont, and told him: "We do not need women on a fifty-fifty basis in the armed services."

Taylor wasn't going to take that one. But as she began to object, Warner thrust out a hand at his wife, telling her again: "You don't have a vote at this table."

"Don't you steady me with your warning hand," Taylor warned Warner right back. The vote at the table was taken and Warner's proposal was approved to be presented to the other Republicans by a vote of four to two.

I set off for the press area at a dead run and banged away at the typewriter in great haste. Deadline was only fifteen minutes away. My last line of the story was: "Taylor, her mouth in a grim line, did not speak."

Then I hustled for a telephone and dictated the story to a *Newsday* editor. It was a pay phone that wasn't in a

booth. I saw a couple of Republican staffers staring at me
and apparently listening hard, but I didn't care about that.
To me they were only a couple of more readers for my
story. "That sounds okay," the editor said to me when I
had finished.

I was a happy reporter. Nothing like a fun, off-beat story
on what had promised to be a dull day. There was going
to be a dress-up dinner and dance in that same ballroom in
just a couple of hours. My wife and I went back to our
motel—there was no room at the inn for most reporters—
and changed, she to a floor-length dress and me to a
business suit.

We drove back to the Tidewater Inn, hung our coats in
the checkroom, and walked into the ballroom. We were
fairly early and I wanted my cigars, which I had left in my
coat. So I excused myself, left my wife, and walked up a
ramp to get them.

As I was turning to walk back down, along came Warner
and Taylor, absolutely resplendent, he handsome and
dashing, she plump but beautiful of face and dress. Below
them the nonpolitical hotel guests who had been sitting in
the lobby rose and gave them a spontaneous round of
applause. They paused to acknowledge it.

Before such splendor I slipped to one side of the ramp to
let them go by. But they didn't pass. To my amazement,
they were approaching me.

"Hey," Liz said to me. "Black sweater."

I pointed at myself. "Me?" I asked.

"Yeah," Liz said. "You. Black sweater. I understand you
wrote a snarky story about me today." She raised a lovely
forefinger and began poking me in the chest. I was
thrilled.

"Snarky?" I managed to blurt, to myself thinking, what
the hell is 'snarky'? Whatever it was, it didn't sound good.

"Yeah," Liz said. "Snarky. And black sweater," I heard
her say, "I want to tell you, I don't like it."

I gathered my wits. "Wait a minute, wait a minute here," I said. "Did you actually read this story you say is snarky?"

"No," Liz admitted. "But I was told about it."

"Who told you?" I asked.

"My staff," Warner said.

Oh, I thought, my audience at the telephone. Aloud I said: "Well, I really don't think it was snarky. Now, I was on deadline and I may have sounded excited when I read it, but I don't think either of you looked bad in this at all."

They did not seem convinced.

"Look," I said. "I don't have it with me now. But I promise I'll bring it back to the inn with me tomorrow and you can read it. Then if you think it's snarky you'll certainly be right to be angry. But," I continued, "think of it this way. Your little argument today put this conference on the map. I could never have gotten a story about it in the paper if it hadn't been for you, and neither could anybody else."

Warner and Taylor began to smile.

"You know what else happened today?" I said to them. "There was a big prison break out west. And Senator Howard Baker's plane was forced down. Engine trouble." There was a gasp from them, for he was a friend. "Don't worry," I added hastily. "He's okay. But you see, this conference didn't have a chance if it wasn't for you."

Liz stepped around Warner and put her arm through mine. Warner came around to my other side and we linked arms. Together the three of us proceeded down the ramp and into the ballroom.

At the threshold Liz paused in dismay. "I'm the only one in a long dress," she said.

"Not so," I said. "There are others. May I introduce you to one?" I led Warner and Taylor across the room to my wife, who looked stunned as we approached. "Liz," I said, "meet my wife, Jean. Jean, meet Miss Taylor. And," I added quickly, "Senator Warner."

We all chatted for a few minutes and then they walked away. The next morning I put on a white turtleneck sweater and brought my story to their table. "Hey, black swea . . ." Taylor began and then said, "You changed your sweater."

"I did it on purpose," I said. "Here's the story. I'll come back in an hour and you can tell me what you think. My editor said it was yar." I remembered "yar" from a Katherine Hepburn movie. I think it referred to a boat.

"Yar?" Taylor said in the same puzzled way I had said "Snarky?" the night before.

"Yeah," I said. "Yar." I left the story and walked off.

When I came back those at the table—Warner, Taylor, and all the rest—told me that they thought it was not a snarky story after all. Taylor said it was okay except for one thing.

"I've been trying to put my mouth in a grim line all morning and I just couldn't do it," she said.

"Well," I said, "you may not have been able to do it this morning, but you did it very well yesterday afternoon." Then I said: "Now you have to do me a favor." Warner and Taylor looked startled. "Please autograph this story," I said.

Liz grinned. With a pen, she drew human lips. "Grim line Liz," she wrote. Warner contented himself with a dash. "Hooray! —John," he wrote. I framed the article and it hangs on my basement wall to this day.

9

REAGAN

EVERYONE KNEW THAT THE SATURDAY NIGHT DEBATE BETWEEN THE two Republican presidential contenders was going to be the greatest political event since Watergate. It was the upstart frontrunner, George Bush, against the former leader, Ronald Reagan, who had been closing the gap fast.

In 1976, when he had lost to Gerald Ford, I thought that Reagan also had lost his race against time. But in 1980, in his sixty-ninth year, there he was again, aging yet ageless, the easy leader in the competition for the Republican nomination until Bush had upset him by winning the Iowa caucus. Now, on February 23, 1980, just four days before the New Hampshire primary, there would be a debate between these two, face to face, and never mind the rest of the Republican pack.

This was the stuff that was sure to lead every paper in the country. The winner of this debate probably would be the winner of the Republican nomination for president.

That Howard Baker, Bob Dole, John Anderson, and Phil Crane were so angry at being left out just spiced up the action even more. Baker and Dole had even filed a complaint with the Federal Election Commission.

For days almost every reporter in New Hampshire had been calling the telephone company to arrange for personal phones to be installed in Nashua High School so they could be sure to get the word out. That is, every reporter except me. The *Newsday* editor in charge of my work had told me that no one from the paper would be assigned to cover the debate on Saturday night.

There wouldn't possibly be time to make the paper, he said. The Sunday paper was tight, he said. A lot of stories. He told me I could go to the debate and watch and maybe work some of it into my Monday piece. But as for a deadline job for the next day? "Don't even take a type-writer," he said.

Stupidly, I followed his advice. All I brought was my pad, my pen, and a tape recorder. I got to the high school more than an hour early, but I still had to park more than a half mile away. The tension began right there. The men and women who were going to be the audience did not walk into that school—they marched. They weren't smil-ing much either. Half of them wore Bush buttons and the other half wore Reagan buttons. They looked as if they were ready for hand-to-hand combat.

By the time I got to the high school I had found out something else. Just a couple of hours earlier Reagan had changed the rules of the debate—he had invited Dole, Baker, Crane, and Anderson to participate.

A few days before, Reagan, trailing after losing to Bush in Iowa, had been desperate for a one-on-one with Bush. But then, within the previous forty-eight hours, a survey by Reagan's pollster, Dick Wirthlin, had found that he had surged to within two points of his rival. So now it was Reagan who had "the big mo." "Now we've got a one-on-one debate that we don't need," a Reagan aide told me.

But Reagan could not back out. Although the official debate sponsor was the newspaper *Nashua Telegraph*, Reagan had wanted the confrontation so much that he had even paid the $3,500 it cost to rent the high school gym. So Reagan had to debate. And at the last minute he invited the others. But now it was Bush who wanted a one-on-one, and he wasn't about to yield to any pack of lesser rivals whose presence could confuse the judgment on who might be the winner.

The other candidates were not about to be put off either. One by one they came to the high school and were taken to a kindergarten set aside as Reagan's holding room and then into a small office to talk things over.

Jim Baker, Bush's campaign manager, came into the kindergarten to protest. He began to argue with John Sears, who was running Reagan's campaign. They sat down for the argument, two men each bigger than six feet, trying to get comfortable on kindergarten chairs.

Baker left without convincing Sears. Then Howard Baker suggested that Bush himself be brought into the discussion. Emissaries were sent, but Bush wouldn't come. Jim Baker said he would not let him. "It would be five against one," he said.

Senator Gordon Humphrey, the New Hampshire Republican, was dispatched to tell Bush personally that if everybody got into the act it would be good for the party. "Don't you lecture me about the GOP," blazed Bush, who had once been Republican national chairman. "I've worked a lot harder than you have to build the Republican party."

Humphrey came back. Reagan was telling the other candidates that if they were not allowed to debate, "we'll all walk out and I won't debate."

The Reagan staffers were about ready to tear out their hair. "Governor," Humphrey whispered to him, "if you don't debate you will lose this primary."

"We'll all be in this together," Howard Baker said.

"Yeah," Dole said. "Let's go on. Hell, I've been kicked out of better places than this."

I was standing in the gym, near the front. It was nearly 8 P.M., a half hour after the debate had been scheduled to start. Bush strode in and half of the crowd of two thousand cheered him lustily. "Bush, Bush, Bush," they shouted. "Reagan, Reagan, Reagan," the other half shouted.

Bush took his seat. Then in walked Reagan, trailed by the four other contenders. He sat and the four stood behind him. The place sounded like the arena for a hockey play-off.

Through the noise J. Herman Pouliot, the publisher of the *Nashua Telegraph*, tried to introduce everybody on the podium. Then he said that the four guys standing up— Howard Baker, the Republican leader of the United States Senate; Bob Dole, a powerful senator and former vice presidential candidate; John Anderson, a congressman and a member of the House Republican leadership; and Congressman Phil Crane, a darling of the right—had not been invited but that since they had insisted on crashing this party, he would allow them to make brief statements at the end of the debate.

The crowd went nuts. So did Reagan. He kept hollering that he wanted to speak. The moderator, Jon Breen, who was the executive editor of the *Nashua Telegraph*, tried to stop him.

"Will the sound man please turn Mr. Reagan's mike off?" shouted Breen, who also had been Jerry Ford's New Hampshire press secretary when the president faced off against Reagan back in 1976.

And that's when Reagan, the red spots on his cheeks deepening, came out with his famous roar: "I am paying for this microphone, Mr. Green."

The crowd shouted its glee. So did Baker, Dole, Anderson, and Crane. "Nazi Germany, Nazi Germany," Dole kept hollering at Breen. No sound man wanting to keep his health would have dared obey the editor's order.

"Give them chairs, give them chairs," the crowd began

to chant. Breen said he would not. So two senators and two congressmen turned to march out.

Dole paused to whisper into the ear of Bush. "George," the senator said, "there will be another day." He turned to Breen and whispered to him too. Breen shifted in his chair at the words. "I think I said 'shucks,'" Dole told me later.

Reporters raced along with the four ousted candidates. They stopped outside the gym for a press conference. Dole called Bush "an elitist." Anderson said Bush displayed "a kind of arrogance." Howard Baker said that Bush was trying "to reinstate closed door politics."

Reagan aides who had trotted along with the reporters were ecstatic. In New Hampshire they had been trying to portray Bush as the preppy rich kid on the block.

Inside, Bush, somewhat rattled, and Reagan, angry, confident, and triumphant, were debating. But that did not matter. It was the spectacle that counted. That and, for me, a telephone. Forget a typewriter.

I walked into the room where the private phones for reporters had been set up. "Could I by any chance . . . ?" "Not now" was the appropriate answer over and over as my colleagues fought to meet their own deadlines. I ran into the hall. There was a pay phone at the end of a corridor.

A pay phone and a long line. I got on the end and began writing my story on my pad in longhand. I still could make the final edition. I knew it. There was now only one man ahead of me. I didn't know him but he had the tags of a reporter. A reporter from a California newspaper.

Three hours time difference! Terrific! Sure, he said, go ahead. When I called, only the news editor was left on the desk. "On a scale of one to ten this is a twenty," I shouted.

"Okay," she said—she believed me!—"Start dictating."

I made the final edition. I don't think Ronald Reagan could have been happier.

* * *

The primary came three days later. In the afternoon, a few hours before the polls closed, Reagan ended months of bitter infighting among his staff by firing his three top advisors. A little later he found out he also had wiped out George Bush in the New Hampshire primary. Once more Reagan was the leader of the Republican pack. It was a place he would not give up again.

At 3:30 P.M. on Sunday, July 13, 1980, Ronald Reagan landed at Metro Airport in Detroit to claim the prize he had sought for twelve years—the Republican nomination to be president of the United States.

Behind the barricades a line of television cameras recorded the landing, but there were only a few reporters and perhaps a half dozen dignitaries waiting in the isolated area of the airport.

And there was his stepson, Michael Reagan; Michael's wife, Colleen; and their two-year-old son, Cameron. It was clear that Cameron was particularly close to his father. He stood and listened to his dad pointing out the big planes on the ground. He held his father's hand. Then finally Michael picked up Cameron and pointed to the sky, to the plume-trailing dot getting swiftly larger, and told him that his grandpa was coming in for a landing.

Michael put Cameron down as the jet landed, holding his son's hand tightly. Cameron began to wave at the jet. Michael waved with him. Cameron stopped waving and Michael did too.

When the jet rumbled to a stop, Michael and Colleen and Cameron were waiting. Ron and Nancy Reagan walked down the plane's stairs and were handed a big bouquet of flowers by one of the VIPs. The soon-to-be presidential candidate shook hands all around.

Michael carried Cameron to his grandfather. Reagan tried to take him, but the little boy turned away, burying his head in his father's shoulder. Michael soothed him and tried again. This time Cameron wailed his protest.

Reagan looked pained. Nancy seemed to be annoyed. With a severe face she grabbed Cameron, talking to him firmly. It did not seem to do much good. The protests grew louder and the little boy was handed back to his father.

Reagan made a three-minute speech to the television cameras. Then, swiftly, the motorcade formed up. The Reagans got into cars and were swept into the city, down to the mammoth maze of the Detroit Plaza Hotel. Reagan stepped out of the limousine and was engulfed in a frenzy of love.

The interior balconies of the Detroit Plaza were jammed with cheering people. Five stories high at the hotel's center is an open concrete labyrinth of ramps, rails, and levels, and not a space of it was unoccupied. Every person, it appeared, was responding to the cheers led by California Lieutenant Governor Mike Curb five floors below.

"R-E-A (pause) G-A-N. R-E-A (pause) G-A-N."

Teenagers were so enthralled with the chant that they were leaping into the air. Middle-aged men and women wearing elephant hats and battery-powered blinking Reagan buttons solemnly joined in the shout.

Now he was on the scene and waving his arms and grinning, the movie actor and the politician combined into the near-perfect public image. "Nancy and I were just flying by," he said into the microphones, "and we thought we'd drop in."

The crowd roared its love. Michael Reagan, Cameron in his arms again, stood next to his adoptive father. Again he tried to hand the two-year-old to his grandfather. This time Cameron didn't shriek. Instead he again quickly turned away and buried his face in the shoulder of his father.

"My grandson doesn't see me in the flesh," the sixty-nine-year-old Reagan said to a man standing next to him. The open microphones caught his words and flung them up and down the five levels of the Detroit Plaza Hotel. "Only on TV," Reagan said into the live microphones. The adoring crowd did not seem to hear. "I had a dream last night," Reagan said. "I dreamed Jimmy Carter asked me why I wanted his job. I told him I didn't want his job. I wanted to be president." Again the great throng shouted its love and admiration. Except Cameron, who kept his arms tightly around his father's neck.

He came slowly down the aisle of the chartered Boeing 727 in his tailored shirtsleeves, both hands clasping a large glass bowl filled with colored candies.

Hesitantly, almost shyly, he stopped at each row of seats and held out the bowl to the reporter-occupants. "Jelly beans?" Ronald Reagan offered.

In his campaign both Nancy and Ron did their absolute best to try to make the reporters happy. Ron set aside two hours a week for individual interviews. He would sit in the front of the plane and try to answer a reporter's questions for about ten minutes at a pop.

Most of the time, though, he wasn't very big on walking down the aisle to feed the reporters. Nancy did that. At just about every stop one Republican organization or another would give her a box of candy.

Mrs. Reagan would give the candy to the reporters. She would come done the aisle holding that box out and thrusting it at us, row on row. Most of us hated it.

It was bad enough to be stuffed with airplane charter food, and now Nancy was giving us chocolates. We were afraid to say no. One thing was for sure: none of us wanted Nancy Reagan to get mad at us.

But time after time, sometimes three times a day or worse, the chocolate-covered cherries, the bon-bons, the solid brown chunks of candy kept coming. And we had to keep eating. Something just had to be done.

So I gave it my best shot. As Mrs. Reagan presented a box of candy to me at chest level I smiled—sweetly, I thought—and said: "Mrs. Reagan, now I know why everybody up front [which was where she, her husband, and the staff sat] is so thin and everybody in the back is so fat. You're fattening us up, Mrs. Reagan."

Nancy's smile became an instant scowl. Uh oh. Trouble. Big trouble. "That's not fair," she exclaimed. "That's terrible. I give to the people up front too. How dare you—"

"A joke," I interrupted in a panic. "It was a joke, Mrs. Reagan. Truly. I was only joking."

The scowl disappeared. "Oh, oh," Mrs. Reagan exclaimed.

"May I have a chocolate, Mrs. Reagan?" I asked. "They really look very, very good." I seized one, popped it into my mouth, and began to chew. "Terrific," I said through the melting candy.

Later a tougher reporter got Mrs. Reagan in trouble over her candy distribution. Judy Bachrach, who worked for the *Washington Star*, wrote an unflattering feature about this generous though annoying habit of the candidate's wife and the fear of rejecting chocolate while flying. She also wrote that Mrs. Reagan had piano legs, an observation with which I would disagree.

I don't know whether it was the candy or the legs, but I was told that when Mrs. Reagan read the article she broke down and wept. But she was the wife of the candidate and she would hold her head high, no matter what. Besides, she had the advice of Joe Canzeri, a canny consultant for both actors and politicians who was now a member of the plane-riding staff.

So the next day, Nancy Reagan came down the aisle of the plane, a box of candy firmly in her grasp, stopping at each row of seats as usual. But a sign had been taped to the box. It read: "Take one or else." We laughed. And we took one.

Now, although Reagan did not walk to the back of the plane very much, he did his best to show that he was one of us. Once, when the jet was coming back into Dulles for the weekend, in the Washington, D.C., area where the Reagans were staying and where nearly all the reporters lived, a pillow fight erupted in the back of the plane.

Pillows were yanked down from the overhead compartments. The flight attendants protested, but all that happened was that they got socked with pillows too. Suddenly there was Reagan standing in the aisle.

The plane was in its fasten seatbelts–descent pattern, and he was standing there with a big grin on his face and a couple of pillows in his hands. He threw them at us. Behind him stood two grim-faced Secret Service agents, one of them holding the back of Reagan's belt.

We knew what that meant. That was really the end of the combat. Gingerly, we flipped pillows toward him so he could catch them. Then he heaved them at us.

He made other appearances too. Every time the 727 took off, a tape would play Willie Nelson singing "On the Road Again." And just about every time there was a takeoff Reagan would go campaign bowling.

He would stand at the curtain that separated his section from ours and roll a piece of fruit, usually an orange, down the aisle. If he could hit anywhere near the back door, we all applauded.

Every time he did this, the photographers would lean out of their seats and take pictures. They figured they would have a sensational shot if he fell and they wanted to be ready for it. Reagan figured the more pictures the better. So he always went bowling. A couple of days before the election, on Halloween night, he came out to bowl with a small pumpkin.

A TV cameraman propped up a rubber mask of Jimmy Carter to give Reagan a better target. "Wait until I get a watermelon," Reagan roared. Instead of Willie Nelson, another country-western singer was on the loudspeaker, chanting a campaign song. Reagan began to jig in the aisle in time to the music. Then as the plane soared he moved forward and hurled the pumpkin. He had great aim. The Carter mask was resoundingly smacked.

I was flying with Ronald Reagan from Los Angeles to Dallas on Friday, August 22, 1980. When we left Los Angeles on board the chartered stretch jet known as *Leadership 80*, I was a professionally neutral, personally liberal, Jewish journalist. A couple of hours after we landed in Dallas I became a right-wing Christian journalist. Let me tell you how this happened.

About forty minutes after we took off from Los Angeles, a couple of Reagan's young aides came walking down the aisle, giving out copies of the speech he was going to deliver that night to a fundamentalist rally that had been organized by the Religious Roundtable of Evangelical Christians.

Los Angeles to Dallas is a long run and I had plenty of time to read the speech over very carefully. In it Reagan attacked the separation of church and state. He said that if he was elected president he would, by God, put religion into government.

He also distorted a controversial course being taught in the elementary schools called "Man, a Course of Study," to what to me was an aggravating extent. I knew something about the controversy because my wife, as copresident of an elementary school PTA, was involved in it.

I looked at this speech with personal scorn. "I bet," I muttered to myself, "that this guy doesn't even believe in Darwin's theory of evolution." That thought kept circulating within me as I typed out an early version of an article for the Saturday paper.

In due time the plane landed in hot, muggy Dallas, and the reporters were put on buses and shipped to a hotel across the street from the convention center where the rally was going to be held.

Reagan, it was announced, would hold a press conference at the hotel before he spoke. Now, the burning issue of the day was Reagan's proposal that the United States in some way recognize Taiwan. This was not something that was making the folks in Beijing feel very comfortable. In fact, George Bush had been sent by the Reagan forces to China to calm those people and reassure them about his running mate's intentions.

So the traveling press was primed to ask Reagan about Taiwan. Lyn Nofziger knew this and had hit on a device to make things easier for his boss. He had invited the reporters from all sorts of religious publications who had been covering the Religious Roundtable meetings to attend the press conference too.

And there we were, religious and secular, mixed up together. But the traveling press was tough and got on Reagan's case quickly with difficult questions about U.S.-Chinese relations. Reagan was desperate for a change of topic. Maybe he didn't know who I was when he saw my upraised arm and pointed at me.

I gave him a change, all right. "Governor," I asked, "do you have any doubts about the theory of evolution?"

Now there was Reagan, facing a room half-filled with religious reporters, about to go across the street to address an evangelical rally where charismatics were worshipped. There was only one thing he could say.

"I have a great many questions about it," he said. "I think that recent discoveries down through the years have pointed up great flaws."

Next to me, Ken Bode, with NBC at the time, was so

excited he couldn't sit still. "Oh, follow, follow, follow," he kept whispering to me.

I was going to follow anyway. Out of the corner of my eye I was happy to see my friend Nofziger glowering at me as if he wanted to kill me. "Governor," I said, "then do you think that the theory of evolution should continue to be taught in the public schools?"

"Well, it is a theory," Reagan said. "It is a scientific theory only and it has in recent years been challenged in the world of science—that is, not believed in the scientific community to be as infallible as it once was. But if it was going to be taught in the schools, then I would think that also the biblical theory of creation—which is not a theory," he amended hastily—"but the biblical story of creation should also be taught."

Mine was the only question to be asked about the theory of evolution. This was great. I rewrote my story to lead with it. I thought that Reagan doubting Darwin made a very nice piece indeed.

As for Taiwan-China, so what? I had written that one before and Reagan really hadn't said anything new. It was old news. I relegated it to a single paragraph in my article.

Most of the other reporters did not share my judgment. They led with the latest Reagan quotes on sticking to his guns about recognizing Taiwan, figuring that was a bigger gaffe than evolution.

But the reporters in the room did want to know who had asked the questions about evolution. They went up to Jim Brady, the press secretary, and asked him. Brady didn't know, but he figured he had to tell them something. "Ah," he said, "you know how it is, with all those right-wing religious journalists there, the governor had to say what he said. It was some right-wing Christian journalist who asked the question."

I didn't find out that he had said this until after we got on the plane, which was way after we had crossed the

street to the rally and listened to some charismatic de-
nounce homosexuals and drug users in the same breath.
He also had said that it was time for "God's children to
come out of the closet" and go after the homosexuals and
the Communists and the liberals.

I must say that I felt a little uneasy when I heard him say
the word *liberals*. But I felt better once we were back on the
plane and found out what Brady had said. I walked up to
him. "Do I look like a right-wing Christian journalist to
you?" I asked.

Brady never corrected his mistake. But during the
campaign, whenever he would get a little peeved at me he
would stare at me and mutter, "Right-wing Christian
journalist."

The press conference in Dallas wasn't the only event
where Reagan stumbled. In the first couple of weeks of the
general election campaign he also managed to stir up a
fuss when he called the Vietnam War "a noble cause" and
when he criticized Carter for beginning his own campaign
in the town that gave birth to the Ku Klux Klan.

Most of his trouble was the result of ad-libs. Stuart
Spencer, Reagan's old consultant who had enraged the old
politician-actor when he went over to Jerry Ford in 1976,
was totally forgiven and brought on board to shut the
candidate up. Spencer acted as a kind of official gag, doing
his best to force Reagan to follow the script. He was not
always successful. There was, for example, the wonderful
moment when Reagan insisted that "trees cause pollu-
tion."

A couple of days after he said that, *Leadership 80*
was flying over a forest fire. Jim Brady and Ken Khachigian, just about the best speech writer in the Republican
party, took one look and then spoke with one voice.
"Killer trees, killer trees," they shouted. In front of the
reporters, too.

When Bill Casey, running the campaign out of its

Virginia headquarters, found out about this indiscretion, he was furious. There was nothing he could do about Khachigian—Ken was the ace speech writer and he just had to be kept on board. But Brady? Never mind his intelligence and quickness and rapport with reporters. Press secretaries were cheap and plentiful. Casey literally grounded Brady for two weeks as punishment, making him work at campaign headquarters during that time.

It wasn't Jim's or Ken's fault, but Reagan's fear of firs and other bark growths resulted in the most wonderful campaign sign I have ever seen in more than a generation of covering campaigns. On October 13, just as the smog was lifting over southern California's Pomona Valley, we came into Claremont Men's College for a campaign appearance and saw it—a banner tied between two trees. CHOP ME DOWN BEFORE I KILL AGAIN, it read.

So much for killer trees. But things could have been a lot worse.

How much worse became evident on a couple of occasions when Ford joined the campaign to show his support for Reagan. In 1980 the former president was returning Reagan's 1976 cold shoulder with a warm helping hand. Ford may have given Reagan a big boost. But some of the things he did must have made the Reagan camp think they were really lucky that the proposal for a Reagan-Ford ticket at the Republican National Convention had never worked out. If Ford had become the vice presidential candidate, there would be no telling how many mistakes might have been made. There was trouble as it was.

The first problem came in Chicago when Reagan, in a speech, revealed that if he was elected he would freeze social programs, give the Pentagon so much money that the generals and admirals would feel they were in a candy store where everything was free—and at the same time cut tax rates 30 percent over the next three years.

After saying this Reagan had dinner in his hotel suite

with Ford, who hadn't bothered to listen to the speech. And during this meal Reagan neglected to mention his brand-new plan to Ford. They talked about other things, and then Ford went downstairs to hold a news conference.

Naturally the reporters asked him about the big new economic plan. Ford seemed dumbstruck. He as much as said that such a proposal would be nuts. He said the reporters had to be wrong, that Reagan simply wouldn't have come up with a screwy scheme like that. Reagan's advisors, sitting in the back of the room, broke into a cold sweat. "I don't think at this stage we can see down the road what the economic situation will be," Ford said.

Something had to be done. Lyn Nofziger hustled onto the little stage in front of Ford. He tried to give the former president the hook. "I'm sure President Ford is quite tired," Nofziger interrupted. "He just can't take any more questions."

But Ford hadn't been questioned by a gang of reporters in a long time. He wasn't about to be shut up. "Nonsense," the former president said. "I haven't seen my friends here for awhile. I'd be happy to take some more questions." Nofziger looked as if he would be happy to strangle Ford. But he slouched back to a corner of the stage and said nothing more, just watching in anguish while Ford blissfully kept tearing apart Reagan's great new economic plan.

I don't think we saw Ford for a long time after that. He and Reagan did speak together at a rally in Texas, and then in the closing days of the campaign he boarded the plane again to stump with Reagan through the Midwest.

At an airport rally Ford got on a platform in a hangar and began to speak to hundreds of people standing pressed together. "Everybody please be comfortable," Ford said. "Please take a seat." There wasn't a chair in the place.

It was contagious. Later that same day, in Battle Creek, Reagan amazed the crowd by pledging "further tax increases for the people of this country." He paused. "Did I say increases?" he asked.

In Pontiac it was Ford's turn again. "Turn out Carter when you go to the polls on November 5," Ford demanded. That would have been a day too late. The election was November 4.

But they could be quick, too. When hard-hat hecklers shouted "Bonzo, Bonzo" at Reagan, he replied: "They better be careful. Bonzo grew up to be King Kong."

All of that happened on November 1, and Reagan was feeling pretty good by then. Ford was feeling so good that he told me that on the whole he'd rather be in a stadium somewhere watching a football game.

A couple of weeks earlier, though, the Republicans had not been at all comfortable. Reagan had been leading, but President Carter was coming back. The private polls of the Reagan camp showed the president to be only a couple of points behind.

Carter desperately wanted to debate with Reagan to show off his superior mind. Reagan had been ducking. But now it was the Republican candidate who needed something to get the campaign moving again. The call was up to Reagan.

Like every other reporter, I really wanted to find out what he would do. On the plane a few people were even making bets about it. All of the reporters were worried that someone would get the debate story first.

Now, for reporters who don't work for *The New York Times* or the *Washington Post*, life is a little tougher. Politicians leak so that it will be to their benefit. They figure they won't get much national publicity out of an exclusive story in papers like *Newsday* or the *Chicago Tribune* or the *Atlanta Constitution*.

So on October 15, when the campaign plane landed in

the dark in Detroit, I walked up to a certain very senior Reagan campaign official with whom I was friendly. "Hey, Joe," I said, "I bet a cameraman twenty bucks that Reagan won't debate Carter."

As I said, this guy and I were friendly. He didn't want me to lose money. "If I were you," he answered with a laugh, "I'd do my best to lay off that bet."

Oh, boy! I could not wait to get to the hotel and start writing.

But wait a minute. There was a problem. "Hey," an editor said, "he didn't actually say there would be a debate, did he?" I had to admit that he had not. "Let's tone this story down," the editor said.

So the lede read: "Ronald Reagan, clinging to a narrowing lead in the race for the presidency, is suddenly giving signs that he may be willing to debate President Carter on national television after all."

It was better than nothing. And it was certainly better than the way I handled the writing of the debate, which took place in Cleveland on October 28.

I was supposed to write an analysis but, although I should have learned from covering the 1976 debates, I made the very basic mistake of deciding to watch this confrontation live inside the hall instead of from a television screen. It is such a different perspective.

In the hall it was obvious that Carter was putting Reagan on the defensive with his superior knowledge of the issues of war and peace, strategic arms limitations, nuclear proliferation, and so forth.

I did not know that on the screen the viewers were seeing what amounted to a different debate. On TV Reagan had belted Carter out of the presidency not with knowledge but with one-liners—by asking Americans whether they were better off in 1980 than they were in 1976 and by wisecracking, "There you go again."

I mentioned what Reagan had said in my article, but I also wrote that Carter had made Reagan play his game. The closest I came to being on point was to write that Carter could not deliver a knockout punch. Besides not watching the debate on TV, I totally forgot that people wanted a change and that all Reagan really had to do was show he could stand on the same platform with the president and not get chewed up.

But I finally learned. Unless the assignment was to write a feature story, I never again covered a presidential debate as a member of the live audience.

It was the last day of the campaign. Reagan began it by playing Peoria. He stood on the warm, windy street in front of the courthouse, laughing with thousands at the jokes of Bob Hope, applauding the words of his running mate, George Bush, and those of Jerry Ford.

Not Reagan, not Bush, not Ford said a word about the fifty-two hostages being held in Iran. Carter's struggles to get them released had held the Democratic president captive as well—dragging him down nightly on the television newscasts. What was scaring the Republicans, right up to the final day of the campaign, was that somehow Carter would win their release and instantly regain his popularity, and that the voters, in their joy, would vote for him again.

So in Peoria the big three of the GOP did not want to say anything about the hostages. Then Senator Charles Percy, an Illinois Republican who was a senior member of the Senate Foreign Relations Committee, spoiled it. He didn't hide his feelings.

Percy stood in front of the courthouse too, acting as a warm-up speaker for the stars. "Under no conditions do I feel the Senate, the Foreign Relations Committee, or the people of this country will tolerate a hasty decision on the hostages that would require somehow paying ransom or get us involved in a war with Iran and Iraq," Percy said. In the audience Reagan staffers winced as they heard Percy speak. But the senator kept right on.

"The fifty-two hostages are members of the diplomatic corps," Percy said. "They must come back with honor. They have waited a year. They can wait a few more days."

After that rally was over we started flying west. We ended up in a shopping center in San Diego. Some young guy in a stovepipe hat and a very loud voice kept heckling Reagan. "What about the Equal Rights Amendment? What about ERA?"

Now back in Detroit, under the direction of the Reagan forces the Grand Old Party, which had been the first political party to endorse equal rights for women, had become the first political party to come out against such a concept. Women's organizations were outraged, and Reagan had been heckled throughout the campaign. Not even his statement that he would appoint a woman to the Supreme Court seemed to satisfy his tormenters.

On election eve in San Diego, though, among all of those conservatives, Reagan finally had enough. He stood on the stage in front of the microphone and looked down in anger. "Aw, shaddup," he bellowed at the lone heckler. The words, carried by amplifiers, echoed through the big shopping center.

When he got back on board the campaign plane, the reporters were ready. We had our tape recorders primed to the right spot.

"Well," Reagan beamed at us, "this was so much fun let's do it all over again."

The reporters all pressed their recorders' play buttons. Up and down the aisle, all that could be heard was Ronald Reagan hollering "Aw, shaddup," "Aw, shaddup."

"Hey," Reagan protested. "Everyone wanted to hear the

speech." We reporters hit reverse on the recorders and the play buttons again. Reagan finally grinned and made us stop with: "That was one of the pleasantest lines I spoke during the campaign."

He moved down the plane, making small talk and shaking hands with the reporters and the television technicians. It was then that he told us of the long-ago murderous assault on his person by Bonzo, the chimpanzee disguised as a male.

But the story, once told, did not disturb his humor. A lot of people asked him to autograph their Secret Service press passes and he happily obliged. I thought about it and decided it would be bad form.

With anecdotes and wine and handshakes, the jet cruised north to Los Angeles. Reagan went home and we reporters were bused to the Century Plaza Hotel, where election night headquarters had been set up.

The next morning I went with a small group of reporters out to Pacific Palisades to watch the Reagans vote where they lived. This was such an exclusive neighborhood that there were no commercial or public buildings that could be used as a polling place. Instead the people of the 1376th Precinct voted in 1980 at the home of Sally and Robert Gulick on Sorrento Street. "It's my civic duty," Mrs. Gulick said when I asked her why she had made her house available.

She had just said good-bye to Dodger baseball announcer Vin Scully, who had cast his vote. Lawrence Welk had come and gone, but Sylvester Stallone hadn't voted yet. We reporters amused ourselves by looking at the precinct's voting list.

Patti Davis and Ron Reagan, two of the Reagan children, also were registered there. Patti was registered as American Independent, the party that had supported George Wallace in 1976. Ron was a registered Democrat.

The Reagans arrived in a limousine at about 10 A.M. The walk up to the Gulicks's front door was roped off to keep the reporters to one side. Pieces of tape had been stuck near the threshold to show the Reagans where to stand after they voted so that the television and still cameras could take their pictures from the best angles.

The Reagans pulled the levers and came out and stood at the tapes. "Where are the children?" I shouted at Reagan. Reagan cupped his hand to an ear. "What?" he asked.

"The children," I yelled. "Ron and Patti. Aren't they voting?"

"What?" Reagan asked.

"Can't you see he's deaf?" a Reagan aide hollered at me. Mrs. Reagan scowled at the aide.

Reagan made a decision. He left the tape and walked up to me. "Now," he said. "What did you say?"

I repeated the question. "They're not voting here," Mrs. Reagan interrupted.

"Do you think you're going to win?" another reporter asked.

"I'm too superstitious to answer anything like that," Reagan answered.

Mrs. Reagan nudged her husband and whispered into his ear. "Cautiously optimistic," she whispered.

"Yes," Reagan said. "Cautiously optimistic."

Someone else asked whether he wasn't more optimistic than that. "No," Reagan said. "President Dewey told me to just play it cool."

The Reagans kissed each other. She got into a car to go home, and he got into his limousine to go to a barber shop. Aides insisted later that he paid $7.50 for the haircut.

That night, of course, Reagan walloped Carter, the margin stunning even his own advisors. At his headquarters at the Century Plaza Reagan shook hands with Red

Skelton and said what the winner is expected to in every drama: "There had never been a more humbling moment in my life."

Then he got into his limousine and went back home to Pacific Palisades. It was definitely a Hollywood ending.

After I wrote my story I got a bottle of wine and went up to my room. Carter had conceded before the polls had closed on the West Coast. I watched developments on TV as a couple of veteran Democratic congressmen from California went down the tubes because Carter had quit early and voters figured there was no use in going to the polls.

Late the next morning, I got on the telephone to be interviewed on a New York City radio show that featured *Newsday* reporters. My friend Bob Greene, *Newsday*'s great investigative reporter, was on with me and speaking from New York. He and I quickly tangled on what kind of a president Reagan would be.

"Environmentalists better watch out," I said. "The poor better watch out. The old people better watch out. Children better watch out."

These were not good words for a supposedly objective reporter, but I was really wound up. I had broken the code. Reporters deal in facts. We are supposed to leave public opinions to columnists and to editorial writers.

Greene tried to cool me down by asking me if the Reagans would set a new style for Washington. "Yeah," I growled. "When he voted yesterday he was wearing a shirt that looked like it had been cut out of a tablecloth from an Italian restaurant."

There was no unsaying it. I certainly didn't hate Ronald Reagan. He was a politician of tremendous charm and magnetism who had a wonderful way with words. I also liked nearly everyone on his staff.

Covering Reagan was a grand experience. When Reagan was involved, all the stories lent themselves to drama and emotion and frequently, the unexpected. But I always had the feeling that presidents should station themselves in the middle of the road to preside fairly over the country. It was okay for members of Congress to go to the right and the left—in fact, it was obligatory—535 differing voices representing the differing views of America.

But to me, a president should represent consensus. Reagan didn't do that. And it was Reagan's radically right-wing view of the world that on a personal level I found so difficult to take. Still, I don't think readers would ever see that in my articles.

All the reporters covering the campaign knew Reagan didn't work very hard and that he liked issues presented to him on a single page with proposed solutions at the bottom (they were called mini-memos).

His imagination frequently overcame the facts. He frequently made stories up and told them as if they were the truth. We always reported that whenever we could confirm it. He also would stretch the truth.

For example, as he frequently said, he indeed had majored in economics at Eureka College with sociology as a co-major. Guess how many teachers were in the Eureka College economics department. That's right. One. Guess how many teachers were in the Eureka College sociology department. That's right. One. What's more, they were the same one.

For all his campaigns and during his eight years in the White House, it seemed pretty clear that Reagan, more than almost all politicians, hired staffers to do his thinking for him and to come up with ideas for him. Visitors to the Oval Office would often come out with stories that showed that the complexities of government seemed not only to bore Reagan but to be beyond him. They would discuss issues, and he would respond with anecdotes.

Yet the presidency itself, with Reagan's hired hands doing the work, moved at a revolutionary rightward pace. And when it came to enunciating the ideas proposed by his assistants, to give them global impact, to sound a call to arms, there was no one who could match Ronald Reagan. And that ability remained through all the scandals and destruction wrought by his administrations—from the Environmental Protection Agency to the Interior Department to the climax of the Iran-contra affair.

Nothing unfair about reporting any of that, both the good and the bad, which all of us did. But opinions voiced by a reporter on the day after the election, opinions of what sort of a president Reagan would make, was walking the line toward editorializing.

Now during the campaign, I really tried to write colorful but balanced copy. I know I usually do this successfully because both conservatives and liberals will tell me that they think the stories I write are fair.

At the same time, I think my job is to write the truth—and that may hurt. In 1968, I wrote a story about sitting with Hubert Humphrey in a hotel room. We were watching the Democratic National Convention nominate him for president while antiwar protesters and reporters were being beaten up by the Chicago cops in the streets below.

"There's my little Donna in the front line," called Humphrey as he saw his daughter-in-law on TV at the convention. "Bob [her husband] never lets her get out of sight. There she is, my cute little blondie."

When his wife, Muriel, appeared on the screen, Humphrey's excitement grew. "Oh, I wish she was here," he shouted. He kissed his hand and pressed it against his wife's image. Then he bent and kissed the television screen with his lips. "Aw, I want to give her a big kiss," he said.

He said other things like that as well and I wrote it all in my story, mixing it with his concern for the riots and the rioters. Bill McIlwain, my managing editor, read it and sent it on to Long Island via Western Union. "I let it go," he said to me. "But, God, you must hate Humphrey."

"I love him," I said. "I hope he wins."

"Then why did you write that?" McIlwain asked.

"Because it was the truth," I said. McIlwain shook his head. "God save us," he said.

But to me, the truth is what must and should be written. There's a problem there too, of course. Reporters, like everyone else, sometimes have different ideas of what is important about a speech or a committee hearing or a presidential news conference. That's why it's good to have many reporters from different news organizations covering a major event. Among all of us, perhaps, a reasonable representation of the truth may come out.

There are times when I don't write at all. I didn't write what I saw when I went down to the Reagan press room the day after the 1980 election expecting to find staffers filled with joy. Instead I found a half dozen junior aides who had flown on the plane sitting disconsolately outside the staff room.

"They told us all good-bye," one said. "They said thank you very much and that was it. We don't have any jobs. We don't even have any money to get out of town."

"See Lyn," I said.

"We're waiting for him now," the young man said unhappily.

Nancy Reagan still didn't like Lyn Nofziger, mainly for the same reason she didn't like him before—because of the way he dressed. During the campaign Nofziger's response was to look worse and worse.

Toward the end of the campaign he could have passed

for a homeless person. He took to wearing a coat that looked like a Salvation Army reject. On the coat he pinned a huge button. "I Love Nancy," the button read.

The day after the election Nofziger collected the dismissed staffers and went to work. Every one of them got money to go back home. Every one got a job in the new administration.

10

CORD OF WOOD

NINETEEN EIGHTY-ONE WAS A GREAT YEAR IN WASHINGTON. IT WAS terrific to have a secretary of interior who had fought to open public lands to mining, oil, and timber interests; to have the former executive director of the Moral Majority as the guy who directed federal activities for nonpublic schools; to have an antiabortionist to direct the Office of Adolescent Pregnancy Programs and a critic of the food stamp program to direct the food stamp program. Put that together with a budget that mashed up just about all social programs but increased defense spending, a president who hated the federal government and who was forever mixing up fact and fiction, a Republican Senate and a Democratic House, and you have a wonderful year.

Maybe not so wonderful for poor people and environmentalists and such, but terrific for the Pentagon and reporters. For the generals and admirals it was like being in a heaven where weapons systems grew on trees. As for the reporters, we don't do well on stories that say that all planes landed safely today and relate how everybody loves one another.

I wrote a lot of Reagan stories, covered the big fights in Congress, and worked on political articles. There was much running around and many long hours, but I enjoyed it. And in early 1982 the pace actually picked up. Senator Harrison (Pete) Williams, a liberal Democrat from New Jersey, the last of the Abscam defendants, was fighting to stay in the Senate and out of jail. The Senate wanted to expel him, but he wasn't about to go quietly.

It was a hot story, and I was the reporter covering it for *Newsday*. The copy desk was sending me into rages almost every other night, though, the way the editors were changing my stories in what seemed to me to be various silly and gratuitous ways and, it appeared, actually writing in mistakes.

At midnight one Thursday, Tony Marro, my old colleague, my old bureau chief, and one of the reporters who had broken the Abscam story but by now the managing editor of *Newsday*, called from Long Island and asked me to read him the first few paragraphs of the next day's piece. I did, he made a couple of small suggestions, and then he told me how pleased he was with the story. I finished it up and went home, the end of another fifteen-hour stint.

When the papers came into the bureau the next day, however, I found that my article again had been revised by the copy desk, the import of the story changed—together with many of the words of which I had been so proud. I was so angry I couldn't get myself to sit down. On the phone Tony promised that he would try to find out what happened, but he couldn't calm me.

I paced in the bureau, finally took a walk, and tried to ease up by buying a couple of books. As far as work was concerned, it was going to be a slow day, the kind of day best spent catching up on expense accounts and plotting next week's strategy. The Senate had gone home for the weekend and I didn't have to write a Williams story. In fact, at this point I didn't want to write a Williams story.

Then, at about two o'clock, the national desk called. Former Senator Jacob Javits, a politician whom I had covered for years and who now was suffering from Lou Gehrig's disease, had been rushed to a hospital. His death could be imminent. But the editors had checked and there was no obit ready. Could I please write a two thousand–word obit today?

I wanted to say no. I was bitter about the copy desk, that constant, consistent destroyer of stories. And I was so very tired. But Javits—I liked Javits, he was a tough politician of great intellect and wisdom, and he had fought hard for many, many great causes. No one at *Newsday* knew this proud, public, but lonely man the way I did. I told the editor I would write the obituary.

It took a long time for me to do this. I didn't wind up my work until two o'clock in the morning. By this time there was no one left in the bureau, of course, except me. I punched the buttons that sent the story to the computers in Melville, New York, and got out, looking forward to the weekend. As I was walking down the garage stairs to my car, I began to feel something I hadn't felt for years—not since I had lost the seventy pounds covering the House Judiciary Committee's impeachment of Richard Nixon. I began to feel vague twinges in my chest, most definitely angina pains.

I figured I needed a good night's rest. I tried to think about something other than work. By the time I pulled into the carport at my house it was nearly three. The pain had long since disappeared.

I went directly to bed. But at 7:30 I was awakened by an awful stomachache. I sat up with it for awhile and then went back to sleep. But an hour later I was up again. It was getting worse.

I thought about this for a minute, then got out of bed and took a shower. The pains would not go away. I dried and looked at myself in the bathroom mirror. I felt this was a formal occasion. I spoke to myself aloud. "Myron, my boy," I said solemnly to my reflection, for it was a solemn occasion, "this is not gas."

I don't know why I shaved, but I did. I don't know how I got myself dressed, but I did. I worked my way downstairs and found my wife, an early riser, in the kitchen. "Jean," I said, "don't be alarmed but I think I'm having a heart attack." Then I said in what I prided myself to be a calm voice, "You'll have to drive to the hospital because it hurts too much for me to drive."

A neighbor took our two youngest boys, Danny and Larry. My oldest son, Morris, a teenager, jumped into the car with us. Running red lights, we got to Suburban Hospital in less than fifteen minutes.

Morris wanted to support me but I felt that would be embarrassing. I walked into the emergency room myself and stood at the entrance to the treatment area. A couple of nurses were there. They were talking to each other. They didn't pay any attention to me.

Finally I interrupted. "Excuse me," I said, "but I think I'm having a heart attack."

They led me to a leather gurney and I stretched out. Swiftly a technician came along with an EKG machine. "Yes, sir," he said, "that's a great diagnosis. You sure are having a heart attack."

Suddenly I was the center of a great deal of medical attention. The world seemed to be collapsing on top of me. Oxygen tubes were being stuffed into my nose. Needles were being jabbed into my arm. And my stomach and chest were hurting like hell.

My wife stood nearby. She didn't look happy. I had to do something. I waved her over. "Call the national desk," I gasped at her.

"Yes, yes," she said.

"Tell them I want them to get in touch with Javits," I said.

"Right," she said.

"Tell them to tell him that I want him to write my obituary," I said. "Maybe we can have a twin-out."

Well, I thought it was funny. But Jean didn't seem to appreciate it at all. Neither did the cardiologist. "Listen, you son of a bitch," he said. "If you got any ideas of going out on me, forget it. I'm not gonna let you." That was how Dr. Augustus Aquino and I met. It is a relationship that turned out to be entertaining, warm, most pleasant, and, fortunately for me, of long duration.

But right then I was hurting. To me it seemed to be hours before I was moved into the cardiac intensive care unit. That was where I found out how lovely morphine could be—indeed, what a lovely place it was for someone who suddenly felt so weak he couldn't even lift his arms.

I was in the hospital for more than a month. When I came out I wasn't even allowed to drive a car. Finally Dr. Aquino gave me permission to work at the office—but I had to stay in the bureau and I wasn't permitted to be there more than four hours a day. I couldn't walk more than a few yards without feeling pains in my chest.

This went on until early June, when, under Dr. Aquino's guidance, I went to Fairfax Hospital to undergo quintupal bypass surgery.

I hoped it would be the key to recovery. With time on my hands, I had worked the phones in the office well enough to come up with a couple of nasty stories, one of them about Senator Alfonse D'Amato, the rough, tough, take-no-prisoners Republican from New York. I had known him from my days in Nassau County and, personally, we got along quite well.

On the Friday of my last week before I was to go into the hospital, about four days after the story he hated had appeared, D'Amato called me. "Hey, Mike," he said, "I just want to wish you well and tell you that I'll be praying for you."

"Why, Al," I said, truly touched by the call. "That's really sweet of you."

"Naw, naw," D'Amato said. "You're just saying that. There's gonna be a lot of people praying for you. But when a sinner like me prays for you. . . ." The rest was lost in mutual laughter.

On Sunday, the day I was supposed to leave for the hospital, I asked Jean to go to a distant book store and buy me a couple of novels. While she was gone I went into the backyard and smoked the last Cuban cigar in my possession. It was the last time I ever smoked.

The operation did give me a new life. It was tough at first, because there was some pain and the orders were to take daily walks to avoid blood clots. Twice I fainted while doing that. Several times I visited the emergency room in the middle of the night with ripping pains across my abdomen that turned out not to be heart attacks.

But the operation was great. After awhile the pains disappeared. I was riding a bicycle again and lifting light weights.

Once more I was able to drive a car. After I stopped smoking I regained the weight I had lost. But I was easing into my job again, going up to the Capitol and out to the White House on some assignments.

Again I was covering Congress, my beat for so many years. Short and stout and balding, my pockets bulging with tape recorder and pad and pens and old press releases, I rushed through the familiar statue-lined corridors of the Capitol.

Again I was wearing clothes that I hoped would make the lawmakers and their staffs remember me. Once I loved brightly colored ties, but not after the death in 1970 of our eight-year-old daughter, Margaret, of Reye's syndrome. Ever since, my wife has found herself unable to wear jewelry and I have not been able to bring myself to wear anything but black ties. After a time, a friend suggested that I might want to try black bow ties.

So now I wear clip-on black bows and compensate by supporting my pants with the gaudiest suspenders I can find. Equipped with these trademarks, once more I was cracking bad jokes and bellowing my questions at the news conferences in the tones taught me by my basic training sergeants back in 1956 when I was a draftee in the U.S. Army. I was back.

By October of 1982 I felt so good that I was ready for the tougher test. I asked and was permitted to go on the road again, to write stories on political campaigns in California and in Illinois. I came back to Washington elated and none the worse physically.

Once I got used to the scar on my chest, my view of life had changed only slightly. For one thing, I tried not to write long obituaries on Friday nights any more. For another, I tried with minor success to avoid raging at the changes editors made in my copy.

Gradually, through the post–heart attack years, I finally came to take the advice of Homer Bigart, the two-time Pulitzer Prize–winning correspondent for *The New York Times* who was one of my campaign trail companions during the 1964 Bobby Kennedy—Kenneth Keating Senate race.

Bigart watched me fume about something some copy editor had done and then approached. "K-K-Kid," said Bigart, who sometimes stuttered. "D-don't read your copy. I d-don't read mine. I give it to 'em p-p-poifect. What they do with it is *their* business." So by and large, I no longer read my articles when they appear in the newspaper. It helps keep my blood pressure down.

The fourteen-hour days continue and the deadlines get earlier and earlier. None of this seems to bother me. My old training on rewrite helps and I can still churn out the copy, trying to write stories the way I would tell them to friends.

Sometimes, I think of my uncle Hymie, a wonderful, funny, lively man who would have the family collapsed in laughter with his jokes and pranks. In the 1950s, he had a heart attack. Back then, there was no bypass procedure to rescue him. Because of his new physical limitations and his increased awareness of mortality, I saw him change into a sober, cautious person who moved gingerly through life for a few more years until another heart attack proved fatal.

But my bypass seemed to have rescued me, at least for the time being. It gave me the physical renewal denied to my uncle Hymie. And I made a promise to myself that I would not be frightened by a heart attack, that I would live my life—with some prudent but minor changes—the way I wanted it to be.

In November of 1982, on election eve, when all of the House of Representatives and a third of the Senate was being put to the test, I went out again, this time with the Democratic speaker of the House, that target of Republican opprobrium, Thomas ("Tip") O'Neill.

In 1981 Tip O'Neill was the only thing the Democrats had going for them. The Republicans had the White House and the Senate, and the last place for the Dems to do anything at all was the House of Representatives. There, of course, the Democrats still held control. And there, as speaker of the House, the Tipper did his best to draw the wagons into a circle.

O'Neill became the symbol for the Democrats, which some people thought was unfortunate. He is a great big guy, overweight, with a shock of white hair, a ruddy face, and a nose that is a copy of W. C. Fields's.

His face is a caricature but his brain is quick and his heart is liberal gold. He did not like to go on TV, which was a drawback to a party that needed someone of national stature to speak out. And since he was a liberal he couldn't help Democrats in the South much either.

The Republicans, particularly Ronald Reagan, made him a target, especially when he battled the White House over its cuts to the poor and the old and its bonuses to the fat cats of America and its appeals to the public greed.

One guy who thought O'Neill was too tempting to ignore was a freshman Republican congressman from Long Island named John LeBoutillier. Now, most members of the House, especially freshmen, know better than to attack the speaker except in unusual circumstances.

But LeBoutillier was a brash young man. He made Tip O'Neill his number-one target. One day he got up and made a witty speech.

"Tip O'Neill is like the budget," the Republican newcomer said. "Big, fat and out of control."

The speaker refused to say a word. "LeBoutillier?" his spokesman, Chris Matthews said. "The speaker wouldn't know him from a cord of wood."

LeBoutillier may have been emboldened by the general silence. He printed buttons and bumper stickers. REPEAL O'NEILL they said.

LeBoutillier was also an athlete, a good pitcher who was on the mound for the annual House Republican vs. Democrat baseball game. The first time he pitched, which was in 1981, he won.

Now, in 1982 he also was thinking about winning a second term in the House. At the same time he was going up to Boston to campaign against the invulnerable O'Neill.

And O'Neill still wasn't saying a word. On Long Island Bob Mrazek, a Democratic Suffolk County legislator, decided to run against LeBoutillier.

After he got into the race, all of a sudden Mrazek started to raise a lot of money from Massachusetts. Fund-raiser after fund-raiser seemed to be arranged in Boston and the surrounding area.

O'Neill mentioned that if Mrazek would win, he thought he would get a seat on the House Appropriations Com-

mittee, one of the most powerful committees of Congress.
Most House members have to hang around for ten years
before they get a shot at such a membership. But now the
Tipper was saying that first-term input on the committee
might be good for the House.

Otherwise the speaker didn't comment on the situation.
Of course, one of his most savvy advisors, Leo Diehl, was
calling Mrazek just about every day to find out what else
he might need, but nobody knew about that at the time.

On election day of 1982, Reagan went flying around the
country to pump up Republican candidates for the House
and Senate. Reporters were flying with him, of course,
and I knew there would be stories concentrating on
Republicans in every newspaper and on every network as
a result.

So, full of physical renewal, I suggested to the *Newsday*
editors that we should have some balance here. I said I
would like to go out with O'Neill. The editors said okay.

To tell the truth, the speaker wasn't doing much. He
was going to a senior citizens home or two in the Boston
neighborhoods and he was going to make a campaign
swing with a next-door congressman, Nick Mavroulos,
who needed help winning reelection about as much as Ted
Kennedy did.

Still, O'Neill was on the stump and I made the best of it.
Late in the day, in between senior citizens homes, he
called me over and invited me to sit down.

"Let's go through these House races together," he said.
"I've been studying them some." He went through a list
quickly, getting to New York in about two minutes.

"You work for a Long Island paper, don't you?" he
asked. I said that I did.

"This fella, LeBoutillier," he said slowly and with emphasis. "I think he's going to lose."

The speaker was most definitely right. Much to Le-
Boutillier's surprise, he did lose to Bob Mrazek.

LeBoutillier's staff was stunned. They didn't know what had hit them. In the speaker's offices on the second floor of the Capitol, still no one said a word. Not until the day came for the annual House Republican-Democrat baseball game.

"Mr. Speaker," Matthews said in front of about fifty reporters. "Today's the day of the baseball game. The Republicans are going to have to get another pitcher. You know, John LeBoutillier lost."

O'Neill looked blank. "Who?" he asked. Then he roared with laughter.

Several months later O'Neill was dining in a Washington restaurant. A young man was in a group several tables away. He knew the speaker, but in truth the speaker did not recognize him.

So the young man made a most polite gesture. John LeBoutillier sent a bottle of wine to the speaker's table with his compliments.

11

FRITZ

I WAS RIDING ON A BUS WITH STEPHEN KING IN THE BEAUTIFUL LAKE country of New Hampshire. The bus was part of the motorcade of Gary Hart, advancing on one small town after another as he tried to win the 1984 first-in-the-nation Democratic primary in New Hampshire.

Hart wasn't on the bus. He was riding in a car. But he was always telling the big contributors and the celebrities who campaigned with him to ride on the bus. He said it was wonderful to do this just to observe the behavior of the reporters. He thought that we were strange, maybe even nutty, and that watching us was very entertaining.

King was wrapped in a big black overcoat, sitting by himself. We were all a little shy as we watched him, at least I was. Considering my salary, even though it's not bad for the newspaper business, I have the greatest respect for anyone who actually can get rich by writing.

So there we were, moving through the mountains, looking at the lovely icy scenery, and doing other odd things, like writing stories on our laptop computers and reading newspapers. Then King started gesturing. He was gesturing at me. I pointed a finger at myself in disbelief. Yes, yes, he nodded, patting the seat next to him. Obviously he wanted me to sit next to him.

I moved up and I sat. King pumped my hand. "I just want to tell you," he said, "what a wonderful job you did on that spread on me in *See* magazine. "Those pictures you took, Ira, were just wonderful."

I tried to interrupt, but he kept on praising me, saying how glad he was to see me again. Finally I was able to stop him. "Excuse me," I said. "But I'm not Ira."

"You're not Ira?" he said.

"No," I said. "I'm sorry, but I'm a reporter, a writer, not a photographer."

King obviously was embarrassed and he said so.

"That's okay," I said. I thought I would try to build on our Hart-inspired reputation of eccentricity. "Just think of me as 'Not Ira,'" I said. "Only kidding." I said hastily. "My name's Mike."

I got up to go back to my seat. "No," King said. "Sit here." We began to talk. I got his autograph. He started giving autographs to the whole bus.

I asked him why he had decided to back Hart instead of Walter Mondale, the front runner to win the Democratic primary.

"Let me tell you," he said. "I was doing promotion work for *The Shining*, which had just come out as a movie. I was in Detroit and you know how Detroit was—it looked like a city that was bombed out. It was terrible.

"Someone asked me if I wanted to meet the vice president, you know, Mondale. He was having a reception at the Detroit Plaza Hotel. I said sure. I go there and there's this reception line. I kept thinking to myself, What should I say to a vice president? What can I say?

"In front of me the people were saying, 'How are you, Mr. Vice President?' and he kept saying, 'I'm fine.' But I wanted to say something different. So I shook his hand and said, 'Mr. Vice President, isn't the demolition in Detroit just terrible?' And he said, 'I'm fine.'

"I think that's when I decided to be for Gary Hart."

The Hart caravan stopped in a small town. The senator shook hands, and King hugged a toddler and signed autographs. "If you don't support me," Hart warned the crowd, "Stephen will scare you to death."

"I'm not America's resident spook," America's number-one horror writer told the audience. "The real American resident spook is in the White House right now."

We all got on the bus again. A dozen reporters waved newly bought King paperbacks under the writer's nose. He signed them all.

Traveling up to New Hampshire's lake country was a rare experience. Most of the time the candidates fight it out in the southern part of the state, because that's where most of the population lives. They ballyhoo their forays up north into the White Mountains, but more than 80 percent of the time they hang out around Concord, the state capitol, and Manchester, a grimy riverside city, and Nashua, near the Massachusetts border.

Reporters coming into New Hampshire try to get motel rooms near those three cities, with Manchester being the preferred place because it is in between the two others.

I love covering presidential primaries in New Hampshire. It's not that this all-white, no-big-city state has absolutely no relationship to most other states; it's not that it feeds like a leech off Massachusetts while bragging that it doesn't tax its own people; it's not that it has been for more than a generation under the influence of the *Manchester Union Leader*, which many reporters regard as sort of the *National Enquirer* of the right wing.

No, it's none of those things. It's not even that outside of the cities it's a physically beautiful place. It's simply that for some reason strange things happen in New Hampshire during presidential primaries, things that just don't happen elsewhere. And by that I don't just mean that New Hampshire voters, particularly in the primaries, have a streak of contrariness that frequently makes them do the unexpected.

In 1984, for example, I decided that there might be a story in going out with the door-to-door canvassers for Walter Mondale. Canvassers for presidential candidates in New Hampshire are almost always college students. There are few adults willing to risk pneumonia by going door-to-door in eighteen-degree weather just to hunt for votes. Except, of course, reporters. And they're not hunting for votes, only for stories, as I was in late February 1984.

So having made the necessary phone calls to the Mondale press operation, on February 25 I found myself in a car with three young canvassers, the second auto in a two-car caravan, heading out to Manchester's Ward Eight. That's when two of the kids told me that they really were for Ronald Reagan.

"I guess you don't see it too often," said Mark Hall, who was nineteen, a Virginian, a student at the University of Hartford and a registered Republican. "Republicans out campaigning for Democrats."

"It's not exactly that we're against Mondale," said Jerry Cook, who was also nineteen and a political science major at the same school. "I mean it's obvious that we're somewhat for him because we're working for him."

They said they were in New Hampshire because they wanted to get involved in presidential campaigning. At the University of Hartford they looked at the bulletin board and saw that only one campaign operation was offering a free round-trip bus ride to Manchester to anyone willing to work. That was Fritz Mondale's.

So Hall and Cook put on Mondale buttons and got on the bus, joining the Mondale army of more than six hundred students. Hall and Cook said they didn't like the bus ride very much. They were riding with a group of Yalies who didn't talk to them or anyone else who wasn't from Yale. The Elis, they said, were just sitting there reading *The New York Times* and not having any sort of a good time during the two-and-a-half-hour ride to Manchester.

This was their second day of canvassing. The first day they grabbed the brown lunch bags marked "bol chee" and "sal chee" but which each also contained a banana, took a can of soda pop, and moved out to the wards.

"It's fun," Hall said. "I mean where else are you going to work all day, hardly eat anything, and then sleep on the floor of Mondale headquarters without a pillow, just a blanket, walk five blocks to the YMCA to take a shower in the morning, and walk back with your hair wet? But it is fun."

The two cars stopped on Seames Drive in a middle-class Manchester neighborhood. The canvassers had been told that the cards they carried bore the names and addresses of undecided voters and voters who had declared for other candidates.

Eric Fillman, a twenty-one-year-old Philadelphian and the team captain, who was unaware of the Republicanism in his midst, split his six canvassers into groups of three. Chris Setaro, eighteen, of Danbury, a student at the University of Connecticut, joined Hall and Cook. "I like Mondale," Setaro insisted. "I'm going to vote for him."

"Mondale? Aw, c'mon, Chris," exclaimed Hall as the three made their way to the first house.

Hall rang the doorbell and grinned at the elderly woman who answered. "How ya doing?" he asked. "I'm Mark and this here's Jerry and Chris." He asked her if she had decided on a candidate to support for the primary. "No, we haven't," the woman answered. "I'm busy cooking." But she did accept a Mondale pamphlet.

On the cold, windy Sunday, many people were not home and only a few of those who were said they were for Mondale. "Yesterday we got John Glenn and Gary Hart [canvassers]," said Mary Long as she talked to the boys at her front door. "I've already made one person happy. I'm voting for John Glenn."

She wouldn't take the pamphlets the three tried to press on her but assured the two young Republicans and one young Democrat: "I won't vote for Reagan." That provoked a roar from within, from her husband Gary. He said he would vote for Reagan for sure. "We've got months to work on him," Mary Long assured the canvassers.

Walking back down the street, Hall said he was feeling a little funny about it all and having to repress some GOP impulses. "One of the hard things about working for Democrats but being a Republican," he said, "is that you have to talk about Democratic issues. When they say 'Reagan' you want to say, 'all right,' but you can't. You've got to talk Mondale."

Soon it was time to head back to headquarters. "Really, I'm out here just to get a feel for what it's like," Cook said.

"It's a good experience to be doing this," Hall said. "I called my dad up and I told him and he said, 'What!' and then I explained to him that Mondale is the best Democrat, and he said, 'Well, when you look at it from that view, you're right."

All six canvassers met up again. I took them all to lunch at McDonald's, which they said they liked better than "sal chee.' Then we went back to Mondale headquarters in Manchester. I shook hands with the boys there and they got on the bus to go back to Connecticut with the no-fun Yalies.

The next day, primary eve, Elm Street, which is the main street of slightly grimy Manchester, was turned into a very long stage set where several political movies were being filmed at the same time.

Teenagers and adults grouped on the sidewalks, holding the placards of their favorites on high and chanting ditties like "Hollings, Hollings, he's our man, if he can't do it, no one can." The local radio stations were filled with commercials. The eight Democratic candidates themselves stumped through the streets, plunging into stores and saloons they had visited a dozen times before. And each, no matter how hopeless his cause, was trailed by the heavy-artillery television cameramen and the infantry of reporters with tape recorders and notepads at the ready.

All were worried about the weather reports of a blizzard the next day, primary day. And the blizzard indeed did strike the state, even as the voters of New Hampshire struck, interrupting Walter Mondale's march toward the Democratic presidential nomination by bestowing a stunning upset victory on the long-shot contender, Senator Gary Hart of Colorado.

Walter Mondale fought back, of course, but every time he thought he had Gary Hart down and out, the contender from Colorado would come back. Hart had no money and in too many key states no political organization to speak of, either. But he hung in there, right up to the last primary. Mondale finally had to win the nomination mainly by simply declaring himself the victor and having nearly all of the Democrats in Washington say they agreed with him.

He might have been better off losing. Mondale was a whole lot smarter than Reagan and he turned the president into coleslaw in their first debate. But Reagan had the love of the people and the money and the organization of the Republican party. There was nothing much that brains could do about that. Against Ronald Reagan, Fritz Mondale was a featherweight.

Mondale knew it, but he wouldn't give up and neither would his staff. Back in 1964, in the disastrous closing days of the Goldwater campaign, I remember the Bloody Marys served at breakfast to help his aides get through another day. In 1972 I remember the quarrels that broke out in the McGovern camp among some of his assistants in the closing days.

But Mondale and his people put up a defiant front. In the last weeks of the campaign he would fairly strut from one side of the platform to the other, his thumb upraised in defiance and the sign behind him reading WE'RE GONNA WIN. The crowds came out to cheer him in those days, thousands upon thousands of shouting men, women, and children. The local politicians, who are in the habit of shunning losers, made an exception for him and crowded next to him.

And Mondale sped on, from city to city, from state to state, for a cause he knew was hopeless. I remember the two campaign planes landing in Quincy, Illinois, one night in late October. It was near midnight, but behind the airport fence more than two hundred supporters had been waiting in the dark to see him. Mondale heard their cheers and began to walk toward the fence. Some of the traveling reporters, weary from the campaign pace of an underdog and knowing they would be wakened before dawn, loudly urged him to get into his waiting car and go to his hotel immediately.

Mondale stopped and looked at them. "We have thirteen days to go," he said. "Try a little dignity. Follow my lead." Then he went to the fence and shook hands.

We had about four hours' sleep that night and then dragged ourselves to the buses. The sun was just coming up over the frosty, corn-stubbled fields when our caravan pulled into Buzz Neisen's farm, but cars already had filled all of the makeshift parking spaces.

The farmers in their baseball caps mobbed the big shed in front of the pig sty. In the shed a makeshift platform had been put up in front of some bales of hay so that the Democratic candidate for president could speak. Dick Durbin, the local Democratic congressman, was there, as was the state attorney general, Neil Hartigan.

Mondale climbed onto the platform and stood in front of the farmers in his pinstripe suit and red tie.

"When I first campaigned in 1948, I rode on the Truman train even though I wasn't old enough to vote," he said. "In that campaign, they wrote Harry Truman off. Couldn't win. Hopeless. They stopped taking polls, he was so far behind.

"But they forgot. Out everywhere in those little farm homes, everywhere in those little stores on Main Street, in those little churches, people were thinking."

The farmers stood very quiet in the shed and watched as Mondale curled a hand as if he were grasping something. "They weren't hollering or making noise," Mondale said. "Then quietly, by the thousands and then by the millions, rural America went to the polls and they voted old Harry Truman back into the White House.

"I ask you to do the same thing now. Think it through. See what you see. Ask who you trust."

In the crowd, Janet Warren, thirty, a Mondale supporter there with her year-old daughter, listened and said, "I think he is going to have a hard time here."

On Mondale went, across the Mississippi Valley and beyond, rolling through green October woods, crossing the Mississippi, not stopping for the night until the city of Milwaukee was reached. "I'm here today to ask you to trust me," Mondale told about fifty Missouri farmers on the way. "Trust is everything to me. I'd rather have your trust than your vote. But I'd like to have both if I could."

He could not win their votes. His own polls told him that. But he kept on with the campaign. In the final days he charged from coast to coast and on the last day he flew from sunny Los Angeles to freezing Mason City, Iowa, and finally home to Minneapolis.

There, in the Minneapolis–St. Paul airport, he spoke of home and the long months on the campaign trail and the man who had guided him throughout his political career,

Hubert Humphrey, dead from cancer more than half a decade ago.

"For thousands and thousands of miles," Mondale said to the hometown crowd, his voice echoing in the big, dirty airport hangar. "Through long days and long weeks and long months and now long years. Through all the debates, through all the campaigns and speeches. Through all the pains and heartaches, I can hear you and I can hear Hubert pushing me on," he said.

"When I got tired," he said, "I could hear him say, 'Give it another whack.' And I did."

The next day he was clobbered at the polls, winning only his home state of Minnesota—and that barely—and the District of Columbia. His staff broke down and wept at last, though one of them tried to josh Mondale, pointing to the candidate's homes in Minnesota and the District of Columbia. "You won everywhere you owned property," he said to Mondale.

In public Mondale himself would not weep. "I am at peace with the knowledge I gave it everything I've got," he said. "Do not despair. This fight did not end tonight. It begins. Let us fight on. . . ."

He walked to an anteroom and stood watching the crowd walk out. Only then did his smile disappear and his eyes fill with tears. The next day he announced that he was taking himself out of elective politics forever.

12

BITBURG

WE FLEW BACK TO WASHINGTON TOGETHER, THE REPORTERS AND Mondale, on the campaign plane that had carried us so many thousands of miles. It was a very exciting trip, not so much because Mondale worked his way up and down the plane, chatting, shaking hands, and posing for pictures, but because the captain of the charter felt he had to honor the gallant loser in some way.

So as we approached National Airport, the captain, Ralph Slater, announced that he intended to pay homage to Mondale by buzzing Washington, D.C. He hadn't told Mondale about this—it was supposed to be a nice surprise.

The thought that this might be a more final finale than we anticipated was a little much for most of us. Seat belts—reporters despise the things—were actually securely fastened, but not before many of us went diving for doubles and triples of the small airline bottles of booze that we hoped would not be our last toast.

Slater brought us down to two hundred feet and zoomed over the airport. I looked up and saw the Washington Monument looming overhead. Bridges seemed to be next to our wingtips. Still, we all cheered him as we went. We didn't have much choice.

"It was a great tribute to someone who had worked very hard," Slater said after he landed the plane. "It was just something I felt needed to be done."

There was another surprise for me when I walked back into the bureau. A correspondent from Albany was coming to Washington on permanent assignment. The editors wanted to put this talented reporter to work in a high-profile post right away.

They figured that someone who covered a state legislature could pick up on a congressional beat right away. So they had an easy solution. I was no longer *Newsday*'s congressional correspondent.

But the bureau chief was taking care of me. For me he had something in mind that was an even higher-profile beat. I was now the White House correspondent.

For years I had filled in at the White House whenever our correspondent there was otherwise occupied, sometimes for months at a time. But it had never before been a full-time post for me.

It was an assignment I had always wanted, particularly with Reagan in the presidency. He was a man I had covered in two campaigns, a man I had studied and had written scores of stories about over a period of nearly ten years. I was elated.

Now I felt I really belonged in the theater seat with the little brass marker reading NEWSDAY. The seat is on the left-hand side about four rows up in the small arena that is called the White House briefing room.

Murderer's Row is the front row of seats. That's reserved for the reporters from the networks and the wire services. Because they're in front, and because the press secretary considers them to be the most important, they get to ask the most questions.

During the Reagan administration, unless a reporter represented *The New York Times*, the *Washington Post*, the television networks, or, on rare occasions, the *Wall Street*

Journal, he or she had just a slightly better chance of getting inside information on a solo basis than the tourists who tromped through the White House by the thousands every day. The privileged reporters, however, would be stuffed with leaks as if they were geese for the fattening and given so many trial balloons that they could float.

To defend against all of this, the reporters had formed themselves into mutual protective organizations of five and six persons each. Then as a group each organization sought interviews with various White House personages.

For me these organizations were a new development. When I went to the White House as a regular in 1985 and my friends working there told me about them, I exclaimed, "They're tongs"—after the old Chinese protective societies. The name stuck, and tongs they have been called ever since.

Of course, covering the White House can be very easy. All a reporter has to do is listen to the daily briefings provided by the White House press secretary, accept the handouts, write down the president's words, and ship it all out to the editors. If it is from the White House, the great funnel through which all of the world's events are filtered, the story is almost sure to be featured right up front. Write White House stories regularly and you are a star, regardless of your competence or your inside information. But although the president's men and women would like to have it that way, I have never met a White House correspondent willing to accept a handouts-only fate.

In late February of 1985 a combination of circumstances gave me a chance to strike on the story that to me is the pride of my career.

That was when Jim Klurfeld, my bureau chief, had lunch with a friend of his and mine who was a Reagan administration official. In the bureau Jim told me that our friend had learned that Reagan had decided against visiting a Nazi concentration camp on his coming trip to the annual economic summit in Germany in April.

The decision was particularly significant because this was a trip that coincided with the fortieth anniversary of V-E Day. West German chancellor Helmut Kohl, the summit host, wanted to limit the dramatic reminders of the capitulation of Nazi Germany as best he could.

The year before, in 1984, he was particularly hurt when he saw all the other leaders of the western alliance gather in Normandy to mark the fortieth anniversary of D day. He and the heads of the Italian government were the only ones who had been left out.

Now Kohl wanted to be part of the old alliance as well as the new. Somehow, after forty years, there had to be a way to make the world forgive—at least to set aside—the fact that in waging war it was his country that had executed twelve million civilians, among them six million Jews, in a systematic attempt to exterminate a whole people from the face of the earth.

Kohl did not want any reminders of that. And seeing that he was a loyal ally, the White House and the State Department were willing to help in this regard. Now, there had been a story in the West German magazine *Der Spiegel* that Reagan might visit the World War II concentration camp at Dachau. But there were also stories that the West German government had been telling the White House that this might not be such a good idea.

And now Jim had been told that Reagan agreed with Kohl. I try very hard not to let my personal feelings intrude into my work, but this was a decision that really got to me. I am old enough so that as a child I lived through World War II and I had personal memories of how the Allies had not exactly acted heroically in trying to save the lives of Jews headed for the Nazi death camps.

I remembered that Franklin Roosevelt had turned back a shipload of Jewish refugees fleeing from the Nazis. I remembered reading stories about how the Turks, under British orders, had towed a leaking yacht filled with nearly one thousand Jewish refugees into the open sea. The yacht, which had been intercepted while heading for Palestine, promptly sank. There was only one survivor.

After forty years I still remembered both the horror of the mass murders by the Nazis and the indifference of the Allies toward the slaughter.

All the instincts of old-time reporters are to submerge our opinions, to suppress our views. At the House and Senate dining room press tables, sitting only a few yards from those we cover, we are blunt in our opinions and we swap speculations with glee. How long will it take for this independent new senator or that maverick new House member to be swallowed by the establishment? How can the president and the senators who despise each other privately be able to deal with each other and act as each other's advocates? But in print and on the air, impartiality is the watchword.

Often, we are so detached from ourselves that we don't think that we are involved in our own surroundings as participants. In 1984, when Senator Gary Hart's campaign jet caught fire and seemed to be going down, a network television crew on board sprang into action by filming the flames.

But there are occasions when detachment deserts us. In 1985, the decision of the president to shun a concentration camp on the fortieth anniversary of V-E Day was something that had to be told. Once again the United States government—even though it had good relations with the government of Israel—seemed to be turning its back on one of the most heinous crimes in human memory. True, it was history now, but it would be another horror to let the world forget.

Yes, this was a story with a cause and I was emotionally involved. But I didn't feel that I was being less than impartial. This was not being an advocate. This was being a reporter doing his job. The administration was trying to ignore the Holocaust, an event that just could not, should not, must not be ignored. I would do my very best to see that it did not happen.

Jim told me he could not write a story from what he had been told. Our administration friend had given him the information with the agreement that it was off the record—which means that it could not be used from him. It could only be used if someone else verified it.

At the White House my first big interview was coming up. It was with a "senior administration official" and I would be one of a group of five correspondents. But this was my shot to verify the tip that Reagan would shun a visit to a concentration camp. Nearly all interviews with White House advisors were with "senior administration officials," which meant that the information could be used but that the sources couldn't be named. When interviews were on the record and we were allowed to use names, hardly anything worth using was ever said.

On March 5 I was among five reporters led by a secretary up the ramp to the upper press office, through another door, and into the inner halls of the White House. We were ushered into an elegant office and asked to seat ourselves around a polished wood conference table. Our tape recorders were at the ready. This senior administration official was a very senior administration official, so senior that an assistant White House press secretary was on hand to monitor the interview.

Immediately I asked him about the possibility of the president not visiting a concentration camp on the coming trip.

The official confirmed this and then, to my amazement, said: "Look, it's forty years ago. We all recognize what has happened. Most of the people in Germany were not even alive when this happened. It's an atrocity. The German people understand this. They know it. It's regrettable. We can never bring back the dead. Isn't it time we went forward from here, honoring our dead, remembering what happened, but not constantly bringing it up?"

I figured it would be kind to give him something of a hint as to what might happen. So I asked him whether he didn't think such an attitude might not offend other Americans, particularly Jewish Americans.

But this very-senior administration official waved off the very idea. "There are other horrors," he answered. "We don't celebrate massacres of Indians, which we perpetrated ourselves, and we should remember that. But we quickly bury that in our conscience." And then he said, "I'm not condoning what the Germans did or anything else, but what we're saying is we're over there for an economic summit."

The four other reporters at the table were interested but had their own questions to ask, and they turned to different subjects. After all, our time was limited. But I was amazed. After all of the stories and all the books I had read about White House insensitivity toward Jews and the Holocaust during World War II, as well as State Department anti-Semitism during that era, I thought presidents might have learned something. Here was an administration that treated Israel with great sympathy and yet thought of the Holocaust as a relatively minor, and politically aggravating, event.

The White House did have an aide who was Jewish and who was assigned to look after Jewish affairs. But there weren't any other Jews in senior positions at the White House to sensitize the insensitive.

The problem was not only with the White House. We five reporters came out of the meeting agreeing that we had a good story. But it didn't get major play.

The *Houston Chronicle*, for example, ran the account by its correspondent on the inside pages. I was told by editors on Long Island to keep my story short—about four hundred words. *Newsday*'s New York edition, then just starting and with a circulation of under 50,000, did put my brief account on a premier page for a tabloid, page five. But in *Newsday*'s Long Island edition, with its circulation of 500,000, the story was cut even more and put on an inside page.

I got a single call about it. This was from an official of a Jewish organization who was puzzled that there hadn't been a bigger reaction from either the public or the press. But there the stories were. They lay there like announcements about the cancellation of a garden show.

A presidential news conference was coming up. For such events there are reserved seats for the news organizations that have correspondents who regularly cover the White House. Jim had told me that he and I would alternate using the reserved seat. This conference was his turn.

We always discussed what questions might be good to ask if the reporter in the seat is recognized by the president. On March 21, the day of the press conference, I suggested to Jim that he might want to ask Reagan why he had decided not to go to a concentration camp. He said he thought that was a fine idea.

Sure enough, Reagan called on him, and Jim asked the question. Reagan gave an answer similar to the response of my very-senior administration official, but he left out the Indian massacres. He said he wouldn't visit a concentration camp because it would "reawaken the memories . . . and the passions of the time."

After the press conference Jim rushed back to the office. I urged that a separate article be written on the president's concentration camp decision. There were the usual hasty telephone discussions with the editors up on Long Island and it was decided—just one story, and wrap in the concentration camp response as part of it. I wasn't happy.

"Believe me," I said to the editors who had rejected the idea, "this is something that won't go away."

Jim put Reagan's answer high in the story, in the third paragraph. The next day, the *Washington Post* did have a separate article about the president and the camp.

For a few days there was nothing more. And then there was a development from a most unlikely source. The White House Correspondents Association is basically an organization whose main function is to arrange for an annual black tie dinner that hopefully will be attended by the president. But when I became a White House regular I discovered that the association does some other things. Among them is to send a White House correspondent on the major advance trips.

Advance trips are taken by White House aides weeks and sometimes months ahead of the official presidential journey. These aides are supposed to review every phase of the coming tour of their chief, eliminate all possible pitfalls, and develop opportunities to bring greater successes to the trip.

The White House correspondent accompanies these aides so that he can tell his reporter colleagues back in Washington what they can expect—from the trip itself to the types of telephones to the comfort level of the hotel rooms. The information is distributed in a written memo that is put out on a not-for-publication basis.

The memo from the correspondent about the trip to Germany came out about two weeks after the press conference. It was a lulu.

In it there was a mention that the president was planning to visit a small cemetery in the village of Bitburg, a cemetery that was filled with a few German civilians and many German soldiers who had been killed during World War II.

The memo did not say anything about any SS being buried at the cemetery. But as far as I was concerned it didn't have to. The Wehrmacht had fought for the government of Nazi Germany by and large with great enthusiasm. And now we had a president of the United States who was going to mark V-E Day in Germany by honoring German World War II dead and shunning a visit to a concentration camp.

I thought it was a terrific story. True, it was off the record—but only for the moment. I knew that any one of several friends in the administration would be willing to put this on the record for me by telling me about it in their own words.

But when I approached a key editor I was informed that there was no interest. "It's an old story," I was told. I was ordered to carry through on the editor's pet project—an interview with Reagan's barber.

Time was short. Reagan was heading out to his California ranch, and I was one of the reporters going to Santa Barbara to cover him from a distance of forty miles. I begged and pleaded to be allowed to write the Bitburg story. No dice. I threw my car keys the length of the bureau and then went and talked to the barber.

After that I tried to prove that Bitburg had never been in the papers before. I asked two lobbyists for Jewish organizations about it. They were startled at what I told them. "Please don't tell anyone," I said to them. "I'll take care of it."

Although the memo had gone out to all of the White House regulars, there had been no stories about the little cemetery. Clearly I had the corner on the interest, if not knowledge, of Bitburg.

A researcher in the *Newsday* library on Long Island checked the files for me and said she couldn't find any stories that had been written about Bitburg. I spoke with a second and more senior editor, who said that the story was interesting and definitely should not be abandoned but that the clips should be checked further.

It was time to fly to Santa Barbara. I went out on the press plane, which was filled not only with reporters but with our families as well. My wife and the two younger of our three sons were with me.

On the plane I decided it was time to take additional action. I spoke with other correspondents about the cemetery and about my deep personal anger about the visit. Some thought that Reagan's stop there was not such a good idea; others told me they thought it wasn't significant.

In Santa Barbara the routine of the California White House became all-involving. I didn't know what to do next. Then on April 11 White House spokesman Larry Speakes mentioned that he would announce the schedule for the president's trip to Europe.

Until he said that, April 11 had all the promise of being a slow day. In fact, I'd told my family that we would drive to Los Angeles. But when Speakes made his announcement, I knew we wouldn't be going anywhere on this day.

During the Reagan administration the White House press room was in Santa Barbara's Sheraton Hotel, right next to the beach. The TV correspondents could do their standups with the palm trees in the background, and we all got the benefit of specially installed wire service tickers and telephones with the operators stationed right in the room to help out.

Of course, the president was never anywhere in sight, but some senior staffers were quartered in a posh hotel up the road, and the traveling tongs would invite them out to lots of wonderful meals and lots of sometimes quite revealing talk.

On this day, April 11, Speakes stood in the front of the Sheraton Hotel press room and ran right through the schedule. I didn't try to interrupt. At the end he asked if anyone had any questions. Naturally, there are always questions.

I had a seat way in the back and the wire service and network correspondents were in the front, as usual, so it was awhile before Speakes recognized me.

"Larry," I asked, "who's buried there [in the cemetery]?"

Speakes seemed puzzled but not at all disturbed at this question. "Who's buried there?" he echoed.

"Yes," I said. "Are they Germans or Americans?"

"Both, I think," Speakes answered and immediately sailed on to the next hand. I knew damn well that Speakes was wrong, not only because of the memo but because I had read somewhere that the Allies never would bury their dead next to Germans. I stuck my arm in the air again, in vain.

But then Speakes recognized Owen Ullman of Knight Ridder News Service. And Ullman told Speakes he thought he was wrong. So Speakes said he would check. He called to an assistant press secretary, Mark Weinberg, who had been in the advance party, and asked him to do so. Weinberg cheerfully agreed.

Ullman urged him on, saying he was very interested in the answer.

"I am too," I called.

"I'm not," another correspondent shouted. Indeed, out of boredom, two of the three networks had packed up their cameras and left.

The routine questions, none about Bitburg, continued. Then back came Weinberg. Only German soldiers buried there, he reported. "Only Germans, huh?" repeated Speakes.

There were so few people in the room who seemed to get the point. I rose to my feet. "Larry," I said, "he's paying homage, apparently, to the defenders of the Third Reich while ignoring the victims of the Third Reich. Is there any way to directly address that?"

The Santa Barbara residents and hotel guests who trooped in daily to see the show of a White House briefing, stood on the sidelines, staring at me. And Speakes didn't look as if he were on automatic pilot anymore.

"Mike," he answered, "I've addressed it and the president has addressed it. 'Nuff said." He didn't bother with a formal ending of the briefing. He just cut off the questions by marching swiftly from the room and out of sight.

And we didn't bother to follow. We just looked at one another and then leaped for the telephones.

I called my national desk, my ego busting out all over. I told the editor what the story would be and then blurted proudly: "I feel sort of responsible."

One of the two *New York Times* reporters sitting in front of me turned and regarded me with icy eyes. "I don't believe you," he said scornfully.

From Santa Barbara we telephoned every Jewish and veterans organization we could get to speak with us. We called the West German Embassy. And then we pooled our quotes. *The New York Times* quoted my question about paying homage to the defenders of the Third Reich but didn't identify me by either name or newspaper. Nothing personal. That's the policy of the *Times*.

No matter about that. No matter about a lost exclusive. No matter about anything now. Bitburg was on its way. During World War II, so many had looked the other way as six million Jews were slaughtered. But although they had been in their common graves for forty years, this American president would not be able to do as he had planned—to ignore those victims again.

It took four days of uproar before the White House made a move. On April 15 Speakes announced that the Reagan advance team was flying back to Europe, this time to look for a suitable concentration camp for the president to visit. Not a camp with ovens or gas chambers—Reagan, his aides said, found something like that to be too distasteful.

So the team settled on Bergen-Belsen, evil enough with its record of tens of thousands of deaths from starvation, disease, and various brutalities. But there were no gas chambers there, no ovens.

Speakes readily admitted that the president had changed his mind because of the protests over his planned visit to Bitburg. But Reagan himself was dodging and twisting. He said he always had been willing to visit a concentration camp but had decided against it "because of my mistaken impression that such a visit was outside the official agenda."

Of course, that's not what he had said when Jim Klurfeld had asked him this question at the March 21 White House news conference. At that time Reagan had said that he wasn't going to visit a camp because he didn't want to reawaken "the memories and so forth." He had said it was "unnecessary" to emphasize "the guilt feeling imposed" on the German people.

The overseas bureaus of the television networks had swung into action. Only CBS had bothered to hang around at the April 11 briefing by Speakes in Santa Barbara, when the Bitburg visit had been revealed. NBC and ABC had been so bored that they had packed up and moved out.

But a couple of days later all three networks had hurried reporters to Bitburg. There they soon discovered what the White House advance team had missed: buried at the cemetery among the regular soldiers of Nazi Germany were members of the elite corps of killers of the Third Reich—the SS.

There was another explosion at this, of course. Now Reagan was not only going to pay homage to the defenders of the Nazis, he was going to offer the respects of the United States to the SS, the organization that not only bore the main responsibility for the systematic murder of twelve million civilians, half of them Jews, but that also had massacred American GIs taken prisoners at Malmedy during the Battle of the Bulge.

On December 17, 1944, eighty-six American soldiers of Battery B of the 285th Field Artillery surrendered to the four thousand SS troopers of Kampfgruppe Peiper. Then the GIs were grouped together and shot down with pistols, rifles, and machine guns. When the wounded tried to run, they too were shot dead. The killing continued the next day, with Kampfgruppe Peiper SS troopers murdering Belgian civilians—men, women, and children alike—about 150 of them in all. After the war the SS commander, Joachim Peiper, was held at the Dachau concentration camp where so many thousands of Jews had been murdered. Peiper was tried and then shot.

But Reagan would not change his mind about going to the cemetery where SS who had fought in the Battle of the Bulge were buried. West German politicians were split bitterly on the issue. So were West German newspapers. The conservative newspaper *Die Welt* said that a Reagan refusal to go to Bitburg would cause the "deepest concern" in Bonn and would be "a heavy blow to German-American relations." The independent *Suddeutsche Zeitung* condemned the coming visit as "foolish . . . designed to soothe the lachrymose Germans and free them from the mark of Cain."

In the U.S. Congress, in Great Britain's Parliament, in France, and in Belgium, the anger and the outrage continued. But Reagan still couldn't figure out what was so bad about going to the cemetery. On April 18 he told a group of editors at the White House, "I think there's nothing wrong with visiting that cemetery." Then the president said that the two thousand German soldiers who were buried there were "victims of Nazism too . . . just as surely as the victims in the concentration camps." Once again he set off a reaction that was heard around the world.

The next day the president of the United States sat anguished in his own house as a living voice from the Holocaust spoke of terror, death, and flames and pleaded with him to shun the cemetery at Bitburg. "That place," Elie Wiesel said, "is not your place. Your place is with the victims of the SS."

In the Roosevelt Room of the White House, the television lights shone down. Wiesel's face glistened with sweat, the perspiration of heat and of the moment. He was there to receive a medal from the president. But he was also there to tell Reagan, face to face, what he thought of his plan to lay a wreath at a cemetery where more than forty of the SS lay.

"The issue here is not politics, but good and evil," said the novelist, the professor, the survivor of Auschwitz and Buchenwald. "We must never confuse them, for I have seen the SS at work and I have seen their victims."

Reagan sat on a chair behind Wiesel. His face was taut, his lips tight, his brow furrowed.

"They were my friends," Wiesel said. "They were my parents. Mr. President, there was a degree of suffering and loneliness in the concentration camps that defies imagination."

But two hours earlier, the president had been on the telephone with Chancellor Helmut Kohl. Reagan had made a commitment. He would not change his mind.

In the press briefing room the appearances by Speakes in front of the reporters became an intense daily duel. Constantly we pressed him for his reaction to the protests. At first Speakes answered. But then there was a change of White House tactics. Speakes decided that if he didn't say anything, we'd have less to write about. So he refused to respond to any questions about Bitburg.

That didn't stop us from asking. The fencing, in which I was a leading combatant, became a spectator sport.

White House aides and television technicians would troop into the press room to listen to the Bitburg battles.

"I'm starting to feel a little sorry for them," one correspondent muttered to me after a lively exchange.

But I was thinking about Franklin Roosevelt and World War II. "I don't," I said.

The attempt by Speakes not to say anything was starting to get under our skins too. "He's gravestonewalling," my friend Jerry Watson of the *Chicago Sun Times* said before one briefing. Since Watson couldn't stay, I told him I wanted to borrow the line. "Be my guest," he said.

So when the briefing began and Speakes again refused to answer any questions, I stood up and said to him: "You're gravestonewalling."

The effect was lost because of some chatter among those sitting in murderer's row. Speakes simply didn't hear me. He turned to ABC's Sam Donaldson and said, "Be quiet, Sam, and behave yourself."

"I just want to hear what Mike said," Donaldson answered.

"You're gravestonewalling," I called to Speakes again.

"I'm what?" Speakes asked.

And this time everyone in the press room—maybe eighty reporters in all—answered in a loud chorus: "You're gravestonewalling."

Speakes did not seem to appreciate this sally. "It's all right for you to make jokes," he said. "You don't get quoted afterwards."

"C'mon, Larry," said Leslie Stahl of CBS. "Smile. Smile."

"One Bitburg question," I said.

"You have asked nothing but questions about Bitburg for the last ten days," Speakes said.

"Larry, that's just not true," I said.

"Oh yeah?" Speakes said. "Name me just one question that didn't have to do with Bitburg."

"Just the other day," I said. "I asked how many contras were buried at Bitburg."

Down the corridor at the Oval Office Reagan was standing fast. He rejected a resolution from the Senate that he not visit the cemetery; he rejected another resolution from the House; he ignored the protest of his friend, Prime Minister Margaret Thatcher. He ignored a petition signed by nearly one hundred members of the British Parliament.

With Speakes not talking, my White House tong got together for lunch with an official of the West German government. He said he didn't know what the fuss was about. For twenty-three years, he said, American, French, and German military officers had been laying wreaths at Bitburg and other cemeteries in at least once-a-year ceremonies. He did allow that such a rite has a slightly different meaning when it is performed by the president of the United States. I wrote that story too, but by now it made as little impact as the article I had written about the very-senior administration official comparing the Holocaust to American Indian massacres.

In West Germany Kohl survived a censure attempt by his opponents in Parliament who accused him of triggering "an impairment" of U.S.-German relations.

Anti-Semites began to speak up. The West German magazine *Quick* declared that "the influence of Jews . . . supported by the power of the big media" was to blame for what was happening. Then Jewish groups called for a day of mourning if Reagan went through with his visit to Bitburg.

On April 30, 1985, Reagan flew off to Bonn. He left at night with a farewell from angry protesters at the White House gates and cheers from his secretary of state, George Shultz. "That great act of reconciliation" is what the secretary called Reagan's determination to lay a wreath at the cemetery.

Congressman Gary Ackerman, a Queens Democrat, who was among the protesters at the gates, had another view. "This visit to Bitburg is a gesture of reconciliation with the Third Reich and not with the German Federal Republic," Ackerman said.

All night long the huge jet filled with reporters sped over the Atlantic, followed by Air Force One. A White House trip is unlike any experienced by a commercial flier. The food and the wines could be the prize cuisine of expensive restaurants. Flight attendants provide instant service, and on this journey the two-level plane seemed specially built for comfort. At about midnight nightcaps were offered and pillows and blankets.

I was much too excited to sleep, but I wasn't the only one. All of us were anticipating a great drama to come. The president and the leaders of the western alliance would be gathering in Bonn, but to tell the truth a lot of us didn't care much about that meeting.

For days a half dozen of us had been checking out maps of Germany, looking at the distances between our destination, Bonn, and the little village of Bitburg. Some of us knew we were going to work the next day, but still we couldn't sleep.

When the jet landed on May 1 we hurried to our rooms. They weren't in hotels but were incredibly small staterooms on two handsome German riverboats anchored on the Rhine.

The six of us met on the dock, hailed two taxis, and off we rushed to an Avis rental car agency in downtown Bonn. I had never before been in Germany. And for one thing, I didn't know that Germans were not very big on automatic transmissions. The last time I had driven a car with a manual transmission had been in 1967. But that was all Avis had in Bonn.

So we started out. It wasn't easy. I didn't think I could

get back the knack at all. Larry O'Rourke of the *St. Louis Post Dispatch* got behind the wheel and gave it a valiant go, but the car kept stalling, sometimes in embarrassing places. Finally Jerry Cahill of the *New York Daily News* took over. The technique came back to him quickly, and we set out down the autobahn for Bitburg, less than one hundred miles away.

We drove through Remagen, where the Allies and the Germans had fought so bitterly at a bridge spanning the Rhine. We looked, but we couldn't see the bridge or what was left of it. On we went, through the Eifel Mountains with their impeccable brown chalets, past the dark forests and the broad fields, green and fresh in the chilly rain.

And then we came to Bitburg, the Bitburg about which we had written so many stories, the Bitburg of the White House Correspondents Association memo, the Bitburg of all the angry briefings at the White House and the State Department. The Bitburg of words was suddenly there, solid with Hansel and Gretel chalets and little shops and narrow picturesque streets, Bitburg, a suddenly renowned town of 12,200.

Until Reagan decided to visit, Bitburg had been best known as the staging area for the German army offensive that became the Battle of the Bulge. In Germany it also is known for its brewery, which produces a locally consumed beer known as Bitburger. In fact, the solid brewery had been just about the only building left standing, the building where Bitburg's sixty remaining residents had taken refuge, when the tanks of General George Patton's Third Army came rolling in on February 26, 1945.

Forty years later there was no sign that the town had ever suffered such damage. We drove slowly through the narrow streets, hunting for cemeteries. We found one quickly, but it was reserved for civilians. We asked citizens on the streets. There was also a cemetery reserved for

Jews, very well tended, a passerby told us. No, we said to him, we wanted the military cemetery.

Finally in the late afternoon we found it. The cemetery was crowded with nearly as many living as dead, for May 1 is a holiday in Europe. For miles around Germans had come to take advantage of their day off by walking among the graves of what had become their nation's most famous cemetery. It was a very small place, and its two thousand graves were close together, each marked with a stone cross flat against the ground.

Fresh white carnations were on every grave. For the forty-nine SS dead—we could tell they were SS because their crosses plainly said so—there was something special. For nearly all of them there were pots of blooming flowers.

In death as in life, they were the elite. Many of the SS graves were in a single row at the very front of the cemetery. And on May Day, propped against a tree near those graves, was a big green wreath festooned with the national colors of Germany—bunting of red, black, and gold. Words in German were inscribed in gold on the bunting.

Among the six of us reporters at the cemetery only Leo Rennert, the Washington bureau chief for the California-based McClatchy newspapers, understood German. Leo, who is Jewish, had been brought up in Austria and as a child had watched as Adolf Hitler himself paraded down the streets of Vienna. He survived the Nazis and the war by being hidden by sympathetic Christians led by a heroic Catholic priest in a small village in Belgium.

"To the Waffen SS," Leo read from the bunting. "They were born as Germans. They lived as fighters. They died as heroes."

We scattered around the cemetery, trying to talk to any and all of the visitors we could. Most of them were older people. Everyone we met said that Reagan was right to come here. They said there weren't that many SS buried here and that, anyway, a lot of young Germans had been forced into that organization against their will.

"The controversy seems to come from Jewish people," said Hans Friedrich, a seventy-year-old Bitburger who had fought the Russians, served in France, and wound up as a prisoner of war in Texas after his capture as a member of Rommel's Afrika Corps. "They are very strong in the United States," Friedrich said. "They are in industry, management, the banks. They have the money."

Karsten Sander, nineteen, the same age as many of the soldiers buried at Bitburg, explained that in Nazi Germany there were good SS and bad SS. He said the good SS were the Waffen SS buried at Bitburg. "We should feel anger about the SS who ran the camps," he said.

Just outside the cemetery grounds Werner Pies, forty-two, the second deputy mayor of Bitburg and a school-teacher, agreed with Sander. "The very bad people who did cruelty are not here," he said. I asked Pies what he teaches his pupils about Hitler. He said they were too young for history. I asked him what the older children are taught. "Now we have a very normal relation to our history," he said. "Hitler was Nazi. Terror, terrorism, and so on."

It was getting into late afternoon and we were tired, hungry, and suffering from jet lag. We went to a small wurst shop a few blocks away. We talked to the woman who served us, Mary Ann Becker, fifty-two, who also said that Reagan should go to the cemetery. Then she said: "I worked for Jewish people for twenty years. They got their mind. I got my mind. The Jewish people are good to everybody. They know how to make money. There was hate for it. The Jewish people are always good, always good."

By the time we returned to Bonn it was night. We just had time to file our stories and then catch the last half of a Bavarian welcome for the benefit of the White House reporters accompanying the president. The oom-pah band was very good, there were dances by nimble folk in leiderhosen and Tirolean hats, and the beer was simply wonderful. A German correspondent took me aside and interviewed me about my thoughts about his land. I told him I saw rebirth and renewal everywhere.

The next day, May 2, I was up before 6 A.M. For I was a member of the White House pool, chosen to follow the president at a very respectful distance through a few activities and then to report back to the hundreds of our colleagues just what we saw.

Although it was early in the morning I was late for the rendezvous. I hurried off the boat and along the sidewalk. It was so early that there was not a moving auto to be seen and not a civilian pedestrian either. There were just hundreds of German soldiers and police officers, all armed with automatic weapons, standing around and waiting.

The traffic light was against me but I only had about five minutes. I jogged across the empty street, my plastic press passes clicking together around my neck.

"Halt!" A young policeman, a grease gun slung from his shoulder, stood angrily before me. "The light," he said. "You crossed against the light."

"I'm sorry," I said. "I'm late."

"This is a terrible thing," the policeman said. "It is something that is against the law."

"I'm very sorry," I said and added with sudden inspiration, "I must go to my meeting with the president of the United States."

The cop stepped back, his face softening. "You have done wrong," he said. "We must set an example for the children."

I looked up and down the street. Not a child in sight, only the soldiers and the police.

"I promise I will never do this again," I said, "but I musn't keep President Reagan waiting."

The cop stepped aside and I moved on as he shouted after me, "Remember the children."

I just made it. We were taken to a small park next to the Rhine where we had to wait in line for an hour while the police frisked each of us in turn. It was a beautiful day. I waited with the other newsies looking for the president's helicopter. He was to be greeted in the park by a variety of important West German officials and then was going to several parties and meetings at the Bundestag, where we were to try to observe him.

The helicopters droned in. I watched the president get out. The band was playing. It was so enjoyable. I kept watching. Suddenly I turned. My colleagues of the pool had vanished. I was the only reporter watching!

I rushed toward the bus in the motorcade, hoping it was the right one. It was not. I stood on the sidewalk and watched them all zoom off without me.

I had missed the pool. What a disgrace! But the next stop, the Bundestag, was only three blocks away, surrounded by a thicket of German police and soldiers. I ran down the sidewalk to the first barricade and presented my very special pool pass. The police looked at it as if it was a soda cracker. "Passport, please!" a policeman said.

Passport? Passport? I had every press pass in the world. But not my passport. The Secret Service had collected all of the passports of the reporters accredited to the White House, saying that if they were presented in a mass it would make it that much easier for us to get in and out of the country.

"Sorry," I said. "No passport." The policeman did not seem to think that this was very funny. Furthermore, he seemed to understand about as much English as I understood of German. "I left it back in my room," I lied.

I retreated on foot to the U.S. press center, where I found White House aides who did understand English. I was very mad. I stomped into the Secret Service office and yelled and protested until my passport was produced and returned to me.

The White House aides, a couple of them, were sympathetic. They got me a car and a West German driver and told me I would be reunited with the pool. This did not happen, however, for more than two hours, at the pool's very last stop of the day, witnessing a presidential courtesy meeting with a West German official in his mansion in downtown Bonn.

I watched Reagan come out and then, with the rest of the pool, boarded the correct little bus for the trip back to the press center. On the way back, however, the bus was stopped at a police barricade.

A West German policeman boarded us, his grease gun dangling from his shoulder. "Passports, please!" he said.

The eyes of the Secret Service agent accompanying us hardened into little slits. He shook his head. "No passports," our guy said.

A second German policeman came on board. This one had unslung his grease gun. "Passports, please!"

"No passports," shouted UPI's Helen Thomas from her seat.

"No passports," other reporters hollered.

I simply could not resist. "Officer," I purred, reaching into my pocket. "Here is my passport."

"Very good, sir," the cop said. He stood aside to let me pass.

"So long, Helen," I called. "I'll be sure to write." But I didn't move.

The Secret Service agent was talking into his wrist and then turning to argue with the cops again. In a couple of minutes the German walkie-talkies began to talk too. The cops listened and they let us go. I made sure to keep my passport for the rest of our stay in Germany.

Back at the press center we discovered that Kohl had been trying to find German opponents of the Nazis to accompany him and Reagan to Bitburg. He could find only one—Colonel Bertolt von Stauffenberg, the son of Count Claus von Stauffenberg, who had planted a bomb in Hitler's conference room in July 1944 and was executed along with more than five thousand other Germans accused of plotting against the führer. Von Stauffenberg said he would go only because "I am a soldier," but he also said that he found this task to be "repugnant." His brother, Franz Ludwig, a member of Parliament, refused to go. So did Alfred von Hofacker, whose father had been hanged by the Nazis with piano wire. "I would feel like I was being used as a fig leaf to hide someone's embarrassment," von Hofacker said.

Both Reagan and Kohl also were looking for prominent Jews to go to Bergen-Belsen with them. They were having a hard time with that too. Bergen-Belsen, said a bitter Kalman Sultanik, vice president of the World Jewish Congress, would be "Judenrein" on the day of the visit. "Judenrein" was a word coined by Adolf Hitler and his Nazis. It means "Jew-free."

In the press center that night Bob Timberg of the *Baltimore Sun* asked me if I wanted to fly to Bergen-Belsen the next day, twenty-four hours ahead of the president. Another *Sun* correspondent, a *Boston Globe* correspondent, and their translator had chartered a small plane. A fourth person could cut the costs of the flight. I was delighted but I was worried about covering the economics part of the economic summit. Bob Reno, *Newsday*'s economics columnist, told me to relax. He volunteered to take care of everything, setting me free to go.

Once again I got up early to take a taxi to the airport, where I met the other travelers. A couple of hours later we had landed and had taken another taxi to the camp. Lager Belsen it was called, Camp Belsen, Bergen-Belsen.

There are low walls of stone, green with age, that go on and on, surrounding enormous mounds covered with heather. Suddenly the walls rise up, treble in size, and display their engravings. HIER RUHEN 2,500 TOTE. APRIL, 1945. "HERE LIE 2,500 DEAD."

The walls rise up again and again. HIER RUHEN 1,000 TOTE. HIER RUHEN 800 TOTE. HIER RUHEN 5,000 TOTE.

This is the place where at least 50,000 Jews, gypsies, and others died. They did not perish in the ovens. They did not die in the gas chambers, for there was none of that in this camp. Instead they died of starvation and disease.

To us the words on the stone monument in the middle of the camp were a silent shriek. EARTH CONCEAL NOT THE BLOOD SHED ON THEE.

There were so many tears, so much death here. I had never before been to a concentration camp and I wept as I wrote in my pad, trying to go about the business of being a reporter.

I thought of Bitburg, where Hitler's men lay under their individual tombstones that identified them by name. I looked at the mounds at Bergen-Belsen, where the dead had been swept into anonymous heaps.

There were individual tombstones in Lager Belsen, but a small engraving explained what they were—symbolic, not marking any bodies. HERE REST MY PARENTS AND BROTHERS AND SISTERS AND GRANDMOTHER, read one, the stone of the Steinbach family. The death camps where they had perished were listed. Auschwitz. Ravensbruck. And of course, Bergen-Belsen.

There are no more original buildings at Lager Belsen, for the British burned the camp to the ground in May 1945, trying to stop a typhus epidemic. But there is a museum called the Document House, which was opened in 1966.

Inside, the pictures on the wall show that at Lager Belsen there was little difference between the living and the dead. At Lager Belsen, all were skeletons and all were without hope.

When we arrived in the Document House, there were other visitors, and they were working too. In a corner a makeshift table was covered with a green cloth. There were plastic dishes and candles and a bottle of wine. The Torah was on a nearby chair, and there was a small stack of prayer shawls. Here Rabbi Avi Weiss and Rabbi Ronald Schwarzberg of the Hebrew Institute of Riverdale in the Bronx planned to celebrate the Sabbath. They told me they were doing this to tell the president what they thought of his visiting Bitburg.

"Any president who places a wreath at the graves of SS murderers and equates them with the victims here is burying the past," Weiss said. "That is not morally right. That is morally obscene."

On the wall behind them there was a picture of the sign the British had put up after liberating the camp in April 1945. THIS IS THE SITE OF THE INFAMOUS BELSEN CONCENTRATION CAMP. . . . 10,000 UNBURIED DEAD WERE FOUND HERE. ANOTHER 13,000 HAVE SINCE DIED. ALL OF THEM VICTIMS OF THE GERMAN NEW ORDER IN EUROPE AND AN EXAMPLE OF NAZI KULTUR.

Hermann Funk, forty-two, on a business trip from South Africa to Germany, stared at the pictures of skeletons by the thousands lying in open fields. "I think it's perfectly dreadful," Funk said. But he thought that Reagan should go to Bitburg. "I think there's nothing wrong with it," he said. "The reason is to further the relationship, not to honor SS soldiers."

On another wall there was a picture of Anne Frank, sweet-faced Anne Frank, the teenage girl who hid in an attic and whose diary became a classic. She and her sister died at Bergen-Belsen only a few days before the British came.

I looked at the statistics on display. In February 1945 there were 22,000 inmates at Lager Belsen. In February about 7,000 died. In March 1945 there were 41,520 inmates. In March 18,168 died.

I walked down the flagstone path again and stared at the mounds. Heike Komarreck, twenty-three, a Berliner, said that what she was seeing was "beyond imagination." Her husband Andreas, also twenty-three and a mechanic, also was horrified but said it was all right for the president to go to Bitburg.

The mounds at Lager Belsen end in a long wall inscribed with tributes in twenty-two languages. The other reporters were impatient. They had to get back to Bonn, and of course, like me, had to file stories.

We walked out, past the juniper, birch, and pine trees that now grow around Lager Belsen. Near the camp the guns still speak, for there are a NATO military base and an artillery range located next door. The Second Panzer Division was based there and some British and Dutch units as well. I saw a half dozen soldiers walking solemnly through Lager Belsen.

Then we were rushing for the plane. I wrote my story on the ride back to Bonn.

The next day, a Saturday, I asked Speakes at his regular press briefing if he had any comment about the SS veterans reunion at Nesselwang, Bavaria. A reporter who had interviewed some of them had written that the old SS fighters felt that they had been rehabilitated to a certain extent by Reagan's decision to visit Bitburg.

Speakes said he wouldn't comment on that. "I'm not a spokesman for the SS," he said.

Nor would he comment on another story that a member of the local Bitburg welcoming committee to greet the president had served in the SS. He was named Fritz Gasper, chairman of the Bitburg Rural District Council, and was reported to have been drafted into the SS as a teenager.

While Speakes was conducting the briefing, there were protest demonstrations in four German cities. Police had to ring the U.S. Embassy in Paris as protection against yet another protest.

But the next day, Sunday, the president of the United States went to Bitburg. First, however, he flew to Bergen-Belsen.

It was a damp day and the stone paths at Lager Belsen were cold and wet. On Saturday morning West German police had dragged off about thirty-five French Jews who had gathered in the Bergen-Belsen parking lot to await Reagan's arrival. The police put them in a bus and took them away.

They gave the two Bronx rabbis, Avi Weiss and Ronald Schwarzberg, until Saturday night before ordering them from the Document House. The police walked into the museum where they were conducting services but waited until they concluded before escorting them out. The cops said they were unarmed, but twenty police cars were outside.

All the same, when Reagan came to the camp there were about twenty demonstrators to meet him, American demonstrators, some weeping, some shouting. "Come back, please, Mr. President," they called as Reagan, ignoring them, walked by. "It's a free country," he shrugged when a couple of us asked him about this later.

The demonstrators told the reporters that Reagan was putting Nazi soldiers on the same level as Nazi victims. They carried a sign: CROCODILE TEARS PROFANE THE VICTIMS.

Except for some of the reporters, Kalman Sultanik was right. Bergen-Belsen was virtually Judenrein. I, among other correspondents, went looking for those of the Jewish faith among the hundreds of invited guests who were stationed near an obelisk that stands in front of the memorial wall. I found a butcher at a U.S. army base who felt it was his duty as an American to be there.

And we found the Israeli ambassador to Germany, Yitzhak Ben-Ari. "Members of my family died in this place," Ben-Ari said. "Personally, I believe it is the right thing to give a sign and Bergen-Belsen is the right sign. I believe the new Germany can be trusted." But aside from the butcher and the ambassador, there were no Jews to be found among the audience.

The president's armor-plated limousine had moved up the pedestrian path of the camp, past the heather-topped mounds with their engravings proclaiming them to be mass graves.

Helicopters clattered overhead. Police and soldiers ringed the grounds. The limousine moved past the engraved metal warning, VISITORS ARE REQUESTED TO OBSERVE THE DIGNITY OF THESE MEMORIAL GROUNDS AND TO REFRAIN FROM DISTURBING THE PEACE OF THE DEAD.

The limousine stopped at the Jewish monument in the middle of the camp. Reagan and Kohl got out with their wives and examined the English inscription. ISRAEL AND THE WORLD SHALL REMEMBER 30,000 JEWS EXTERMINATED IN THE CONCENTRATION CAMP OF BERGEN-BELSEN AT THE HANDS OF THE MURDEROUS NAZIS. EARTH CONCEAL NOT THE BLOOD SHED ON THEE.

Reagan walked to one of the biggest mounds. The script prepared by the White House called for him to do that, and a network pool television camera was in position to record his reaction. He stared somberly at the inscription HIER RUHEN 5,000 TOTE.

Then he walked to the obelisk, where he picked up a green wreath and placed it at the foot of the plinth.

It was time to offer prayers for the dead. But there were no rabbis in this place. So the prayers were said by Catholic bishop Josef Homeyer and Lutheran minister Tielko Tielemann.

In front of the obelisk the president began to speak the words of an address created by the great Republican speech writer Ken Khachigian. His voice, low and somber, choked slightly as he referred to "all these children of God, under bleak and lifeless mounds, the plainness of which does not even hint at the unspeakable acts that created them. Through it all was their faith and a spirit that moved their faith."

And his voice choked again when he spoke of Anne Frank. His wife Nancy wiped a tear from her cheek as her husband said, "Somewhere here lies Anne Frank. Everywhere here are memories, pulling us, touching us. . . . We can and must pledge. Never again."

Then he was off for his plane and the two-hundred-mile flight to Bitburg. He was well guarded, but we reporters weren't that fortunate. Put in buses heading for German military helicopters, we were surrounded by angry young men and women, Germans protesting Reagan's decision to go to Bitburg. They couldn't get at him so they tried to get at us. Whistles squealed in the European version of the Bronx cheer, and stones were hurled against our windows.

But the buses kept moving out and the police eventually began moving in. Within a few minutes we had left the stone throwers behind and had reached the helicopters.

At Bitburg, once again the buses from the landing point had to make their way through crowds of demonstrators. The streets of the little village were packed, some of the spectators there to cheer and others to boo. Many who were there to shout their anger were Jewish. They were from France and from England and from the United States. The Jewish War Veterans were protesting, and with them were members of local city councils from New York and New Jersey.

At the cemetery an honor guard of U.S. Air Force and maroon-bereted German paratroopers was waiting. There was no heather inside, nothing but the individual green graves, each and every one bright with daffodils, geraniums, tulips, roses, gardenias, and other flowers. The wreath extolling the SS had been removed.

Reagan and Kohl had come up with a public relations surprise. Also waiting for them was ninety-year-old

General Matthew Ridgway, a hero of World War II and Korea. And next to him was a hero of the Luftwaffe, seventy-one-year-old General Johanner Steinhoff, credited with shooting down three hundred Allied planes during World War II.

It was difficult for most of us to see. Reporters and dignitaries were lined up on one side of the cemetery six deep. Reagan and Kohl walked inside and were greeted by a few civilians. A West German government press aide told me that Fritz Gasper, the local council chairman who had served in the SS, was not among them.

To a solemn drum roll Reagan, Kohl, and the generals walked along the side of the cemetery to the front, where a tower, one hundred feet high, was the landmark. Directly opposite the tower are a half dozen of the SS graves, in the front row.

In silence Reagan, Kohl, and the generals put their hands on two big wreaths. Four German paratroopers hoisted the wreaths onto hooks in the tower wall. The chancellor and the president stepped back, their heels less than three feet from the SS graves.

The president's jaw tightened. Kohl wiped away a tear. A German bugler played his army's version of taps, "I Had a Comrade."

The old generals shook hands. Then they, Reagan, and Kohl walked back down the side of the cemetery and out the gate. They had entered and left in eight minutes.

The wreath Reagan had placed at Bergen-Belsen read: THE PEOPLE OF THE UNITED STATES OF AMERICA. But the White House didn't have the nerve to put something like that on the wreath Reagan placed at Bitburg. That one, made of white lilies, pale yellow roses, blue iris and red gerbera, read only: THE PRESIDENT OF THE UNITED STATES.

Reagan did not speak at the cemetery. Instead the motorcade traveled down the road to the big U.S air base outside Bitburg, a base filled with U.S. servicemen, their wives, and their children. And there, after an enthusiastic welcome, he delivered a second speech. "We can mourn the German war dead today as human beings, crushed by a vicious ideology," he said. "How many were fanatical followers of a dictator and willfully carried out his cruel orders?" the president asked. "And how many were conscripts, forced into service during the death throes of the Nazi war machine?"

He spoke of a sixteen-year-old German soldier, Hans Vincent, who was buried at Bitburg and said he mourned him in the same way he mourned Anne Frank. "We do not believe in collective guilt," Reagan said.

And he also told a story about a German mother who he said during the Battle of the Bulge gave shelter to three American soldiers who were lost behind enemy lines. Then, the president said, there was a knock on the door of her little house, and when the woman opened it she found four German soldiers waiting there.

The woman, he said, warned everybody that they could not shoot each other, and they all ate dinner together— after she had said grace. Reagan said the Germans and the Americans stayed the night together. The next day, the president said, the German troopers showed the Americans how to return to their own lines. "Surely," the president said, "we Allies in peacetime should honor the reconciliation of the last forty years."

To the American reporters it sounded like another one of those incredible Ronald Reagan stories that the president would relate, not on the basis of truth but to justify his actions and to make his audience feel good. But to some German reporters this was sensational stuff, sentimental, religious, filled with good deeds by Germans in war, the very symbol of reconciliation. THERE WAS A GERMAN MOTHER blared the lead headline of one German tabloid.

The next day about five thousand young Germans sang "The Star-Spangled Banner" for the president and cheered him when he addressed them at Hambach Castle. Never mind that in Israel the politicians didn't feel the same as their ambassador to West Germany, who had attended the ceremony at Bergen-Belsen.

"There is no reconciliation with nazism," said Defense Minister Yitzhak Rabin. "The historic mistake of President Reagan was in equating murderers with victims. For this, he will not be forgiven either by enlightened humanity or by the Jewish people."

But in picturesque Hambach the young West Germans were serenading the president with the U.S. national anthem. A jubilant Bernhard Vogel, premier of the Rhineland Palatinate, exclaimed that the president had visited "a concentration camp *and* a German military cemetery." The cheers rang out for that as well.

But perhaps for the president, the most significant applause came aboard Air Force One—spontaneous hand claps from his staff on Sunday night for his performance as everybody flew back to Bonn. Ronald Reagan beamed his thanks with a broad smile.

13

AT THE SUMMIT

BITBURG WAS QUICKLY FORGOTTEN. SOME WHITE HOUSE AIDES brought back bottles of Bitburger beer as souvenirs, and once, when I took a few days off, Speakes noted my absence at a press briefing by saying, "Waldman's vacationing in Bitburg this week." But little was spoken or written about the White House disaster.

The president's staff, realizing that nothing makes people forget a calamity more than the production of a new extravaganza, decided to have Reagan stump the country to propagandize for a new tax code. Numbers are dull, but if there was anyone who could bring them to life it was the old Hollywood king of the Bs.

Reagan had just started on this great crusade in early June, a couple of weeks after his return from Europe, when something happened that was a lot more exciting than taxes. A TWA jet was hijacked by Moslem terrorists and flown to Beirut, where thirty-nine American passengers were held hostage.

Of course, all of the lead stories on television and in the newspapers were now on the new crisis and the efforts of the White House and State Department to win the release of the hostages.

At such a time getting inside information—hard enough

when things are routine—becomes a job that is almost impossible for most reporters. The networks, the *Times*, and the *Washington Post* are given some inside tips because they are used by the White House and the State Department to send out signals. But for the rest of us there is only silence.

In a way, the president himself also is prevented from arriving at a full understanding of the situation. For as a rule staffers try to keep hostage families from the president. Meetings like that present presidents with the grief, the tears, the pleas of the relatives.

And when it comes to hostages, presidential staffers do not want to let compassion get in the way of the decision-making process. On top of that, the presidential advisors were trying to maintain an atmosphere of normalcy. So Reagan, right in the middle of the crisis, continued his road schedule, going out to talk about taxes.

But in Indianapolis the relatives of one of the victims finally reached him. In a huge convention center he was standing on the stage, trying to concentrate on tax revision. But behind the blue curtain the hostage's family was waiting.

His thoughts on the crisis made him break into his own speech on the tax code. "We cannot reward their grisly deeds," he said. "We will not cave in."

In front of him duck calls and police whistles shrieked approval. More than five thousand Jaycees, some in red shirts, others in Indian headdresses, stamped their feet and howled their support. "USA, USA, USA."

Behind Reagan, behind the blue curtain, White House Chief of Staff Donald Regan was doing his best to console the family of James Hoskins, Jr., twenty-two, of Indianapolis, a prisoner somewhere in Beirut. When the president finished his speech he ducked behind the curtain to spend five minutes with the Hoskins family, to reassure them that he was doing all he could.

After that encounter Reagan began meeting with the

relatives of hostages as he went out to various cities to whip up support for tax code revision. On June 28 he was in Chicago Heights, meeting in a high school cafeteria with twenty-nine relatives of hostages from the Chicago area. Except for a White House pool, we reporters were kept out of sight in another room. The White House pool did its job, though. It approached Reagan and asked if he was making any progress in his efforts to free the hostages.

"I am not going to speculate," Reagan said. "You know me. I'm superstitious. I never talk about a no-hitter if you are pitching one."

The quote was dutifully included in the written pool report. I took one look at it and became very excited. I knew my man. It is very tough for Ronald Reagan to keep a secret when good news is about to break.

On the plane back to Washington I banged out a story saying that the president had hinted that the hostages were about to be released. Other reporters were far more cautious. They didn't write anything at all like that.

But an editor on the national desk did agree with me and the story ran. The next day came the announcement that the hostages were being freed. I felt triumphant. There were, however, no pats on the back—either from the main office on Long Island or from my friends in Washington. Over and over I heard the same three words. "You were lucky," all of these people said.

Nobody was lucky a week later, when on July 8, a couple of days after welcoming the hostages home, the president made a speech at an American Bar Association meeting denouncing Iran, Cuba, Libya, North Korea, and Nicaragua as a "new international version of Murder Inc." to spawn and sponsor terrorism throughout the world.

Reagan was great. He set hundreds of lawyers to cheering as he denounced those nations as "outlaws" run by "the strangest collection of misfits, Looney Tunes, and squalid criminals since the advent of the Third Reich." He said that terrorists would have to be fought like pirates.

And even while he was saying these tough things, none of us reporters had the wit or the sources to know that right then his men—Colonel Oliver North, National Security Advisor Robert McFarlane, and McFarlane's deputy at the time, Admiral John Poindexter—were wheeling and dealing with Iran to swap weapons for hostages.

We should have had a clue. Secretary of State George Shultz kept talking about shutting down Beirut Airport as a reprisal for the hostage taking. But nothing ever happened about that. I did point out in my story that while Reagan hinted at new antiterrorist legislation, his aides were saying that nothing was in the works. But I never followed through to find out why, to find out what was up.

Of course, we all had other matters to keep us busy, among them the announcement that Reagan was to undergo surgery for colon cancer. And only a couple of days after the president got back to the White House from the hospital, he had to have a cancerous lump removed from his nose—a relatively minor procedure but one that caused an uproar because Nancy Reagan wouldn't let Larry Speakes or anyone else tell the truth—that the skin cancer was skin cancer. Finally Reagan himself broke that news to reporters.

A week later the president and his wife flew to Santa Barbara for a recuperative vacation, trailed by reporters and their families in another plane. As usual the Reagans went immediately to Rancho del Cielo, their mountaintop retreat. As usual we reporters were kept in Santa Barbara, about forty miles away.

For a reporter, covering Reagan in Santa Barbara was a combination of fright and fun. It is a luxury resort, absolutely unaffordable for the average journalist not on an expense account. With an expense account Santa

Barbara is wonderful. At the same time, reporters could enjoy its pleasures only at their peril. They were always worried about the stories their colleagues might be extracting from the White House aides quartered over at the plush Biltmore Hotel up the road. So daily the traveling tongs were on the alert, wheedling, beseeching presidential assistants into lunches, dinners, drinks, anything to try to get a story.

But the president himself was nowhere to be seen. Just about the only report we got on him was from Speakes, who didn't get up to the ranch either but who claimed to be in touch by telephone. "Today the president chopped wood and cleared brush," he would say of the seventy-four-year-old Reagan during most such times. When Reagan was healing from major surgery, Speakes would change to "Today the president took a walk."

Finally I got tired of this. The networks, I knew, kept an eye on Reagan as best they could. I decided I would at least write a story about how they did it.

I told Susan Zirinsky, a CBS producer, what I wanted to do and she was very agreeable. She gave me directions and then made a couple of calls to make sure her people knew I was coming. A British reporter, Mike White, wanted to do the same story, so we went together in my rented car.

The highway part was okay, even though it was through the mountains. But when we got off and started up Refugio Road in the Santa Ynez Mountains, I began to get a little nervous. The road was a narrow corkscrew and there was no guardrail on the outer edge. I could look down thousands of feet as I drove. We went past 3333 Refugio Road, which was the address of Rancho del Cielo—there wasn't much besides a locked gate—and then we came to the turnoff.

There wasn't any pavement there. Only a kind of red-dirt track leading up the mountain, a trail without guard rails whose sole marking was a sign that read DANGER! and warned that the county did not maintain the road and so was not responsible for whatever might happen on it. "CBS built it," Susan had told me.

I started up the track, regretting that I didn't have four-wheel drive but thankful that I was in a heavy car. Refugio Road was tricky, but this latest climb was terrifying, a two-way switchback trail that was so steep I sometimes couldn't see over the hood of the car. But out the side window I could see forests in the valley so many thousands of feet below.

After a couple of miles we finally reached the crest, greeted there by television technicians. They told us to drive up past them and park. This time the car seemed to be in an absolutely vertical position. I couldn't see at all. Mike got out and walked in front, leading me to the flattened hilltop and a parking space.

When I got out I could see what sort of expertise I had as a driver. Some CBS daredevil actually had driven a truck up the hill. In back of it was a sixteen-inch telescope trained on Rancho del Cielo, on a mountaintop three miles away. Looking through the telescope was a television camera. And looking through the camera was CBS cameraman Erik Prentniecks. What the telescope and Prentniecks saw came out on a nineteen-inch television set that was also in the truck.

Without a telescope the craggy mountains of brown and green tumbled into one another everywhere and the blue of the sky was so intense that it merged into the sea without even the horizon to keep them apart. Buildings were few and far between. In this beauty there were some irritations and problems—many hungry gnats and mosquitoes and, on Refugio Road, signs reading: EXTREME FIRE DANGER. PLEASE BE CAREFUL.

I sat in the truck and watched the screen. I saw Reagan's five-room adobe ranch house and a little pond near it. The house had a red-tile roof, and the pond had a canoe moored at its shoreline.

Then the screen showed Reagan walking out of his house. He was wearing brown pants and a white shirt. On the nineteen-inch screen his image was shimmering in the heat.

Except for the shimmer, the president looked pretty good. Bob Jennings, an ABC cameraman, said that when Reagan came out earlier in the morning it was cooler and he wasn't shimmering at all.

Jennings recounted that he saw the president sit on the patio and watch a couple of his hired hands use a little tractor to mow his rather small front lawn. He said Reagan seemed to chat with the workers while the mowing was going on. Of course, since the president and Jennings were a little more than three miles apart at the time, it was tough to figure out what he was saying.

I saw the shimmering Reagan joined by his shimmering wife. Then, just as Speakes had said, I saw them start out on their walk. They strolled hand in hand across the newly mowed grass and headed for the woods. It was not an intimate moment. Six shimmering Secret Service agents trailed closely behind.

The Secret Service called the overlook "Newsie Nob" and the agents used the term in their radio conversations about it. So the camera crews, who also had radios, took to calling their perch "Newsie Nob" too.

Prentniecks said he used to be able to look right through Reagan's picture window and spot the president sitting at a table, drinking coffee and going over his weekly radio speech. But when the Reagans found out about the power of the telescope, they put curtains over the picture window. And they planted a tree in front of the bathroom window just in case.

But there were views that could be even more embarrassing. A couple of years earlier, a day or so after the

Soviets shot down a Korean Air Lines jet that had wandered into their territory, the CBS telescopic camera picked up the president horseback riding with apparently carefree spirit, a little dog yipping happily along behind him.

This was just after Reagan's aides had been telling the traveling White House press of the grief and concern of the president at the downing of the airliner.

When presidential assistant Michael Deaver, who had remained in Washington, saw the pictures on the television news programs, he was said to have flown into a rage. Reportedly he phoned presidential counselor Edwin Meese in Santa Barbara to get Reagan back to Washington. And the president was forced to cut his vacation short and return.

The telescope not only could focus close onto the house, it could also offer panoramic views of the whole 688-acre ranch. When I was looking I saw a helicopter land on the top of the mountain. The president's visitors were George and Barbara Bush. I could look down the mountain on the television screen and see that the Reagans were not going up to the landing pad. But I could see the first couple halfway up the road from their house and at the same time view the little motorcade bearing the Bushes traveling down the mountain to meet them.

After awhile Mike and I left. We went down the hill in my car, praying successfully against brake burnout. Our stories were apparently also great successes, if only because they appeared in several newspapers besides our own. I don't know who read what, but a couple of days after they appeared there was talk that Nancy Reagan had been upset by the accounts of the ability of the networks to keep track of the first family's vacation activities. And NBC announced that it was pulling off Newsie Nob. "There was a growing feeling inside the company that it was an invasion of privacy," said one NBC correspondent.

I didn't agree. Reagan wasn't drafted to be president, he volunteered. When men and women run for political office—particularly for Congress and for the presidency—I think they give up their right to privacy. They are no longer private citizens, they are public men and women, and the voters have every right to know what they are doing. Of course, both reporters and politicians have to exercise some common sense when it comes to coverage and when it comes to behavior.

In Reagan's case, I felt we had a right to know as much about him as we could. And since he didn't come off the mountain or invite us onto it, I thought the networks were doing the right thing. So did CBS and ABC and CNN. They all stayed on Newsie Nob.

At Rancho del Cielo Reagan's health had improved enough so that he finally was able to get on a horse and ride around his spread, a cowboy hat shading his sensitive nose. He threw a big barbecue for the reporters at a Santa Barbara mansion (not his), and, during this only close-up appearance, he seemed a bit frail to me. Yet a couple of days later, on Labor Day, he was leading us back to Washington, stopping in the Midwest to make speeches and looking and sounding as if he were the embodiment of health.

He came back quarreling with Congress about trade and budget deficits and staying on the stump to argue for revising the tax code. But the summit with Mikhail Gorbachev—the very first meeting of the two world leaders—was uppermost in everyone's mind.

I was covering presummit jockeying knowing that I wasn't going to be the reporter *Newsday* would send to the summit in Geneva. Jim Klurfeld, my bureau chief and friend, was our Soviet expert and he was scheduled to make the trip. Not only did I know little about missile throw weights and couldn't care less, but there was also no room in the *Newsday* budget for two to travel to

Geneva. Besides, our European correspondent, Pat Sloyan, would be sharing the work.

But less than three weeks before the president was to fly to Geneva, without warning, Jim suffered a heart attack. He is a man who is as tough and feisty as he is decent and talented and he wasn't about to let his misfortune beat him down. Still, even he couldn't recover from this in three weeks. Geneva was out of the question. I was told I would be his replacement.

So I went to school. Washington experts of every ideology were offering classes in summitry, teaching reporters and columnists about issues and technicalities that might arise in Geneva. I went to three different "schools" —in a nondescript office, in an elegant think tank, and at the Watergate Hotel. I was taught by scientists and politicians and administration officials and conservatives and liberals. I think I learned a lot, but in Switzerland I was able to use very little of it.

It was cold in Geneva and so cloudy that I never got even a glimpse of the Alps. Mainly I spent my time in two buildings—our hotel, where nearly all of the Americans stayed and where the White House briefings were conducted, and the International Press Center, about three or four blocks down the street, where the Soviets held their briefings.

The president's aides turned information on and off like a faucet. The Russians had arrived in Geneva a week earlier and had held daily news conferences to convince the gathering press of the righteousness of their nuclear ways. Not an American official was around Geneva to make a public reply.

When Reagan finally landed in Geneva, though, presidential aides talked anywhere and everywhere and to anyone. That included the traveling tongs. Instead of approaching White House aides and begging for interviews, the aides were approaching us. We had so many invitations to listen to experts that we finally had to start turning presidential advisors down because we were running out of time to write.

The first meeting between Gorbachev and Reagan, the man who had called the Soviet Union the Evil Empire, was scheduled for November 19 in a nineteenth-century lakeside chateau called Villa Fleur d'Eau. The villa had been set aside for the use of the president.

On November 18, in the restaurant of the American hotel, our tong talked to a White House advisor about the imminent first encounter, the opening moments so necessary to establish a cordial relationship. A total of fifteen minutes had been allotted for a private get-acquainted session for the two leaders.

"The president thought a lot about this," the advisor said. "We've made some recommendations on agenda items best tested on Gorbachev at the tête-à-tête. But the president basically said, 'Thanks, but I've got something else in mind.' He's kept it close to the vest.

"We haven't taught him, we haven't tried to prep him for body gestures or language or any opening lines," the advisor said. "How do you do this? I mean, this man has been at this all his life. He's made a career out of using language and gestures and so forth."

I was in the pool to watch the opening moments of the meeting—to see the president actually greet the head of the Soviet Union for the very first time. I was up at dawn and with my colleagues walked down to the International Press Center. There we met reporters from other countries—the Soviet Union, France, Germany, Switzerland, and Czechoslovakia. Special tags were distributed for the event. Then we were driven by bus along Lake Geneva to the villa. We were finding out how the Swiss keep their neutrality. They looked as if they had more people under arms than any nation in the world.

We stood on line in the cold for nearly two hours

waiting for the Swiss to search us. They did not appreciate complaints. When Chris Wallace, then the NBC White House correspondent, mildly protested the long delay, a leather-coated gendarme brought his nightstick up sharply between his legs.

Finally we were all examined and approved to enter. I found, however, that our place was still outdoors, behind the usual ropes. It was 8:45 A.M. Geneva time—2:45 A.M. EST. A brisk breeze gusted off the tossing lake, lowering the wind chill factor of the thirty-degree temperature to a shuddering level. Two Swiss flags flapped from the pier about two hundred yards away at the tree-marked border of the broad ice-crisp lawn.

At 9:45 A.M. the black Cadillac limousine with Washington, D.C., license tags and Swiss and American flags flying from the fenders pulled up the gravel driveway in front of Fleur d'Eau.

Soldiers in camouflage uniforms and grease gun–toting gendarmes watched and shivered in the damp morning. Reagan, wearing a black overcoat and white scarf, and his chief of staff, Donald Regan, got out of the car. The president was carrying a sheaf of papers under one arm.

They walked up the eleven stone steps to the two-story house, more glass than stone, entering through gold-rimmed French doors. Inside I could see National Security Advisor Robert McFarlane pacing restlessly, his strides carrying him past other White House and State Department aides.

Outside the wind continued to gust. I worried about my pens freezing and about my fingers getting too cold to hang onto them.

The president walked to a bay window and looked out at the international huddle of shivering reporters. He gave the thumbs-up sign and strolled away.

Five minutes passed. Then a dozen bulky men appeared. A couple of them stood in front of the ropes. They were standing in front of me! Gorbachev was coming and I couldn't see!

I tapped one of the hulks on the back. It took several taps to make him turn around. "Excuse me," I said. "Could you please move a little?" The man grunted and turned his back on me.

A Czech reporter laughed. "KGB," he told me.

But I was furious. "I don't care who they are," I said. "I gotta see." I tapped the guy on the shoulder again. "C'mon," I said. "Move." He grunted again and stood his ground.

I saw a Secret Service agent approaching. "Could you get these guys to move three feet?" I asked him. The agent spoke to the hulks. To my amazement and delight, they moved. A couple of Eastern bloc reporters laughed in appreciation.

At 10:01 A.M. a black Zil limousine pulled up the gravel drive, exactly one minute late. The Soviet flag was flying from the right fender. A back door opened and Gorbachev stepped out. He was wearing a charcoal-gray overcoat and a gray scarf.

Reagan was already at the top of the stone steps, waiting for him. The seventy-four-year-old president was wearing a blue suit. On this bitter morning he had left his overcoat in the house.

Down the stone steps he came as Gorbachev stared. The Soviet leader swept off his gray fedora, shaped in a style that had been popular in the United States two generations ago, and stepped forward. Eagerly Reagan advanced, a smile on his face, both his hands outstretched in welcome.

Gorbachev seemed a bit puzzled, a little cautious. He said something, and from his gestures the words, whether in Russian or in English, were clear. "Where's your coat?" the Soviet leader seemed to ask the U.S. president.

Reagan's smile became an easy laugh, warm in the icy

wind. "I left it inside," he said. His hand grasped Gorbachev's left arm.

Gorbachev's slight smile began to widen. He allowed himself to be led up the steps. At the top Reagan gently turned him so that both leaders faced the television and still cameras. They posed with their smiles.

Then they turned. Reagan's hand went to Gorbachev's back as he guided him through the French doors. Quickly the Soviet and U.S. aides who had gathered outside to watch followed them in. The welcome had taken sixty seconds.

Inside they sat in wing chairs and posed for pictures for the American press. Gorbachev was wearing a dark-blue pinstripe suit. A reporter reminded him that Andrei Gromyko once said to Gorbachev, "You have a nice smile but iron teeth."

The interpreter translated, listened to the smiling Soviet leader's answer, and then translated again. "It hasn't yet been confirmed," Gorbachev said. "As of now, I'm still using my own teeth. But as to the substance of your question, both the president and I have good grounds to believe we can have a good talk."

The American press left and the Soviet reporters replaced them. They wished Gorbachev good luck. The Soviet leader asked them to offer the same wish to Reagan. They did.

"I hope for the best," Reagan said.

"I join in this opinion," Gorbachev said.

And then they began to talk, for more than an hour instead of fifteen minutes, while their aides waited in the adjoining living room. The talk was supposed to have been about a general overview of U.S.-Soviet relations. It could have been about the weather. What amazed us reporters was that at first we were told there were only the principals and their translators and no one to take notes.

After that they continued with their advisors, breaking

for lunch and then coming back to the villa. At 3:45 P.M. they put on their coats and took a walk, a stroll not on the schedule. They walked across the lawn toward the lake, where there was a swimming pool and a small house. Inside, the fireplace was already warming the living room. There, again with only their interpreters, they sat and talked once more. They didn't stop until fifty-four minutes had gone by.

In the next two days Reagan and Gorbachev met with each other in front of so many roaring fireplaces in so many chateaus and little houses that Speakes quipped: "This is called the Fireside Summit."

They were supposed to be spending most of their time in meetings in the company of their top advisors. Instead they spent most of their time meeting only with their interpreters. I asked Speakes if anyone was taking notes at these briefings. Reagan was a guy who forgot the names of heads of state, a president who went to a meeting of black mayors where he called Sam Pierce, his own secretary of Housing and Urban Development and the only black in the administration, "Mayor," a seventy-four year old who met with the Republican leader of the House at least once a week for years and kept calling him "Bob Michelle" when his name, though spelled "Michel," is pronounced the same as "Michael."

Would he agree to withdraw American troops from Europe and then forget he had done this? Would he make a deal on nuclear arms reduction and be unable to remember the details? Anything was possible. But Speakes, after some hesitation, did tell us that the interpreters at least were taking notes. Which was a good thing, because weeks afterward, Reagan told a high school class that he had, in one of those tête-à-têtes, informed Gorbachev that he wished there would be an invasion from outer space. A threat like that, the president told the Soviet leader, would be something to unite the two of them. I would like to have seen Gorbachev's face when Reagan laid that one on him.

Of course, the Russian and the American diplomatic teams were meeting on the side, but no big deals were closed. Yet what did happen was something even bigger—a thaw in the cold war. There were agreements for cultural exchanges and to hold annual summits.

In fact, by the time the summit wound up just about everyone seemed to be going home happy. This included the reporters, who had written lots of stories, which is all it takes to make us happy. I celebrated by meeting my wife in Paris for a week's vacation. I was at ease with the world. My editors had given me high marks for my work in Geneva and in the previous months. All was well.

But a couple of weeks after that, in mid-December, I was contacted by an editor. "I've got some news for you," he said. "We're taking you off the White House beat. From now on you're covering the New York congressional delegation."

I began to laugh. In the bigger bureaus like *Newsday*'s, covering the local delegation was assigned to the younger, less experienced reporters. I was fifty-three years old and had been a Washington correspondent for eighteen years. "This is a joke, isn't it?" I said.

"No joke," was the answer. "Starting next year, your beat is the New York congressional delegation."

I couldn't believe it. I tried to fight it by appealing to other editors, but I got nowhere. "We knew you wouldn't like it," one editor said to me. "But we figured you'd get used to it."

"Well," I said, "you're half right."

I really did my best, but the next several months were painful. *Newsday* gives in-house awards for various stories, and the announcements are always a couple of months behind. I kept getting prizes for my White House work. Once, the paper published a full-page ad, titled BITBURG, praising me for that event. But I was no longer a national reporter. In terms of Washington experience, in terms of tenure on the paper, and in terms of age I was the senior correspondent. But without any real explanation, I had been assigned the most junior beat in the bureau.

Klurfeld did his best for me and I tried not to disappoint him. He was heading back to Long Island to become editor of the editorial pages. But in his closing months as bureau chief he continued to give me White House assignments, sending me back to California. In Santa Barbara in early April I was among six reporters in a traveling tong who met with a White House aide. We were given an exclusive story—that the United States would take some sort of action against Libya and Muammar al-Qaddafi in revenge for the bombing of a TWA airliner—even though the United States wasn't sure that he was responsible. A few weeks after the story ran, the United States bombed Tripoli.

I had a nice exclusive, but it didn't change my new beat. Jim finally left Washington for Long Island and was succeeded as bureau chief by Pat Sloyan, another friend. Pat told me he would try to help.

He also began giving me national assignments to go along with reporting on the activities of local congressmen. In September of 1986 he sent me to Grand Rapids, Michigan, to cover a three-day forum sponsored by Jerry Ford titled "Humor and the Presidency."

At the forum they told the old stories. You remember them. They were all true. Remember the one about the time Richard Nixon's motorcade stopped short? A police motorcycle leading the way had skidded and overturned, pinning its rider. An anxious Nixon bent over the policeman, who was in agony with a broken arm and likely a broken leg. The president tried to comfort him with small talk. "So," Nixon asked. "How do you like your job?"

Ford was not only the host of this gathering, he was also

the only president, current or former, brave enough to show up.

He said he had invited Jimmy Carter and was told he was too busy putting the finishing touches on his library. He said he'd invited Nixon, who said he was too busy, period. He said he'd invited Geraldine Ferraro, who said she would come but then canceled. He said he had invited then–Vice President George Bush, who said he might come but never did.

The first night of the forum Ford hosted a reception at the Gerald Ford Museum, located on the banks of the Grand River just across from downtown Grand Rapids. I waited to shake his hand and reintroduced myself. I told him that I remembered him best as the Republican leader of the House because when on several Sundays I had called him at home about various news events he had been unfailingly courteous and informative. I told him how much I appreciated that.

Ford obviously was pleased. "And what exactly are you doing now?" he asked.

I stretched the truth. "Oh," I said, "the same as ever. Still covering Congress, still working out of Washington."

The face of Jerry Ford, former president, former congressional leader, ardent golfer, and postpresidential millionaire, suddenly seemed pained and bleak. "So you survived," he said.

I felt awful. "Oh, Mr. President," I said. "You've done so much more than survive."

The subject quickly was changed. Ford led a group of us to a couple of exhibits that recalled his campaigns for elections to the House.

But by then my mind was on something else. With three words Jerry Ford had told me something and taught me something. Washington was still my home and I still had an eye on the events of the country. This had been a good thing to cover. Maybe I was a survivor after all.

14

PICKLES

THE HOUSE AND SENATE ELECTIONS WERE DRAWING NEAR AND narcotics was a big campaign issue. Since New York City was a national drug center, Sloyan told me to add narcotics to my beat—and some politics as well. So I made another trip with Ronald Reagan. And I went down to Florida to cover the Senate election there.

And then, late in the year, Sloyan called me into his office. "You still have to cover a local delegation," he said, "Long Island instead of New York City. But from now on you're our national correspondent for the House of Representatives."

This was not so bad. Half a Congress is better than none. But right away there was one of those sensational Washington developments that made things even better, the kind of stuff that kept popping up all during the time Ronald Reagan was president. The nation was told that we secretly had been selling arms to Iran to try to free the U.S. hostages. Not only that but we were giving the profits from the sales of the weapons to the contras of Nicaragua. And the White House was engineering this after Congress, by law, had banned military aid to the contras.

When Attorney General Ed Meese first made the announcement at the White House and we read the wire service stories coming off the ticker, there was only one thing to do. We reporters laughed and laughed. Even for the Reagan administration this was too nutty to be true.

But it was true, and at the end of 1986 and through half of 1987 it was easily the most luscious story of the time. For me, another wonderful development was that our coverage was being directed by Charlotte Hall, a splendid editor who had come to Washington from Long Island to be our news editor.

When the House and the Senate special Iran-contra committees finally got around to holding their joint hearings, it was her idea to have me write a daily feature story about the testimony, leaving the hard news to others. Once again I was writing articles about the major occurrences of the day. I was delighted.

In fact, Iran-contra stories were taking up so much of my time that I practically forgot about the beginnings of the 1988 presidential campaign. But as it started the editors gave me a piece of the action. I was sent to Denver in April to cover Gary Hart's announcement that he was in the race and went back again to witness Congresswoman Pat Schroeder's tearful declaration that she was out of the race. I saw sex and plagiarism scandals whiz by with scarcely any involvement—although with long-distance phone calls to various old friends I did manage to confirm for *Newsday* that Hart planned to retire from the running after stories about his liaison with Donna Rice.

Then in late 1987 the national desk sent me to Iowa to write a story about Congressman Dick Gephardt of Missouri running for the Democratic presidential nomination.

So I flew out to Des Moines. Gephardt was bouncing around Iowa in a little prop-driven Cessna, going from farm town to farm town and gravely studying the stacks of corn and hay. He was giving this dreadfully dull speech about his economic proposals, which he kept saying would make Asian countries bring down their trade barriers and let America sell its products overseas again. Sometimes, particularly in the early morning, he would open his mouth and his listeners would start closing their eyes.

At 8 A.M., with the temperature at ten below and the wind shrieking across the flat farmland, he would be in some drafty fire hall struggling to explain why it was really important and worthwhile to impose an oil import fee on the people of the United States. He made this a regular part of his stump speech.

Gephardt would say that a tax like an oil import fee reminded him of his childhood, when his mother gave him a daily dose of castor oil. "I hated it," he would say of the medication, "but my mother told me it would be good for me in the long run."

Loreen Gephardt, a sturdy eighty years old then and in temporary residence in Iowa for the duration of the caucus campaign, was asked about this odd habit of administering a daily laxative to her son.

"Certainly not," she said. "It was cod liver oil." There was an immediate adjustment in the stump speech.

When I first walked into Gephardt's Des Moines press office and asked if an interview could be arranged, I was greeted with great hospitality. In the early stages of a campaign, when there is competition to the left and competition to the right and a candidate gets to feeling that an audience of one hundred is a blockbuster crowd, even a reporter from a high school newspaper can get an interview.

Okay, they said. So I got on this little Cessna, having carefully taken my Dramamine first. I sat in a seat directly facing Gephardt. We were so close that we were playing kneesies.

I started asking my questions and he started answering very politely. He seemed like a very nice guy.

Then the wind picked up. The Cessna started getting blown every which way. It was pitching up and it was pitching down. Gephardt was still smiling. Dramamine, I thought, do your stuff. But then the plane dropped fifty feet and my stomach did not drop with it. In fact, my stomach never did catch up with the plane.

I tried to keep asking questions but by this time I really couldn't hear the answers. I was green. I looked at Gephardt. His eyes were getting bigger and bigger.

I looked for an air sickness bag. The plane was not well equipped. Look at it this way, I told myself. If this guy actually does get to the White House you will be able to say that you barfed on a president. How many reporters could say that? How many people could say that?

Gephardt was sitting stock still. "Sorry," I told him. "Can we finish the interview later?"

"Oh, sure," he said. I put my head down. It didn't do much good but I managed to exercise full willpower. Fifteen minutes later the Cessna put down in a small city. Gephardt, who had to speak and eat lunch there, was unsullied. He spoke. I neither listened nor ate. Lunch was Alka Seltzer. I felt better.

I actually got back on board the plane. Gephardt showed his bravery too—he sat down opposite me again. We finished the interview before the plane started rocking again, and I suffered quietly until it landed in Des Moines.

Gephardt is a patient man, a politician who had trained from his boyhood to be a leader. But it is one thing to represent a conservative Democratic district of the southern part of St. Louis in Congress and quite another to be president of the United States.

He is bright and he had a clever campaign team and he

did manage to win the Iowa Democratic caucus. But after that his quest became as uncertain as the flights of the squadron of Lear jets and prop Cessnas he used to ferry the reporters and his staff from state to state.

Some of the younger reporters got so that they couldn't take it—the bouncing, the crowding, the feeling of flying on a very windy edge. Once, a couple of them took a three-hundred-dollar cab ride to our next destination rather than board a Cessna in a high wind. Other times they rented cars rather than fly.

After Michigan caucus night, when he lost once again, Gephardt flew back to Missouri to run for his House seat instead. The competition, with Governor Mike Dukakis, Senator Al Gore, and Jesse Jackson the survivors, moved to Wisconsin. But I went east to New York to prepare to cover the Democratic presidential primary in my home state.

"In New York you got Cuomo number one and Koch number two," David Garth, the political consultant working for Gore, told me when I asked him what impact the outcome in Wisconsin might have in New York. "Then you have the Mets and the Yankees and the Knicks and the Nets and the Reverend Al Sharpton and Tawana Brawley. And we're supposed to know what happens in Wisconsin? People here think Wisconsin is a pair of shoes."

To Garth—and to the other political operatives—politics in New York was "the ethnic game." "The so-called pandering to the Spanish, the blacks, the Jews, the Italians, and the Irish, if we can find them," Garth said. "I'll tell you, WASPs are hard to find. They don't even run for office. We have been the melting pot with nothing melting for one hundred years. And we like it that way. We don't want to know from reality."

Mayor Ed Koch went after Jackson on all fronts, saying

that his domestic programs would bankrupt the country in three weeks, his military programs would leave the country defenseless within six weeks, and that he would end American support for Israel.

I was given a new assignment—shifted to covering Al Gore most of the time. Garth had told me that to win in New York a presidential contender had to be praised by Governor Mario Cuomo, criticized by Koch, and have two million dollars for an advertising campaign. Now I was covering a guy who had been criticized by Cuomo, praised by Koch, and had less than one million dollars for an advertising campaign.

I began following Gore around the state and writing ledes like "It was a beautiful day at the Love Canal," which never got into the paper.

But life was not at all bad. Because I really was covering a very odd couple—Ed Koch and Al Gore—the loudest, fastest mouth in the city and the prep school, Ivy League Washington insider who claimed to be a good old boy from the mountains of Tennessee.

In New York big, handsome forty-year-old Al Gore was David Garth's extremely endangered species, the vanishing WASP. I asked him if not being an ethnic was hurting him. He looked a little puzzled. "I don't think it is a handicap to be of English-American descent," he replied.

Gore really didn't know his way around the city, but he did know his way around politics and he knew how to bloody an opponent. It was Gore who gave Dukakis a cut so deep that he never recovered, turning him into a certain loser against George Bush in November. Dukakis may not have known the wound was fatal when, at a Democratic candidates' debate in Manhattan's Felt Forum, Gore went after Dukakis for a Massachusetts program that gave two-week unsupervised furloughs to criminals, including those convicted of first-degree murder.

Gore didn't mention Willie Horton by name, but he did

say that eleven murderers furloughed under the program had not returned and that two more had killed again while they were out. Gore asked Dukakis if he would install the same kind of program on a federal level if he were to be elected president.

Dukakis tried to dodge and duck, tried not to give an answer, but the crowd hooted and shouted at his evasions. "We have changed our program," Dukakis finally acknowledged. "We will not furlough lifers any more."

Later I talked about the exchange with a friend of mine who was a Washington Republican political consultant working with George Bush. "I think," he said thoughtfully, "that you're going to hear about that furlough program again."

But Gore didn't do himself much good either. Jewish voters were being told to vote for the frontrunner, Dukakis. A vote for Gore, the line went, might weaken Dukakis so much that the despised and feared Jesse Jackson might be able to win in an upset.

Koch took Gore into the streets and tried his best to counter this. He marched next to Gore in a Salute to Israel parade—Dukakis marched separately—and then gibed at Jackson for not showing up.

A couple of days later, the mayor met Gore at Lexington Avenue and Seventy-seventh Street, shaking hands with riders as they rushed into the subway station. Like a big bird, Koch flapped his arms toward the sky and gave the political mating call. "Yoo hoo," the mayor shouted as the crowd began to thin. "Hey. It's us. Al Gore and me. Say hello."

He had beckoned the reporters to stand next to him, the better to record his words. "My lucky corner," the mayor said fondly. Then he whaled away at Jackson for missing the Israel parade. "What he did was an insult to this city," Koch said. "An insult to this city. Can you imagine him avoiding a parade, any other ethnic parade? The St. Patrick's Day Parade, the Puerto Rican Day Parade, the

Martin Luther King Day Parade, the black parade, any
parade that walks up Fifth Avenue? That's an insult to
people."

Two black women stood on the sidewalk and stared
balefully at the mayor. "Next election," one of them
muttered. "That's it."

Koch did not seem to hear her. He was busy shaking
hands and lecturing the subway riders on the importance
of voting for Gore. "You mustn't be afraid," the mayor
said, "as Jesse Jackson was when he wouldn't go into the
parade. You got to be able to take it. Presidents have to be
able to take it."

Gore, standing a little distance away, was shaking
hands too. "The mayor is speaking for himself," Gore
said. "Jesse Jackson speaks for himself. My relationship
with Jackson is good."

I walked back to Koch and asked him why Gore didn't
holler like he did. "Well, they don't do it that way in
Tennessee," he said.

The next day was primary day. Gore decided he'd better
campaign alone. He began by shaking hands with riders
leaving the Seventh Avenue escalator of Penn Station. It
was not a good beginning.

"You really picked a good place to stand," a large
woman shouted sarcastically, as Gore positioned himself
only about ten steps away from the top of the escalator.
"You're blocking everybody."

But Gore stood his ground. He was from Tennessee.
What did he know about Pennsylvania Station and morning rush hour in New York?

Many of those coming up the escalator paused to shake
hands with the senator. This created an enormous jam of
people, since the escalator kept running and the riders
kept rising, their backs to the big yellow and black sign
that reads PLAY ATLANTIC CITY'S BIGGEST JACKPOT.

"You're standing in the wrong spot," a man yelled at Gore.

"Get the hell out of here," another snarled.

But Gore kept shaking hands with the more tolerant commuters, the politician's smile becoming fixed on his face. "I'd like to have your vote and support," Gore said.

"Look what you're doing to the commuters," a woman called. "Move away, move away."

"Thank you," Gore said. "Thank you. Nice to see you."

On the level below, hundreds of commuters began to pile up in an apparently hopelessly struggling mob. "There's five million people downstairs, trying to get upstairs," panted a man who had fought his way up the adjoining stairs. "Move," he shouted at Gore.

"Oh," a woman said to another as she spotted Gore. "He's cute."

"He doesn't care about Israel," another woman called loudly. "All he wants is Jewish votes."

Two black men arrived and, standing about five yards from Gore, began distributing leaflets to the commuters. "Jackson for president," they called. "Jesse for president."

Later, as the voters were going to the polls, Gore went to visit eight and nine year olds at PS 9-M in Manhattan. The children, mainly black, seemed very glad to see him. I knelt behind them and whispered, "Who would you like to see win the primary today?"

A half dozen small faces turned and smiled sweetly at me. "Jesse Jackson," the children choroused.

"Cut that out," an advance man hissed at me.

I smiled at him and turned back to the children. "Do you know that Senator Gore is also running for president?" I asked.

"Oh," a little girl said. "He's nice. Can't they both be president?"

Neither of them could be president. By the time the polls in New York closed, Dukakis had 51 percent of the vote,

Jackson had 37 percent, and poor All Gore, the taste of real half-sour pickles and true bialys still strange in his mouth, had come in third with only 10 percent. Two days later he took himself out of the race. I had to find myself yet another candidate to cover.

15

QUAYLE AND COMPANY

IT WAS HOT IN NEW ORLEANS, A DAY FOR SLOW STROLLS AND COOL drinks, but all the same, some of the Republicans gathered for their national convention were on the run. Others, however, seemed to be at ease. In one part of the city Senator Dan Quayle, unlike Senator Bob Dole, wasn't bothering with any last-minute campaigning to try to get the vice presidential nomination. Then again, Quayle had not been Bush's big rival for the presidential nomination. Dole and Bush hated each other and had hated each other for years; Quayle had no such feelings.

So on August 16, dressed casually, Dan and Marilyn Quayle had no frantic rounds of politicking and speech making on the schedule. Instead they had a leisurely lunch and then began an easy walk through the French Quarter, just like hundreds of other Republican convention delegates.

It was convention time, yet the city was so relaxed that, according to the local papers, the police had abolished the vice squad. Moreover, alcoholic beverages legally could be carried down the street just as long as they were not in glass containers. Signs invited tourists to witness nude female dancing and nude male dancing. A few young women discreetly patrolled the neighborhood until dawn.

Jazz invigorated the humid air of Bourbon Street. On the second-floor porches protected by wrought-iron black railings, residents lounged against walls or sat at tables, drinks in hand, and stared down at the rare sight of Republicans in their city.

Tawdry but alluring stores offered souvenir T-shirts, cups, glasses, and ceramic masks of comedy and tragedy. There was a voodoo shop, where charms and potions could be purchased; and innumerable bars and grand antique shops invited all to consume or look at their wares. I was told that the Quayles were doing the proper thing—inspecting the antique stores.

Suddenly Quayle heard the sound of his beeper—the one the Bush organization had provided him ever since he got on the list of possible running mates. He and Marilyn rushed back to their room at the Intercontinental Hotel, where they made the calls that confirmed that he had been beepered to greatness. Bush had indeed picked him to be the vice presidential candidate. He was ordered to get down to the Riverfront, a shopping center and dock on the Mississippi, as quickly as possible. Don't answer the phone, he was told. Don't even answer the door.

He had no time to prepare a speech. He and Marilyn barely had time to change their clothes. The phone began to ring off the hook. A volunteer tried to handle it. It was impossible.

The Quayles rushed downstairs and got in a car driven by another volunteer. Tom Duesterberg, Quayle's Senate administrative assistant, was with them. The car let them off at the Riverfront, in back of the enormous crowd that had gathered in front of the platform where Bush was going to speak.

Duesterberg had to lead the way, the Quayles following. No one knew who they were. "Hey, buddy," indignant people kept calling at Quayle as he tried to shove through the mob. "Who the hell do you think you are?"

And Quayle, with his vow of silence, couldn't even tell them. He just had to keep pushing and endure the yells, the curses, the threats. By the time he reached the platform he was red in the face, flustered, and excited. When Bush introduced him, the most notable thing Quayle did was to flap his arms, like a big bird.

Afterward, when he and Marilyn got back to the Intercontinental Hotel, they were met by this short guy in a six-hundred-dollar suit. He told them he was Joe Canzeri and that he would be Quayle's deputy campaign manager.

There was not only Canzeri but also a squad of Secret Service agents. They bundled up the Quayles' things and moved Dan, Marilyn, and their stuff out of the Intercontinental. To let the Quayles feel comfortable they let a couple of the Senate staffers come along. The whole group was hustled over to the Westin Hotel, where Reagan had just pulled out.

The Quayles were taken in through the kitchen and whisked up to their fifteenth-floor suite so fast that it took two days for Dan to find out the name of his new hotel. And when he first got to his rooms, another short guy, this one in a rumpled suit, was waiting for him. He introduced himself as Stuart Spencer, Quayle's new campaign manager.

Senator Quayle didn't know it, but he was getting Reagan's old A Team, a couple of the best GOP political operatives around. Spencer was the California political consultant who had led Reagan to victory as governor and then to the presidency in 1980. In 1976, though, he had gotten Ron and Nancy pretty mad by switching sides and joining up with Gerald Ford, to keep the Republican nomination with the president. Canzeri knew Spencer well, having worked in the Reagan campaigns. He also had been an assistant to Nelson Rockefeller. He did show business people too—Frank Sinatra and Evel Kneivel were among his clients.

In the suite Canzeri pulled out a wad of message slips. They were all from reporters, asking that their phone calls be returned. He started reading off the names to Spencer. Canzeri would read a name. "Uh uh," Spencer would say, and Canzeri would ball up the slip and toss it into the wastebasket. It really impressed Quayle's Senate staffers. They knew they were in the big time now.

That night Spencer, Canzeri, and Lanny Wiles, another old Reagan campaign hand, had dinner in the suite with the Quayles and three Senate staffers. "This is going to be different from any Senate campaign," Spencer told Quayle. "In Indiana you gave the same stump speech. Now you can't do that. You'll be going from stop to stop. You'll have to talk water rights and gun control, or in the South it will be defense. So you'll have to rely on your staff."

Of course, presidential and vice presidential candidates do give the same speech over and over. But Spencer figured Quayle wouldn't know that. The team was under orders to take control and that is what they intended to do.

"We know pace," Spencer told him. "We know timing. We know advance. We know scheduling."

And poor Dan Quayle didn't even know how to use a TelePrompTer, the transparent plastic device through which words are scrolled, allowing speakers to read their texts while seeming to be talking from memory. Dan Quayle had to make an acceptance speech. He didn't want to use the TelePrompTer.

"I'll speak from notes," he told Spencer and Canzeri. They were used to Reagan's technique of using four by six index cards, so they agreed. But Roger Ailes, who was handling the media for Bush and who also had worked for Quayle, later persuaded him to change his mind.

The next day the three Quayle children—Tucker, fourteen; Benjamin, eleven; and Corinne, nine—were flown into New Orleans from Indianapolis, where they had been staying with their grandparents. When Corinne started to climb out of the plane she took a good look at the mob of TV cameras, photographers, and reporters. Then she turned right around and tried to get back on the plane. It took her mother, Marilyn, to coax her to come along.

Of course, Quayle had other troubles. Immediately the story of his having joined the National Guard to evade the draft during the Vietnam War became national news—as did speculation that his influential family had used political pull to keep him out of active duty. Spencer, Canzeri, and the rest of the team—all picked three weeks before the convention to manage the vice presidential candidate no matter who was selected—had their work cut out for them.

By August 18 the National Guard story was the talk of the convention. Delegates kept comforting themselves by saying, "At least he didn't go to Canada."

I was still covering Dole and I was amazed that the Bush forces really knew how to rub it in. Not only had Bush denied Dole the vice presidential nomination, he had asked him to be the person who makes the nominating speech for Quayle at the convention. To make sure he did it right, the Bush writers even provided Dole with the speech.

Dole was a hero of World War II. The ribbon of the Purple Heart is on his lapel and he virtually lost the use of his right arm in combat against the Germans. He was going from hotel to hotel giving pep talks to various state delegations. I was among a crowd of reporters who tried to quiz him as he left the Wisconsin state delegation. "The National Guard is very important to us in America and if he got in the National Guard like everyone else there's nothing wrong with that," Dole said.

But, I asked him, what if Quayle had used influence to get into the Guard? Dole's face grew stony as he tried to escape, moving toward a hotel stairway. "That would be different," the Senate Republican leader said.

He reached the staircase and began to descend, his press secretary, Walt Riker, accompanying him. Security men blocked the reporters from following. I leaned over the stairwell. "Isn't it ironic that you, a World War II hero, are nominating him?" I shouted at him.

Dole froze when I said that. Then he continued to walk down the stairs without saying a word. At the landing he stopped and looked up at me. "He's a good man," Dole called. And he continued his descent.

Dole did his duty well. And Quayle made it through his convention speech simply sounding dull. He hit the campaign trail with Bush in the obligatory opening joint appearances on the stump, but the National Guard uproar just wouldn't go away. On August 22 Quayle soloed as a vice presidential candidate. He made a speech defending his military record before the Veterans of Foreign Wars and got a standing ovation.

But the relief didn't last long. On August 23 every television network reported that Paula Parkinson, a beautiful lobbyist notorious for having gotten a couple of Republican congressmen into trouble, was claiming that Quayle had once propositioned her. Quayle denied it.

Just as that was dying down, though, came the front-page stories of his poor grades in college, his enrolling in a program for minorities to get into law school, his reputation as an intellectual lightweight. Quayle went to Huntington, Indiana, his hometown, a hostile press hot after him. The home folks rallied around their man, booing reporters and catcalling as the newsies were forced to ask Quayle questions through a loudspeaker mike. Everybody thought it was a Republican plot, but my Republican friends insist that it was an accident. "It wasn't really planned to have the mike there and get the crowd fired up," one GOP operative told me. "It just worked out that way."

A little after that Quayle went back to Washington, D.C., to get a cram course in how to be a candidate. "We just wanted to get him home," my Republican friend told me. "We just wanted to get him out of the news for awhile."

I began covering Quayle on Labor Day, which by tradition is considered to be the opening of the presidential campaign. The day before Labor Day my oldest son, Morris, was married to Roz Rudo. It was an afternoon wedding. That evening, after seeing the newlyweds off, I changed clothes, packed a bag, and flew to Newark, New Jersey, to link up with Quayle, whose campaign trail task was to look as patriotic as possible.

For the first time since 1968, I was not my paper's lead reporter on a presidential candidate. That was the decision of my editors. They didn't tell me why. I was disappointed but didn't make strenuous objections. An assignment to Quayle was not bad. Here was a guy who was really making news. Besides, I was looking forward to a reunion with my friends from the 1980 Reagan campaign.

Labor Day morning the Quayle motorcade headed out, going down the road and across a rickety bridge to Ellis Island. Dave Prosperi, whom I knew from Reagan campaigns and the White House, was Quayle's press secretary. He had put me in the pool, so I was riding in a van with a few other newsies. All of the other reporters were on a bus.

Except for us and a few park rangers, Ellis Island, the American landfall for millions of immigrants, including my father and his brothers and sisters, was empty. We cautioned the van driver to wait for us and then trailed Quayle, his wife, and their three children into the great hall, whose four bronze domes tower over the island.

There were stacks of lumber inside. Walls were scraped. Old radiators were piled in corners. This wasn't any showplace yet. We shouted questions at the Quayles. They told us that their ancestors had not come to the United States by way of Ellis Island.

After a couple of minutes we walked outside. I tried to ask Quayle another question. Canzeri was so worried by this prospective ad-lib that he tried to hold me back. But I shouted it out anyway, a real toughie: "Senator, if your forebears didn't come from here, then why are you here?"

Quayle was willing to answer that one. "To talk about what America means," Quayle hollered.

Actually he was there because from Ellis Island the Statue of Liberty makes a splendid background for the television cameras. He and his family posed for pictures so that the statue would be looking over their shoulders. Then we took two boats over to Liberty Island, where the statue is located. The Quayles, several accompanying politicians, and the staffers were on one boat and the reporters were on the other. We were told not to worry about our belongings that we had left in the vans and the buses—the motorcade was going overland and would meet us at Liberty Island.

The boats were so close that I was able to shout another question at Quayle—whether this was his first visit ever to the Statue of Liberty. He shouted back that it was.

In the shadow of the statue, the Quayle team had gathered about fifteen hundred people ready to cheer the candidate. They had distributed handwritten signs for the crowd to hold. One of them was held by a turban-wearing Sikh. NATIONAL GUARD FOR QUAYLE it read. I asked the sign holder if he had ever been a member of the National Guard. He said he had not.

The Quayles climbed onto a platform and faced the crowd. All of a sudden the two of them, in unison, swung into action. They clapped their right hands over their hearts and lifted their eyes toward the heavens. Then they recited the Pledge of Allegiance. Their audience followed right along. It was such a socko start that some in the crowd recited the pledge twice.

Then Quayle made a speech explaining what the Pledge of Allegiance means to him. With slightly different words, Red Skelton had done the same thing about twenty-five years ago, and the old comedian had made a record out of it.

For candidates for public office, their opening addresses usually set out the themes and goals of their campaigns. The definition of the Pledge of Allegiance was Quayle's opening day speech.

When he finally finished, the pool reporters rushed for the van. But it was nowhere to be seen. Prosperi joined us in the hunt and then ordered us onto the bus with the rest of the press. We had to hurry to Newark Airport and fly to Detroit.

There was one problem. I had left a bag in the van. The bag held my most important and expensive writing instrument, my computer. "Don't worry," a Quayle aide said, "the van will meet us at the airport."

When we got there, however, there still was no van. A *Time* photographer in the pool was furious. "Listen," he said to the Quayle staffers, "I got five thousand dollars worth of cameras on that thing." That made me feel better. I think my computer cost only eight hundred dollars.

In the empty airport terminal, Quayle staffers stood around. They did not want to offend *Time* magazine. The Quayle aides whispered to the Secret Service detail. The Secret Service detail began talking up their sleeves, where their transmitters were hidden. New Jersey State Police went to their patrol cars to put out bulletins to be on the lookout for a missing Quayle van. Prowl cars were dispatched to the hotel from where we had started out.

Then we remembered that about five hours earlier, on Ellis Island, we had told the van driver to wait. A patrol car was sent back to the island. Sure enough, although every other vehicle in our motorcade had moved out toward Liberty Island, and Ellis Island was all but deserted, the van driver had taken the wait order seriously and literally. He was still waiting.

And so was Quayle and his chartered plane. He waited until the van got to the airport and we were able to retrieve our equipment. Only then did we fly off to Detroit. Quayle was supposed to march in a Polish-American parade in Hamtramck, but one thing that wasn't waiting was the parade. It was over by the time he arrived.

All the same, there was a crowd still hanging around at an outdoor stage. Someone pinned a SOLIDARITY button onto Quayle's lapel. He got on the stage and he was really excited. When a woman in a Polish costume began to sing the Polish national anthem, the senator tried to lip-synch along, pretending he was singing in Polish too.

It was a great, almost bilingual, beginning to the campaign.

For the next weeks I jumped from candidate to candidate, even spending some time with Bush and Dukakis. But it was the vice presidential race that took up more than half of my time.

On the whole I enjoyed covering Quayle more than I did Lloyd Bentsen. That was basically because the Democratic senator from Texas was totally predictable.

Put him on a tractor in Cedar Rapids, Iowa, and he would plough a straight furrow. Put him in a New York deli and he would eat at least some of the nine-inch-thick pastrami sandwich presented to him. Put him in front of cops in Los Angeles and he would say—oops—he would say he isn't in favor of gun control, a very opposite view from that held by his running mate, Michael Dukakis.

After he said that, after we got back on the campaign plane, I asked him a question. "Okay," I said. "President Dukakis is in the White House and Vice President Bentsen is presiding in the Senate. A vote on gun control has ended up in a fifty-fifty tie. Mr. Vice President, would you vote your heart and your convictions or the convictions of the President of the United States?"

Bentsen threw up his hands and started back up the aisle with an "Oh, no."

"C'mon, Senator," I called after him. "You can tell me."

"Okay," he said, looking at the other reporters with their pens poised over their pads. "But I want to whisper it in your ear."

I walked up to him and he bent and he whispered. "Bizzz, bizzz, bizzz, bizzz, bizzz," said Bentsen. "Bizzz, bizzz, bizzz, bizzz, bizzz." Then he straightened up, patted me on the shoulder, and said loudly, "Now mind you tell the other folks here just what I said about this situation." And giggling, he walked back to his seat.

"Well?" the other reporters chorused.

"I will quote exactly," I answered. And I did.

A few minutes later, though, Mike McCurry, who was Bentsen's campaign and press secretary, came back to tell me that of course in such a situation he would have to do the president's bidding.

Now Bentsen was fun, but he was a political powerhouse whose biggest problem on the stump was his encyclopedic knowledge of the issues and his occasional tendency to lapse into Senate jargon when he gave his explanations. He is Cool Hand Lloyd, whose brown eyes turn to balls of ice when he is baited. And he was so smooth that he didn't make much news. Anyway, if my editors were interested in anything concerning the vice presidential campaign, they were interested in stories about Quayle.

Their interest did grow when it was announced that the two would debate in Omaha on October 5. Months before they became vice presidential candidates they had gone on television to debate a labor issue. And Quayle had appeared to take Bentsen's measure.

But to the public Quayle was the lightweight, gaffe-prone draft dodger, and Bentsen was the tough wise man and combat veteran of World War II.

Bentsen's face is a rugged map of more than three generations; Quayle has the smooth, regular features of a young movie star. Bentsen looks old enough to be Quayle's father. If Quayle just managed to stay even in the Omaha confrontation, Bentsen surely would be considered the loser.

"He'll do a good job," Bentsen predicted to me beforehand. Then he got a little edge in his voice. "He can handle the bromides very well," he said. "I'll do my best and that'll be it. He'll be packaged very well."

I switched to the Quayle campaign and asked Quayle the same questions. "There's not a whole lot of preparation to do for a debate," Quayle said to me. "Either you know it or you don't."

In private Quayle seemed to me to be a pleasant, decent, almost sweet-natured man, bewildered at his status as the political laughingstock of the country. His handlers were trying to hide him. In the early days, although he gave individual interviews, he would rarely if ever walk back from the front of the plane to chat with reporters. Off the plane he would appear in high schools or in front of Republican audiences, making shrill speeches attacking Dukakis with such exaggerations that to me the words seemed absurd. Most of the time there was nothing wrong with his delivery, but there were moments when his tongue would betray him. He would do things like misquote Indiana University basketball coach Bobby Knight, saying, "There is nothing that a good offense cannot beat a better offense." Another favorite was calling the Holocaust "an obscene period in our nation's history" instead of Nazi Germany's history.

"If I were choosing someone for president," Bentsen said to me of Quayle, "he wouldn't be on my short list."

"I would say I consider Lloyd Bentsen a friend," Quayle

told me before the debate. "I've been to his house a couple of times on social occasions so I consider him a friend. I think Lloyd Bentsen's a gentleman."

Bentsen's job, McCurry told me, was to "play harmonious background music to the main tune of the nominee." That was what Bush wanted Quayle to do as well, but it wasn't really possible.

"Think of the two weeks of publicity I had," Quayle told me as he discussed the beginning of the campaign. "To be introduced to America in that fashion . . ."

And he was still learning the ways of big-league campaigning. It took him awhile before he discovered he had to walk off an airplane with his wife Marilyn on his left. That way they both could wave with their right hands and then have those hands free to shake as they worked the receiving line on the tarmac.

But that was the least of Quayle's worries. For weeks he and Bentsen prepared for their showdown. Once, on the campaign plane I saw Bentsen look at his black debate briefing book and then rehearse by shouting at the bulkhead. I assume he was rehearsing because his wife, Beryl Ann ("B.A."), who was sitting next to him, didn't seem to be upset or even pay any attention.

In the last few days before the debate the preparations grew intense. Both stopped campaigning to study full time. Bentsen went to Austin, Texas, and used an empty saloon as a rehearsal hall. Quayle went back to Washington and took over an empty suite of legal offices.

Down in Austin Congressman Dennis Eckhardt (D-Ohio) was playing the part of Quayle during the rehearsals. Bentsen's staff had been trying to get their man up for the debate. McCurry had cut out a clipping about how Quayle was making speeches comparing himself with John F. Kennedy.

"Jack Kennedy was almost my same age when he ran, not for vice president, but president," Quayle would say on the stump. "I have almost the same amount of service in Congress as Jack Kennedy and I'm willing to put my legislative record and legislative accomplishments on the table and compare it to him."

The words, of course, weren't Quayle's idea. One of his advisors told me that the Quayle team had been searching around for a way to say that Quayle, although he looked young, was mature enough to be either president or vice president. They thought about having him compare himself to the writers of the Constitution. "Their average age was thirty-seven, if you take out Benjamin Franklin," the advisor said. "But we decided on Kennedy. It was more current."

Down in Austin Bentsen was going through not only rehearsals but also debate preparation meetings. At one of those his old friend and advisor, George Christian, gave him a piece of advice on the Quayle-Kennedy comparison. "I made the statement that I didn't think he ought to let him get away with it," said Christian, who served as press secretary to the late President Lyndon Johnson. "Bentsen didn't answer."

Then, in the saloon, during a debate rehearsal, Eckhardt played his role to the hilt and used Quayle's words in comparing himself to Kennedy. "Bentsen stopped the rehearsal dead cold," McCurry said. "He said something like, 'Does he really say that?' Then he shook his head and said, 'Well, Dan Quayle is no more JFK than George Bush is Ronald Reagan.'"

In Washington Senator Bob Packwood (R-Oreg.) was playing the part of Bentsen for Quayle's rehearsals in the law office. Quayle practiced more days than Bentsen, who hated the rehearsals. The Quayle team thought that a lot of foreign policy questions would be asked. Henry Kissinger gave Quayle a briefing. Quayle went to the White House, where Ronald Reagan gave him a pep talk.

In Austin things were getting testy. "Is this a worthwhile exercise?" McCurry asked Bentsen during a rehearsal.

"It's for the birds," Bentsen answered.

Eckhardt tried to ease matters by wearing a Ronald Reagan mask at the last rehearsal. "Bentsen laughed," McCurry said. "It was the only light moment of the last two days."

In Washington Jeff Nesbitt, who was Quayle's Senate press secretary, was talking about the dos and don'ts for his boss. "He does have to look statesmanlike," Nesbitt said. "But no matter what he does, he's going to look what he is—a forty-one year old. He's got to show he's got twelve years in Congress. He's got to be calm and deliberate. He can't flap his arms, he can't get excited. People have to look at him and say, 'Yes, this man looks presidential or vice presidential.' "

McCurry kept thinking about the movie *The Candidate*, starring Robert Redford, the handsome actor Quayle liked to say he resembled before he switched and started comparing himself to Kennedy. Uneasily McCurry remembered that in the movie the young Redford debates the distinguished silver-haired incumbent senator, Crocker Jarman, and although not so wise or experienced, he still destroys the incumbent with a series of devastating one-liners.

A few hours before the debate the two rivals flew out to their showdown in Omaha.

It was the night of the number twos, but in Omaha this was a top-banana event. Hundreds of reporters were in the city, and special buses had to be used to get them to and from the Omaha Civic Center, where the debate would be held. So many reporters wanted to follow Quayle out the next day that the Republicans had to charter a second plane for them—a development unheard of in the coverage of vice presidential campaigns.

The reporters were taken to the exhibition hall of the

civic center, an echo chamber of a place that was really a giant, faintly aromatic, basement. I think that it was used for cattle shows at least some of the time.

On October 5, instead of stockyard pens, television sets were lined up in front of rows of desks. The local phone company had installed telephones for all of us who had requested them. Free food was available to all reporters, and free pens, free pads, and free cigarette lighters. There were also free souvenir pins. I bought a souvenir T-shirt. BROUHAHA IN OMAHA, it read. The exhibition hall was so noisy that when I tried to send an early story by hooking my computer to a phone, the din repeatedly fouled communications.

Separate large areas were curtained off for the Republican and Democratic dignitaries who would be the spinners. These were the organized squadrons of men and women who waged on behalf of their opposing campaigns the postdebate battle for reporters' minds and favorable coverage. During a debate they would be getting their instructions from political operatives who would give them a general party line to follow. Then, immediately after a debate, they would sally out among us, trying to persuade us that their side had won the war of words.

For *Newsday*, at any rate, no matter what they said would do no good. The reporters writing the stories about the debates were back in Washington. I was in Omaha but my assignment was to write a story about the spinners, not really about the debate.

All the same, I decided to watch the confrontation on television, instead of in person, so I could view it just like almost everybody else. To my eyes, what I saw was appalling for Quayle. His words came out in choppy phrases, with strange pauses in the wrong places. Too many times during the debate he seemed like a talking robot with faulty circuits.

He had been braced for foreign policy questions, but

there were few of those. He had been braced to attack Dukakis more than Bentsen, and that he did. But he had not been braced to answer the obvious and simple question: if some calamity overtook George Bush and Dan Quayle became president, what would be the first thing he would do?

"First—first I'd say a prayer for myself and the country that I'm about to lead," Quayle answered. In front of our television sets we reporters laughed heartily. This was not the best response from a guy who was one of Johnny Carson's main sources of material, from a guy pictured as so dumb that the most popular Democratic campaign button read PRESIDENT QUAYLE?

Five times Quayle was asked the question. And he never could answer it to the satisfaction of the panelists. But the ordeal of those questions was nothing compared to the blow struck by Bentsen.

In his effort to answer the panelists, Quayle had fallen back on the old Kennedy line provided by his staff for his stump speech. "I have as much experience in the Congress as Jack Kennedy did when he sought the presidency," Quayle said.

The silver-haired Bentsen pounced. "Senator, I served with Jack Kennedy," Bentsen said in his cultured, non-Texas accent that resounded with chilling superiority. "I knew Jack Kennedy. Jack Kennedy was a friend of mine. Senator, you are no Jack Kennedy."

Quayle paled at the hit. On the screen he seemed to wince. The shouts and applause from Democratic partisans in the live audience spilled from the television sets into millions of living rooms.

"That was really uncalled for, Senator," Quayle gasped.

Bentsen was not contrite. "You are the one that was making the comparison, Senator," he purred. "And I'm the one who knew him well. And frankly I think you are so far apart in the objectives you choose for your country that I did not think the comparison was well taken."

This was one ninety-minute debate where the time simply flew by. Maybe not for Quayle but certainly for the fascinated reporters watching in the hall.

When it ended, the spinners came charging into our arena. At the first presidential debate at Wake Forest University in North Carolina the Democratic spinners had been in the live audience and had tarried to give Mike Dukakis—a narrow winner in his first confrontation with George Bush—a final round of applause. Their dallying was a dreadful mistake. The Republican spinners, who also had been in the live audience, hadn't waited. Instead, they had rushed across the green, banner-hung quadrangle to the building where the reporters were working and had gotten a vital twenty-minute head start on the Democrats. With deadlines only minutes away, I think the Republicans at Wake Forest managed to sway enough of us so that we reporters—and like it or not, we are the referees in such matters—called the debate a draw.

But the Democrats had learned, and this time in Omaha they hit the floor running with their spin theme clearly in mind. In moments the gigantic basement was a series of human whirlpools—Republican and Democratic spinners encircled by reporters and television cameras, their words clashing as they tried to fight for victory for their champions.

"Five strikes," chortled Congressman Bill Gray (D-Pa.) as he talked about the repeated questioning of Quayle as to what he would do if he became president. "He struck out all five times."

"Five strikes," chortled Congressman Dennis Eckhardt (D-Ohio), who had played Quayle in rehearsals for Bentsen and who had reminded Bentsen of the Kennedy opening. "He struck out five times and then he took the Fifth Amendment."

"We'd say a prayer too," chortled Susan Estrich, the campaign manager for Dukakis.

"Bentsen ran away from Mike Dukakis," pronounced Rich Bond, the deputy campaign manager of the Bush-Quayle campaign.

"He ran away," pronounced Senator Alan Simpson (R-Wyo.).

"A cheap shot," Republican National Committee chairman Frank Fahrenkopf said of Bentsen's Kennedy crack.

"I think he put to rest some doubts," James Baker, the Bush-Quayle campaign chairman, said of Quayle, without any irony intended.

Several television commentators and newspapers, including *Newsday*, called the debate a draw. I myself did not agree. After I wrote my spin story I went back to my hotel and dropped into the bar for a drink. Half of the Republican world and half of the reporters were there. Charlie Black, the Republican consultant, and Jim Lake, a consultant working still another Republican presidential campaign, sat down with my group.

They kept telling us how well Quayle did. A couple of the reporters at the table politely said they agreed. Charlie and Jim are friends and I told Charlie the truth. I told him I thought that Quayle had had his clock cleaned. Charlie said he appreciated my frankness. Then Charlie turned to Jim and said, "Mike, here, is off the reservation."

In his hotel suite Quayle was on the phone with George Bush, who, like the Democratic spinners, used baseball terminology. "Home run," Bush told his running mate. "Home run."

Sweet words from the boss. They were the crowning phrases from what he had been hearing from his advisors, who had been telling him what a great job he had done. He went to bed that night convinced he had won the debate.

It was not until he awoke the next morning that he

discovered that even the Republicans were saying he had fouled out.

In another hotel Bentsen went to bed on the night of October 5 also convinced that he was the winner. He didn't know by how much. When he awoke the next morning he discovered that to the Democrats he had become the folk hero of their ticket.

On a gray Thursday morning the two combatants rose and flew from Omaha—Bentsen to Texas to be embraced in person by Dukakis and Quayle to small city after small city in Missouri—far, far away from George Bush.

I was on the Quayle plane. We were told that he would have no comment. But the airport personnel did not provide the plane with any steps, so he couldn't use the front door to the aircraft. He had to walk up the plane's steps in the rear. And as he and his wife made their way between the reporters' seats, we trapped him in the aisle.

We asked him about his answers to the repeated questions about what he would do if he were president. First he said the question was "important." A little later he said the question was "inappropriate." Then he said it was Bentsen and not he who had ducked the question about what he would do if he suddenly became president.

He said that Bentsen was running away from Dukakis. Then, when he found out that the two of them were campaigning together in Texas, he said they were "sticking together like Velcro." For Quayle it was a very bad day.

Rich Bond was riding the second plane, doing his bit for damage control. At each stop reporters from both planes would meet and swap quotes they had gotten from staffers.

In every city, Quayle delivered a speech written by Khachigian saying that it was Bentsen who had done badly. "He waffled," Quayle said. "He shuffled, ducked, and dodged." The crowds, Republican though they were, did not applaud the lines—in fact, they didn't applaud very much at all.

In Joplin, Missouri, so Republican that there was only one elected Democrat in the entire county, I asked Don Miller, a salesman who was in the audience of about one thousand, what he thought of the debate. "Not much," he said. "Quayle looked like he was scared to death half the time."

I asked if he would vote for Dukakis. "I'm a Republican," Miller said. "I'm going to vote for Bush anyway."

That night Quayle sat in his hotel room and started reading the newspaper commentaries about the debate. One article, quoting an unnamed Bush staffer as sneering that Quayle needed to be "potty trained," was simply too much.

He had been hit with the fact that he, the hawk, had served in the National Guard to duck service in Vietnam and that he had used influence to be accepted into the Guard. He had been hit with the charges of bad school grades and conniving to get into law school. He had been hit with the charge that he might have had a dalliance with Playboy poser Paula Parkinson.

And now there was "potty trained." Then, when he opened another paper, there was conservative columnist George Will writing about not sending "a boy with a sword" into combat.

That was it. Something snapped at that point. Still, he listened as Khachigian, Canzeri, Spencer, and the rest of the team gave him a new pitch. Stand up and be proud to be the guy who is the national target for the rotten tomatoes. Quayle accepted the words as he had accepted all of the other directions. Dutifully, he started saying: "We can stand the attention, we can stand the heat. We're going to stay in the kitchen, and George Bush is going to be the next president of the United States. The voters will vote for him."

But he also had decided to revolt against his handlers. All of a sudden, instead of ducking the reporters trailing him, Quayle was becoming very friendly. He started to stand on the sidewalk and give little five- and ten-minute press conferences.

That night, Friday night, I was designated to be one of the pool reporters assigned to go with him to a fund-raiser in a house in a Tennessee suburb. Except to use a bathroom in the nursery, the reporters were not allowed inside.

We loafed on the sidewalk, looking up the path to the house and the crowd we saw through the windows. Quayle made a speech, which we couldn't hear, and then came out. I kidded him about the T-shirts he was being given each time he spoke at a high school.

Quickly Quayle became serious. "I want to be my own spin doctor," he said to me. "If I come back on the plane, will there be a spin seat for me?"

"Senator," I said, "it's your plane. Every seat is yours. I'm sure there would be one for you."

"I'm going to come back on the plane and spin," Quayle said. He got into his limousine and I got into the van with the other reporters and Dave Prosperi, the press secretary. I told them what Quayle had said.

Prosperi grinned. "The press secretary reserves the right to veto," he said.

When we got to the plane, I made Quayle's offer part of the pool report. Sure enough, as the jet flew toward Washington and home, Quayle, with Prosperi at his side, made his way back to us.

For him it turned out to be a mistake. There were special reporters on board, reporters who wrote long features and interviews for a living, reporters whose repeated requests for interviews had been denied. Now he was coming down the aisle toward them, the long-denied quarry approaching of its own accord. Raw meat at last!

There was a mad rush toward him. I thought the plane would tilt. Reporters were stacked so tightly that there were few who could take notes. Our arms were imprisoned by other bodies. We held up our tape recorders in frozen positions and began to shout.

Quayle really didn't like the questions about his parents and their relationship to the John Birch Society and what that relationship had meant to him in his childhood and so on. And what did he think of Richard Nixon? And why did he sneer at Dukakis as "the liberal governor from Massachusetts?" Was he attacking the whole Northeast? New England? Massachusetts?

"You're out of line," Quayle finally snapped.

"Why am I out of line?" the prime questioner asked.

"Because," Quayle said, "I say you are." Still, Quayle never quite flew into an open rage.

He gutted it out and stayed with us until the plane started to bank over Dulles and it was time for all of us to get back in our seats. He didn't spin anyone toward his point of view but he didn't give anyone a nasty story, either.

"I think there was one friendly question out of the whole thing," Quayle said during an interview he gave me a couple of weeks later. "At the end, as I was going back up the aisle, you said, 'Do you still like us?' and I turned around and I smiled and said, 'Well, of course.' But I think that was it."

On Saturday morning Quayle phoned the Bush-Quayle campaign chairman, Jim Baker. "He told him that it couldn't get any worse," a Quayle friend said, "that the perception of him just couldn't get any worse. Then he said that from now on he was going to talk to reporters when he wanted to."

Back in Washington I immediately was told to cover Dukakis, who was touring New York in a one-day stand.

I followed him out to Long Island and into Manhattan. I went with him up to Boston and I flew with him to Los Angeles for his second and final debate with Bush, this time at UCLA in Los Angeles. As the chartered jet sped west the Democratic whip of the House of Representatives, Congressman Tony Coelho of California, was coaching Dukakis on what he had to do.

"He is a blind date who must prove he can be a welcome guest for the next four years," Coelho said of the man whom George Bush had called "the Iceman." Coelho hinted that he agreed that Dukakis was a kind of a stiff on the stump. "I told him," the congressman said, "'Use your hands, use 'em.'"

Dukakis tried to show off his warm side when the plane landed to refuel in the middle of the night in Fargo, North Dakota. More than twenty-five hundred Democrats had come to the airport to wish Dukakis well. He did his best. He used his hands so much that he looked like the Pope invoking a blessing. He led the crowd in singing happy birthday to Ted Mondale, who is Fritz Mondale's son. He kissed two college cheerleaders on their cheeks after they helped him into a school football jacket.

The crowd cheered all of this lustily, and Dukakis tried out using his hands again by waving before he departed. "You have to practice the plays," Coelho said. "It's how he says it. The body language."

Of course, everyone remembers how things turned out. At UCLA we reporters again were given free pens, free pads, free food, and free souvenir pins. Joe Canzeri, taking time out from the Quayle campaign, briefed the Bush spinners and in a very private ceremony conferred on all of them the degrees of "Doctors of Spin." To each he presented propeller-topped beanies for their heads and toy doctor bags for their hands.

They were inspired, but so were the Democrats. This time advance spinner patrols from both sides hustled into the press room even before the debate began. They would have predicted victory if they could but figured that even we wouldn't swallow that. So they claimed they were giving us a "pre-spin rinse" and presented us with opposing words and papers, each side declaring the other's candidate to be a liar unfit to hold the presidency.

One of the pre-spinners for Dukakis was Senator Al Gore, who had fought for the Democratic presidential nomination himself. I reminded him that he was the politician who had, way back in the New York primary, first questioned the Dukakis prison furlough program—a questioning that Bush had evolved into the Willie Horton ads. "A scurrilous, phony issue," Gore answered with only the slightest trace of a smile.

It was grist for my now-customary spin story, but the material for that article was a very minor part of the evening. Once more the debate—or at least parts of it—proved to be sensational.

Right from the start Dukakis forgot everything Coelho had told him about letting the American people see what a passionate human being he was.

"Governor," was the first question from moderator Bernard Shaw, "if Kitty Dukakis were raped and murdered, would you favor an irrevocable death penalty for the killer?"

There was a small gasp from the live audience, but Dukakis didn't hesitate. "No, I don't, Bernard," he answered. "And I think you know that I've opposed the death penalty during all of my life."

In my mind I could see Democratic politicians all over the country cowering in their chairs and groaning. This guy was such an ice cube he might as well have been answering a question about the budget. Then, instead of talking about his love for his wife, instead of showing his humanity, he started talking about drugs.

Only a few days earlier he had spoken with emotion

about the way robbers had tied and gagged his aged father some years ago. Now he was again the Iceman. He was making Dan Quayle look like an accomplished debater. Right then and there, any faint hope of a Democratic victory disappeared.

The morning after that fatal encounter the Democratic candidate set out on a West Coast sweep in his campaign jet. It was supposed to be a triumphant tour to hail what his handlers had hoped would be a sure debate victory.

When I reached the plane I was given some exciting news. One of the other passengers for this tour would be the actress Debra Winger. Even before *An Officer and a Gentleman* I was one of the millions of males who had been entranced by her—the sexy voice, the gorgeous eyes, the wonderful figure. That she was also a terrific actress didn't hurt either.

And now my celluloid love was off the screen, in close real-life proximity to me. In Sacramento, the first stop of the tour, I saw her standing behind Dukakis on the steps at the state capitol, smiling and applauding for him and for Lloyd Bentsen, who had flown more than a thousand miles just to show up at the event and to speak fewer words than the miles he had traveled.

After the speeches there was another surprise. My friend Francis O'Brien, who was helping Dukakis in the campaign, came aboard the press bus. O'Brien had been House Judiciary Committee Chairman Peter Rodino's administrative assistant during the impeachment proceedings against Nixon, and we had become good friends back then. He had left work in the Capitol to try his hand at movies. He had been the executive producer of *Gallipoli*. So it was nice to see him again. What made it even nicer was that he was squiring Debra.

A half dozen rows back I shouted words at them, any words, trying to engage them in conversation. Francis introduced us. I asked for her autograph. "It's for my sons," I fibbed. "They would treasure it forever." Then I said, "And so would I."

Debra grinned and signed. I talked to her about Skull and Bones, the Yale secret society to which Bush belongs. I told her that the society actually collected skulls and that Bush's father had made off with the skull of Geronimo and donated it to the society. I was desperate to make conversation.

"Myron, shut up," Francis shouted.

"Stop that," Debra said to Francis. "I like Myron. He reminds me of my father." She looked at me and added hastily, "—except younger."

On the plane, when the male staffers, the male Secret Service agents, and the male reporters saw her, they went into a collective ecstacy. And she tried to make us happy. She posed for pictures with the Secret Service. She had bantering words for just about everyone. Then she walked up front where the candidate was sitting and sat down across from him.

Kitty Dukakis, the candidate's wife, strolled back and sat down in my row to talk with Tom Oliphant, the *Boston Globe* reporter. I horned in with some questions of my own.

Mrs. Dukakis was indignant about Bernard Shaw's rape and murder question. "I'm glad I'm not the candidate," she said. "If I were, I don't know what I would do. Of course Michael loves me. Of course he would do something."

After awhile Mrs. Dukakis walked back up front. Tom Foley, who is now the Speaker of the House but who then was the number-two Democrat—the majority leader— came back to chat. He recognized me as a congressional reporter and stopped to talk as I sat in my window seat. Other reporters gathered in the aisle. Suddenly Debra wriggled through the crowd and leaned over.

"What is this, Myron?" she chuckled. "Do you just sit

here and hold court?" This was wonderful. Foley smiled and quietly edged further down the aisle, leaving Debra as the center of attention.

After a few minutes she also left and sat in the reporters' section with Francis O'Brien and another Dukakis aide, Nick Mitropolus. When Debra sat next to him Nick got so excited that he began to thump the roof of the plane with his hand. There were shouts of "Thumper, Thumper." Male reporters thumped along with him. Debra laughed.

Up the aisle, at the front of the plane, I saw that Dukakis himself was on his feet. I gestured to him, beckoning him to come back so that we could talk to him about the debate. I wanted to ask him about what his wife had said about his love and his passion. But the candidate shook his head no.

So I walked over to Debra Winger. "Debra," I said, "Do us a favor. Go up there and bring him back."

"Bring him back?" she said. "Listen, I sat across from him for twenty minutes and he didn't say one word to me. I don't think he knows who I am."

But I remembered. I reminded her of her father. Except younger, of course. "Debra," I said, "you can do it, kid. go on up there and bring him back."

"What am I?" she said. "The sacrificial virgin?" She paused. "Strike virgin," she said.

"Debra," I said. "You can do it. I know you can."

She looked at me reproachfully but started up the aisle. She kept muttering, "sacrificial virgin, sacrificial virgin." But she went. I saw her up there, talking earnestly to Dukakis. Now there was someone who knew how to use her hands when she spoke. It took her only a couple of minutes. She started back, the candidate in tow.

We reporters surrounded him. Governor, weren't you upset by Bernard Shaw's question? Governor, wouldn't you really have done something violent to someone who raped and murdered your wife?

"Aw," Dukakis said, "I've been asked that question a thousand times. It doesn't bother me."

But wouldn't you try to avenge violence on your wife? Kitty was wrong. The governor shook his head no. He said he would let the law take its course. And certainly, no death penalty.

Dukakis went back up front. I made the "O" sign with a thumb and forefinger to my pal Debra. She smiled in appreciation. Francis showed her the papers every presidential campaign plane has on board—a photopcopied daily compilation of every story on the campaign from every newspaper the home office is able to collect.

Debra read for a little while and then moved to my seatmate, Tom Oliphant. His article on Kitty Dukakis in the *Boston Globe* was one of those in the bundle. "You're a funny fellow," she said. "How come the story you wrote is dry? Stories should have a little humor."

Her words hit me right in the funny machine. The news desk was in one of its no-vivid-writing-please phases. If Alicia Patterson, the founder of *Newsday*, were alive she would have been furious.

"Debra," I said, "I'm glad you said that about humor." She looked at me impatiently. "Oh, Myron," she said, "the trouble with you is that you take everything so personally."

The plane flew on to Seattle, where it was raining, as usual. Dukakis made his speech outdoors but in front of a good crowd, in spite of the weather. Debra stood behind him, afterward telling reporters that she was happy she had worn her boots.

On the flight back to Los Angeles she was sitting three rows in front of me. I fished a button out of my pocket, a souvenir of the vice presidential debate, and walked up to her.

"Debra," I said, "on behalf of myself and the other reporters, I'd like to present you with this button for causing the most excitement on a campaign plane since Barry Goldwater put his into a nose dive in 1964."

"Oh," she said. "I've got a button."

"Not this one," I said. She took it, looked at it, and then suddenly pulled me to her. This was impossible. This happened to Richard Gere and Robert Redford, to say nothing of the governor of Nebraska. This didn't happen to short, round reporters in their late middle age.

But it was happening. How wonderful. How sweet. How unimaginable. She kissed me on the lips.

She held the pin high and jumped up and down. "Myron and I are pinned," she called. "Myron and I are pinned."

My heart and my head told me that this was the moment to speak words that would be remembered for their wit, words that might be remembered for awhile—to election day, at least. But there was only one thing I could think to say, and I said it. "Wait until my wife finds out," I said.

"Don't worry," Oliphant said, scribbling in his notebook. "She will."

Back in Los Angeles Debra and I didn't say good-bye. But Debra, you were the best thing that happened to me in the campaign of 1988.

Dukakis flew back to Boston, but I didn't go with him. Instead I went as far east as Denver, to pick up Bush. *Newsday*'s regular Bush correspondent needed a few days off the campaign trail.

I'd covered Bush immediately after the primaries and found him on occasion to be an unintentionally very funny fellow. He would make mistakes. He couldn't remember important names and dates. He would sound like a wimp.

But he sure didn't sound like a wimp now. And there was another development that had begun early but now towered over the campaign. It was the candidate's lofty statements about himself and his bald, outright lies about his opponent.

In Detroit the candidate had mourned the murders of two city policemen. Then he had accused Dukakis of being soft on crime. "We share their grief," Bush said of the policemen's families. Then he brightened. "And now," Bush said, "on to the politics."

He didn't stop there. He went into his "kinder, gentler America" phrases, and then in almost the same breath he demanded tough judges who would hand out the death penalty. Drummers in high school bands banged their approval. The crowds just ate it up.

On the plane a Bush aide was enthusiastic as he talked of the coming visit to New York. "It's great," he said, "there's a couple of dead cops there too."

Flying high and hitting low, Bush jetted into New York to try to seize one of the few remaining Dukakis stronghold states. Bush went to Christ the King High School in Queens, where he put on the commemorative bar of one of the murdered New York policemen, Patrolman Eddie Byrne, and then tossed red meat at five hundred applauding policemen and hundreds more shouting high school students.

"You and I know," Bush roared, "that when the apple rots, you cull it out. Some people need to be taken off the streets and kept off the streets. . . . My opponent is against the death penalty."

All of those New York cops, representing benevolent associations with fifty thousand members, gave Bush their endorsements at the school, whose teacher's union had been broken after a lengthy strike in 1981. Unions were picketing outside as Bush spoke.

Rich Bond, the deputy campaign chairman, said the Bush camp knew what kind of school it was when the decision was made to have the rally there. "We were aware of the community dispute," he said. "We had a choice where to receive this endorsement."

The next day, I left Bush and returned to Washington. After a three-day rest I was out again, this time with Bentsen. Unlike most candidates, who tend to put on pounds during a campaign, Bentsen had become positively skinny.

He wouldn't say it, but he knew the ticket was going down like his weight. At the same time he was in many ways a happy man, secure in his pride, because he knew he was campaigning to rave reviews from the reporters and the politicians in his party. So he was having the time of his life, dashing from city to city in Texas and the border states on a desperate Democratic rescue mission.

His trouble was Dukakis. Quayle might have been an anchor pulling down Bush, but for the Democrats it was the top of the ticket that was the far heavier drag.

"I wouldn't be on a ticket with someone who'd take my shotgun away," Bentsen would say over and over as he stumped through the South. And also, "I wouldn't be on a ticket with someone who is for a weak defense."

On November 1, a week before election day, I flew with Bentsen into Owensboro, Kentucky, which is right on the Indiana border. The powers of the Kentucky Democratic establishment did their best for their old pal, turning out thousands of Democrats for a rally in a tobacco barn. The governor was there, and the Democratic senator, Wendell Ford, and Bill Natcher, the local Democratic congressman.

"Give 'em hell, Lloyd," the crowd shouted. And Bentsen did his best. The Democrats cheered and cheered. And then, I think partly because they knew what was going to happen on election day, the whole audience serenaded him with their sad, sad state song of terrible loss, "My Old Kentucky Home."

Just for the sake of the song my friend, *New York Times*man Warren Weaver, and I began to sing along.

"Oh the sun shines bright on my old Kentucky home,"
we sang, "'tis summer, the—" and Warren and I abruptly
stopped singing and looked at each other in horror. We
both had simultaneously remembered the original racist
line: "'tis summer, the darkies are gay."

But the crowd sailed smoothly on. "'Tis summer, the
people are gay," they sang.

By arrangement I waited in the dark outside of a side
door to the barn until Bentsen walked out. Then I got into
a limousine with him for the five-minute ride to the
airport. I asked the sixty-seven-year-old senator, who is
chairman of the Senate Finance Committee, if he was
having a good time.

"My work, much of it, has been in the field of economics
and finance," he said. "There's not many applause lines in
that kind of speech. So I take pleasure in belting one out."

No candidate will predict his own defeat or the defeat of
his ticket. When I asked Bentsen if he had any regrets he
answered "Absolutely not." He said it twice. "I'm still
working at it," he said. I've got more to do."

I asked him about his plans for the next presidential
campaign in 1992. There was a long silence. "I'm not
worried about that," Bentsen finally said. "I'm just worried about the election, trying to do the best I can in the
last week."

We continued the interview on the campaign plane as it
flew to St. Louis, where he planned to make a late night
speech at Washington University. I dropped off at the
airport. A Bentsen staffer drove me to an airport motel. It
was past 11 P.M. Before seven the next morning I was on a
commercial flight to Memphis, Tennessee, to meet up
with the Quayle campaign so I could complete the reporting on a single story about how the two vice presidential
candidates were winding up their campaigns. By 9 A.M. I
was shaking hands with Dave Prosperi and other Quayle
staffers in the Marriott Hotel in Memphis. Prosperi told

me the schedule. That very night I was going back to Owensboro, for that was where Quayle would be campaigning next.

Owensboro may have been right across the river from Quayle's home state, but I don't think it was a great place for a Republican to campaign. This city was so Democratic that Democratic congressman Bill Natcher was said to stand for reelection rather than run. Owensboro's favorite bumper sticker seemed to be one reading HONK IF YOU'RE SMARTER THAN QUAYLE. And the biggest Republican figure in the state, Senator Mitch McConnell, was so peeved at Quayle's selection as the vice presidential candidate that he wouldn't come to Owensboro to introduce him for his speech. For that Quayle had to rely on Martin Tori, the volunteer the Republicans had put up against the unbeatable Natcher.

Owensboro Republicans may have been few in number but they did teach me some things about the wealth of GOP hospitality. The Democrats gave the press a song; the Republicans presented us each with little overnight bags containing goodies that included Red Man chewing tobacco and, far more intriguing, pint bottles of bourbon.

At night Quayle decided to relax by playing basketball with his staff and reporters. That was when he first saw I was back on his campaign. He seemed happy at my return and invited me to ride with him in his limousine to the college where the game would be played.

"This is great," I told him. "I desperately need an interview with you. Let's do it now."

"Oh," Quayle protested, "not now. I promise—I'll give you the interview tomorrow. Let's just relax." So instead we swapped jokes and small talk on the ride to the college.

The women's volleyball team shrieked its delight when he walked into the gym and then stayed to watch. Quayle is not as good a basketball player as he is a golfer but he is good all the same. The young women sat and cheered as he led his team to victory. Me, I stood on the sidelines and watched.

The next day he toured Premium Allied Tool of Owensboro. After strolling through the factory he stopped to give a speech to about one hundred of the workers who had been assembled for the occasion. He was in shirtsleeves. His staff lounged in the corners, staying clear of the machinery. The Secret Service looked alert. This is the unabridged version of what he said:

"From what I've seen here, we got a very active plant, very active work force. I was impressed with that when I went around and talked to a number of people, found out half your products are exports. Exports particularly from this plant happen to mean jobs.

"Exports translate into jobs. Jobs are what we are talking about. Coming from here, do you all say it around here? From the other side of the river?"

Quayle laughed. The workers didn't. They shifted slightly.

"I'm glad to be on this side," Quayle said. "But as I say, in Indiana we have a number of machine shops like this one. We don't do quite the sophisticated work that you do here, but I certainly want to congratulate you on what we have been able to do.

"You never know on Wednesday afternoon who's going to pop in. Did Lloyd Bentsen pop in yesterday?"

"No," two men called.

"No," Quayle echoed. "Good." He laughed. No one else did.

"I understand he was in town. We were over in Evansville yesterday and so we're back in this area, get on this side of the river and make sure that we shake a few hands and try to solicit a few votes and make sure that the economy is going to expand.

"But we're delighted to be here and maybe what I do if you got time—I don't want you to take too much time

away from the precious workday—I'd like to throw it open
to questions I can answer for you. I don't get involved in
any kinds of wages or job specifications or things of that
sort, but I've got a lot of other answers."

There was a long silence. Then one worker called:
"After your election, will you be back in Owensboro?"

"Will you invite me back?" Quayle asked.

"Yes," the worker said.

"All right," Quayle said. "Let's get through the elections
first and hopefully things will go our way. It looks
reasonably good right now, but reasonably good or looking close is only good in horseshoes. Remember, in
horseshoes closeness counts. In elections, it doesn't.

"So we hope to wake up Wednesday morning—as a
matter of fact, we'd just as soon find out Tuesday night if
the voters will let us know real early rather than keeping
us up all night—at least in Kentucky.

"Now, you fellows—are you on eastern or central
here?"

"Central," a worker called.

"Yeah, central," Quayle said. "So your polls still close at
six—seven o'clock eastern. But Kentucky is like Indiana.
They always battle and see which one is going to be there
first. Part of Indiana—the Evansville area—is on central
daylight. So is the area around Chicago. But much of the
state is on eastern. So is Kentucky. Much of the state is on
eastern.

"So we always fight about who's going to be first at
night. So we'll build a little contest out there to see if
Kentucky can beat Indiana by going for George Bush first.
See who wins that race. Like in basketball, things like
that."

Quayle paused. "Any other questions out there?" he
asked.

There was a slight shifting of feet but dead silence.

"Now's your chance," Quayle said.

No one said a thing.

"Well, if not, thank you for allowing me to come here six days before the election. The six days are going to go very slowly as far as I'm concerned."

I don't want to give the impression that what Quayle said to the workers was the way he spoke all of the time—just some of the time, when he didn't use the words prepared for him by Ken Khachigian or by one or another of his staffers. Not being able to deliver an extemporaneous speech is a problem that is not particularly unique to him—although his unintentional humor is.

At any rate, that very night Quayle gave a perfectly credible and logical red-meat speech to a cheering crowd of more than a thousand gathered in an Owensboro airport hangar. He even used a famous line from his disastrous debate with Bentsen.

"Can you imagine?" he said. "Michael Dukakis said he really is in the mode of Harry Truman and Franklin Delano Roosevelt and John Kennedy. I never served with John Kennedy. But I'll tell you one thing. Mike Dukakis is no John Kennedy."

I was given my Quayle interview in a room in the little Owensboro airport terminal the next morning. We were scheduled to fly off to another city, but there was trouble with the plane and repairs had to be made. Quayle went off to a toy store to buy presents for the birthday of his soon-to-be twelve-year-old son—games including Photon, an electronic gun game in which the contestants try to shoot each other. He was happy because Photon, a $79.99 fad of 1987, cost him only $14.99 in November 1988.

Quayle seemed to me to be a nice guy who was dreadfully wounded at having been made into a national joke. "I thought I knew what the ground rules were," he said, "but I was off by a factor of ten."

But he thought of how the reporters traveling with him

had grown to like him and he said he believed that things had changed. "All the untrue personal statements that have been made about me and about my family," Quayle said. "That's something I wish didn't happen. But it did." All the same, he said he didn't hold any grudges. "It's behind me," he said. "I'm a person who looks forward. I'm a journalist myself. Everyone is prone to make mistakes and misjudgments, as they say. So let bygones be bygones."

Late that evening, on the plane ride back to Washington, reporters asked Quayle how he was going to spend the weekend. Marilyn Quayle answered for him. "Play Photon," she said.

I went out with him again for the final push. At planeside he and the reporters and his staff posed together for a class picture. Just as the photographer said "cheese," many of the reporters clapped their right hands against their hearts—a silent Pledge of Allegiance to mock the Republican campaign patriotism that we felt was nothing more than cynical political opportunism.

I was standing next to Quayle and I saw him wince. The photographer, startled at our sudden, previously agreed on gesture, did not snap the picture. "Oh, you guys," Quayle said sadly.

We would not show any mercy. I felt a mild pang of sympathy, but it was countered by a stronger urge to remain faithful to my colleagues. We kept our hands at our hearts. The photographer shrugged and clicked away. It was a year before the pictures were distributed.

A little later, this time all together, we asked Quayle again how it felt to be mocked and ridiculed from the first day of the campaign to the last. Quayle smiled. "Actually, it's part of our strategy," he said. "We want them to attack the vice presidential candidate and leave George Bush alone."

He was the only member of either ticket who never

appeared on a national television interview show. We asked him why. He had no real answer.

His handlers had tried to protect him from hecklers wherever he went and he seemed to travel to the small cities and the rural areas, where his treatment by crowds would be gentler.

At first Quayle said that he had been in all but two or three of the top television markets. But then, agreeably, he went along with the popular thesis. He tried to make a joke out of it. "Actually," he said, "I think the scheduler back there in Washington has got a dart board in his office. They sort of take darts and wherever they stick they say, 'There's where the vice presidential candidate is going today.'"

I liked Quayle personally. I sympathized with him. Reporters aren't supposed to be merciless. But the obligation is to tell the truth. And that's what I tried to do. I wrote what he did and what he said, the good parts of it and the bad parts of it and the foolish parts of it. Nobody had forced him to accept the vice presidential nomination. He was a public man, and I treated him as a public man.

Now in the final hours of the campaign, he was going back home to Indiana, to love and to applause, where he was introduced as the man who would bring "Hoosier values and Hoosier common sense to the White House . . . good old common sense that comes only from the state of Indiana."

On Tuesday morning, November 8, Quayle was back in his small hometown of Huntington to cast his vote. There was a rumor of a death threat, and the Secret Service seemed especially alert. But Dan Quayle, unafraid, went to his lucky charm.

Some who are superstitious rely on a rabbit's foot. Others may have a particular garment to wear or a lucky charm. Some even visit voodoo doctors.

Not Quayle. His secret magic was to go to his dentist on Election Day to have his teeth cleaned.

Marilyn Quayle insisted that it really wasn't superstition—that election day was simply the first time during a campaign that he could get to his dentist.

But Quayle contradicted her. "It's a little bit of good luck," he said of his appointment with Dr. John E. Regan. "Let's say superstitious. Why change when it worked in the past?"

After going through this lucky treatment, he came walking down the chilly street, showing off his newly cleaned teeth with a grin. About fifty first graders gamboled around him, chanting over and over, "Dan's the Man. Dan's the Man."

Hundreds watched as he walked into the old stone courthouse to vote. Hundreds more cheered when he emerged and walked down the street to the *Huntington Herald Press*, owned and published by his father, Jim, to write the headline for the afternoon edition.

Democratic headquarters was right across the street. As he came out of the newspaper office, from the little Democratic storefront came the mocking amplified strains of the Quayle parody written to the tune of "Back Home in Indiana."

> *I spent the war in Indiana*
> *Getting shot was not for me*
> *I never went to 'Nam, I never saw Saigon*
> *I only watched it on TV.*

If Quayle heard, he gave no sign. He walked quickly back down Jefferson Street in the middle of a roped-off lane. I asked him what he had written for his father. BUSH CLOSING IN ON VICTORY, he said.

"Isn't that a little weak?" I asked.

"What did I tell you?" he answered. "Cautiously optimistic."

He walked down the roped-off open-air aisle, down the street to Republican headquarters. There he was greeted, not by a song but with a gift from his alma mater—a bright-red Huntington North High School letter jacket with his name scripted on it.

Then he made another election day good luck stop—to a café called Nick's Kitchen. It was absolutely mobbed. The staff let a television crew walk in with Quayle. But they barred the writing reporters.

I was pretty sore. When Quayle came out I stopped him immediately. "They wouldn't let us in there," I said. "You're a reporter. Give us a fill."

Quayle obliged, telling us about the few words he'd spoken and how the crowd had cheered. He said that once, about three years earlier, he had approached someone in Nick's who didn't know who he was. "Not this time," he smiled. "They all knew who I was."

We all flew back to Washington then. Bush was in Texas for election night, but Quayle was assigned to the Washington Hilton Hotel for the big national Republican victory party. When Quayle got there in the early evening he didn't want to talk to reporters anymore. He didn't want to make news. After all, it was George Bush's night.

About fifty Hoosiers made him feel comfortable, eating dinner with him in the hotel restaurant. He spent most of his time, though, sitting in his shirtsleeves in his eighth-floor hotel suite, telephoning winning Republican governors and congressmen.

At 12:15 A.M. he came downstairs and gave his victory speech. It didn't much matter what he said because the crowd already was pumped up by the ticket's triumph. And that was a good thing, because Quayle didn't say much.

He thanked everybody for their help and pledged his loyalty and devotion to Bush. And that was that. He had been, as he said, the lightning rod of the campaign. And now he was the vice president–elect of the United States.

16

BREAK A LEG

AFTER THE CAMPAIGN I WAITED FOR THE EDITORS TO DECIDE MY NEW assignment. I worried about my fate, but I shouldn't have. To my surprise and pleasure, once again I was *Newsday's* national congressional correspondent, covering both the House and the Senate. I think it is the best assignment in town. The White House is certainly the glamor beat, but the sum of a reporter's information there rarely goes beyond what the president's staff carefully chooses to say. In the Capitol there are 535 legislators to consult, not to mention literally thousands of their aides.

Most reporters covering Congress work long hours. My workdays are dictated by my assignment. If a congressional hearing starts at 9:30 A.M., I am there no later than 9 to make sure I have a seat and to make small talk with committee staffers to get a clearer understanding of what will take place. But if I'm covering a House floor debate, I might not arrive until after 11—half the time, the House doesn't come in until noon.

No matter when I start, the chances of my finishing before 7:30 at night are slim. The deadlines are at 6:30, and the editors usually want reporters available well after 7 for checks on the story.

Since floor debates frequently continue after 6:30, I will

begin writing on a portable computer at about 5:45 P.M., sitting in a press room just off either the press gallery overlooking the House chamber or the Senate chamber. I will be watching the debate on television while I type.

I will write what I know, pointing the story to what I think will be the result and leaving a blank where I would ordinarily put the vote. For example, on a Saturday night in October 1990, the Senate passed the budget exactly on *Newsday*'s deadline. I had filed an eight-hundred-word story fifteen minutes earlier. I watched the senators vote, holding a phone to my ear, and called in the result as it happened. We made the entire run of our Sunday paper with a full-blown, up-to-date account.

Of course, in these days of 1990 and 1991 there isn't too much going on in Congress that seems to interest news-paper editors. All of the action is in the Soviet Union and eastern Europe and the Persian Gulf. Not many major stories come out of Congress on any of that. But this is a good job, and I'm not complaining.

One day in June of 1989 I was among a half dozen reporters who met with Vice President Dan Quayle. It was the first time I'd spoken with him since election night. He gave us lunch in the vice president's best Senate office—he has three in the Capitol—the one just off the floor of the Senate itself. He was able to answer the questions of all of us on a whole variety of domestic and foreign issues. He spoke with assurance and ease. Best of all for President George Bush, on that day he made no news at all. But to tell the truth, judging just from that single lunch, he seemed far more knowledgable than Ronald Reagan did when he was president.

I'm fifty-eight years old now. There are days I am frustrated as *Newsday*'s news hole seems to shrink and I am ordered to keep my stories to four hundred words or less so they will fit in less space. But then I think of my contemporaries, of my friend in television news who after twenty-five years of service was abruptly fired by a network on the grounds that he was no longer as photogenic as his boss liked. I think of how he looked when he came to visit me in the Capitol, where he had once worked.

I think of how, one by one, so many of the other reporters of my generation have left the daily hunt, going into different businesses as their eagerness and their interest waned, or becoming editors or columnists or bureau chiefs or, worst of all, announcing their retirement. And I think of the longing on the face of Jerry Ford when he spoke of his days in Washington.

Back when I worked for the *Philadelphia Bulletin* I suddenly was assigned to cover the annual banquet given by the organizers of the United Fund. My face, I guess, showed that I didn't think much of the job.

The editor tried to make me feel better. "I want you to get a really offbeat story," he told me. I went out and interviewed some of the banquet guests who were being helped by the fund—the impoverished, the ill, the lame, the halt, and the blind. When I came back I wrote what I thought was a moving story and submitted it.

"No, no, no," the editor who had wanted originality said. "Look. Go back to the clips and look at last year's story. That will give you the right idea."

I took the recommended clipping from the library. It was a straightforward unvarnished account of the dinner, enumerating sums collected and describing self-congratulatory speeches. I followed it word for word, simply substituting names, figures, and quotations. "This is terrific," the editor said. And the story ran on the front page.

The next year the editor said to me, "Mike, you did such a good job last time, go out and cover the United Fund again." I went, then returned to the library for the clip and repeated the process. "Better than ever," the delighted editor said. And again the story was on page one.

To his happiness, I performed the exercise the third year
as well. In my fourth and final year at the *Bulletin* I did it
one more time. On this occasion the editor read it and
began to frown. "I don't know, Mike," he said to me.
"This seems to have lost some of its zip."

One thing I learned then was never to repeat myself on
a story. And one thing I know now, I haven't lost any of
my zip.

In 1989 I covered the fall of Congressman Jim Wright,
the first speaker of the House ever to be forced to resign. The
charges against him, brought by Congressman Newt Ging-
rich, the conservative Republican from Georgia, weren't
much when one thinks of other white-collar wrongdoings.
But they were enough.

Morning after morning we reporters would assemble in
the basement of the Capitol, outside the room where the
House Ethics Committee was meeting in secret session to
debate those accusations. Now, the basement of the
Capitol, in some respects, is like a lot of other basements—
lined with exposed pipes that ooze water onto the unfin-
ished but polished floor.

One morning I slipped on a puddle. After a few
moments I managed to get to my feet and hobble upstairs.
I worked through the day and filed a story. Then I went to
a hospital emergency room. My left ankle was broken. I
was forced to stay home for two weeks.

But I came back, stumping along on a cast, trying to
chase the haggard Wright down the corridors of the
Capitol and hoping to be able to lean against a wall during
the traditional press conferences the speaker holds in his
inner office. He would keep them as brief as possible,
sitting behind his desk to answer the never-ending questions about his troubles and complaining that no one
wanted to know anything about upcoming legislation.

One day in the middle of this, I ate a chili lunch and
suddenly was hit with agonizing pains in my stomach and

chest. I tried to continue the job of reporting for about an hour and then had to give it up. I walked up to Bob Petersen, the superintendent of the Senate press gallery, and told him how I felt. In two minutes, the gallery was filled with police, medics, a doctor, an ambulance crew.

Suddenly, I felt better. But after being the center of so much attention, no one was about to let me walk away. I was carried out of the Capitol on a stretcher, raising my arms and giving the V sign with both hands as I went to reassure my anxious colleagues. I was taken by ambulance to Capitol Hill Hospital and put in cardiac intensive care. I was furious. I had finished reporting a Sunday story and I wanted to write it. Over the protests of my editors, I talked my wife into bringing me the portable computer I kept at home.

In intensive care, I wrote the story. Then I disconnected myself from various monitoring plugs, avoided the nurses, tiptoed to a public telephone and sent the story.

I guess I still have a reputation about getting upset about changes in my story. I found this out after there was a mild panic on the national desk. Carl Pisano, one of my editors, told me later that no one wanted to edit it. If major revisions were requested, no one wanted to tell me. They figured I might have another heart attack on the spot.

So a reluctant editor not on the national desk was recruited. By then, it was determined that I hadn't had a heart attack after all. Two days in intensive care and I was sent home, still wobbly. But now everything was safe. The editor called at home and ordered me to rewrite the story. And I did, rather calmly I thought. Two days later, I again was in the Capitol on the trail of Jim Wright.

In happier days Wright had been solitary by choice, frequently lunching alone in the House dining room and avoiding the comraderie of his colleagues. But in the last weeks he walked the halls, looking for attention from the other Democratic congressmen, looking for eye contact, hoping for support. He looked and he saw more and more of them looking the other way.

After he was forced to leave there was a new serenity in the House of Representatives. The new speaker, Congressman Tom Foley, a Washington Democrat, was so much kinder and gentler than Wright that during a postmidnight debate wrapping up legislative business for 1989 the Republican leader, Bob Michel, introduced a resolution praising him—a resolution that was approved by bipartisan acclamation. So in the Capitol the year came basically to a sweet, do-nothing end.

I see the politicians and my colleagues of the press come and go, driven from Washington by age and by scandal and by ambition as well. Many of the members of Congress and nearly all of the reporters are now younger than I. But some of the veterans remain, still savoring the taste of contemporary history. And I'm still happy to play the great game of covering the next Washington story and the one after that. So I guess Jerry Ford was right. I have survived. For now, at any rate.

INDEX